THE EMPLOYMENT RIGHTS OF TEACHERS

Exploring Education Law Worldwide

Edited by
Charles J. Russo
and
Jan DeGroof

ROWMAN & LITTLEFIELD PUBLISHERS, INC.
Lanham • Boulder • New York • Toronto • Plymouth, UK

Published in the United States of America
by Rowman & Littlefield Education
A Division of Rowman & Littlefield Publishers, Inc.
A wholly owned subsidiary of The Rowman & Littlefield Publishing Group, Inc.
4501 Forbes Boulevard, Suite 200, Lanham, Maryland 20706
www.rowmaneducation.com

Estover Road
Plymouth PL6 7PY
United Kingdom

British Library Cataloguing in Publication Information Available

Library of Congress Cataloging-in-Publication Data

The employment rights of teachers : exploring education law worldwide / edited by Charles J. Russo and Jan DeGroof.
p. cm.
Includes bibliographical references.
ISBN-13: 978-1-57886-934-3 (cloth : alk. paper)
ISBN-10: 1-57886-934-X (cloth : alk. paper)
ISBN-13: 978-1-57886-935-0 (pbk. : alk. paper)
ISBN-10: 1-57886-935-8 (pbk. : alk. paper)
eISBN-13: 978-1-57886-936-7
eISBN-10: 1-57886-936-6

1. Teachers—Legal status, laws, etc. 2. Educational laws and legislation. 3. Teachers—Employment. I. Russo, Charles J. II. Groof, Jan de.
K3748.E47 2009
344'.078—dc22

2008029456

™ The paper used in this publication meets the minimum requirements of American National Standard for Information Sciences—Permanence of Paper for Printed Library Materials, ANSI/NISO Z39.48-1992. Manufactured in the United States of America.

To our wives

Debbie and Christine

With all of our love and affection

Charlie and Jan

Contents

Preface

In light of the growing interest in the international and comparative educational rights of teachers, this edited volume, which covers thirteen different nations, provides an overview for interested readers.

Readers are advised that rather than translate notes and other pertinent terms into English, they are ordinarily preserved in their original languages. We have done this not only because the underlying documents are often unavailable in English but also because translating the names might create difficulties for native speakers who wish to research the relevant material. In addition, since each of the nations covered in this book uses a slightly different system of legal citation, we have left references in their original form rather than attempt to standardize them under one rubric. Finally, we have preserved minor variations in the different forms of English used throughout the world so that readers can get a flavor of how our seemingly common tongue is used throughout the world.

Of course, no single book can ever hope to cover the myriad of legal topics, or laws of nations, addressing the educational rights of teachers. Even so, we hope that these well-written and researched chapters, authored by leading scholars in the field, will serve as up-to-date and ready sources of information to help keep educational leaders abreast of the many changes in the ever-growing area of comparative education law.

Acknowledgments

As with any book, there are a number of people who must be thanked. Four sets of people were very helpful in putting this book together. First, thanks to Tom Koerner at Rowman & Littlefield Education, who was most supportive of this project from its inception through its publication. Thanks also to Paul Cacciato, Maera Winters, and Doug English at Rowman & Littlefield for their efforts in helping to get this book published. Thanks, too, to Jennifer Perkins for copyediting the text. Second, it almost goes without saying that we are grateful to the authors for their valuable contributions to this book. Third, at the University of Dayton we would like to thank Ms Colleen Wildenhaus and Charlie's assistant, Ms. Elizabeth Pearn, for her efforts in helping to prepare the manuscript for publication. Last, but certainly not least, we would like to express our deepest appreciation and love for our wives and for their ongoing love and support, without which none of this work would have been completed.

1

Introduction

Charles J. Russo and Jan DeGroof

Introduction

As well-established as the right to work is in the industrialized world, in many places it is neither as well-defined nor as protected even though signatories to various international treaties profess their adherence to the lofty principles contained in the array of documents addressing what is recognized as a fundamental human right. The right to work is an important human right to the extent that without the ability to support themselves, workers will have a difficult time affording themselves, and their families, the opportunity to enjoy their other rights.

International documents acknowledge the fundamental right of individuals to work but do not explicitly address the status of teachers. Even so, this chapter begins by highlighting relevant passages in international agreements on the status of the right to work as a fundamental human right, while the second section offers a brief reflection on why this right, especially for teachers, is an important issue of which all educational leaders should be aware.

International Documents on the Right to Work

The Universal Declaration of Human Rights (UDHR) (1948) is perhaps the premier international document recognizing fundamental human rights. The first right enshrined in the UDHR is that:

> All human beings are born free and equal in dignity and rights. They are endowed with reason and conscience and should act towards one another in a spirit of brotherhood. (Article 1)

This primary right is to be afforded

> . . . without distinction of any kind, such as race, colour, sex, language, religion, political or other opinion, national or social origin, property, birth or other status. (Article 2)

Further reflecting principles that are at the heart of the American and many other systems of law, the UDHR declares that

> All are equal before the law and are entitled without any discrimination to equal protection of the law. All are entitled to equal protection against any discrimination in violation of this Declaration and against any incitement to such discrimination. (Article 7)

As important as these fundamental rights are, it almost goes without saying that in order to appreciate them, persons must have the ability to work so as to support themselves. To this end, according to Article 23 of the UDHR:

(1) Everyone has the right to work, to free choice of employment, to just and favorable conditions of work and to protection against unemployment.
(2) Everyone, without any discrimination, has the right to equal pay for equal work.
(3) Everyone who works has the right to just and favorable remuneration ensuring for himself and his family an existence worthy of human dignity, and supplemented, if necessary, by other means of social protection.
(4) Everyone has the right to form and to join trade unions for the protection of his interests.

In conjunction with Article 23.4, Article 20 amplifies the rights of individuals to gather freely with groups of their choice even though it does not directly address unions.

(1) Everyone has the right to freedom of peaceful assembly and association.
(2) No one may be compelled to belong to an association.

Two other sections of the UDHR address rights that are of paramount importance to educators who are involved in the teaching–learning process.

Article 18 specifies that "Everyone has the right to freedom of thought . . . ," while Article 19 stipulates that

> Everyone has the right to freedom of opinion and expression; this right includes freedom to hold opinions without interference and to seek, receive and impart information and ideas through any media and regardless of frontiers.

As important as the right to work is, it, like the other enumerated rights in the UDHR, is not always safeguarded in all member nations. Moreover, if the general right to employment is not well-protected or clarified in many settings, then the rights of teachers, undoubtedly the most significant and influential group of individuals outside family members who impact the lives of children and who help to ensure that the other fundamental rights are set in place, are even more precarious.

Of course, the rights of teachers to work freely is well-respected in industrialized nations including such countries as Australia, England (and other European countries), Canada, and the United States. These nations regulate the employment rights of teachers pursuant to a wide array of constitutional, statutory, and judicial mechanisms, at both the national and local levels. These nations also generally ensure that teachers have the right to organize and bargain collectively with their employers over the terms and conditions of their employment. At the same time, these nations have safeguards in place to protect the rights of teachers to speak and teach freely on a wide variety of subjects, subject to appropriate governmental oversight of school curricula and instructional methodologies.

At the heart of principles governing international labor law are the Conventions and Recommendations of the International Labor Organization (ILO), governed by the International Labor Conference (ILC), a body that ordinarily meets annually to consider additions to the ILO. Founded in 1919 with the support of the League of Nations (Gregory, 1988), to date, the ILC has enacted 186 conventions (ILO, conventions) and 198 recommendations (ILO, recommendations), even though not all of these remain in effect.

Most broadly, the ILO is designed to protect the rights of workers in all spheres of human endeavor, even though its accompanying Conventions and Recommendations do not specifically address education. Of course, like other international documents and treaties, the success of the ILO is mixed, at best, because it depends on the good faith of signatories who are willing to comply with its provisions. Even though it is not successful in all situations, the ILO remains the most far-reaching international forum for the resolution of labor disputes.

Based in part on fears that the ILO traced its origins to European socialist initiatives, the United States did not join the organization until 1934, at the behest of President Roosevelt's Secretary of Labor, Frances Perkins (Gregory, 1988, p. 148). Following decades of American indifference to the ILO, the United States withheld its financial support to the ILO as a result of its granting observer status to the Palestinian Liberation Organization. The United States formally withdrew from the ILO in 1977 but re-joined three years later (Gregory, 1988) in the face of criticism of its unwillingness to participate in the organization's activities.

Its status as a signatory notwithstanding, the United States has resisted joining the majority of nations that have largely ratified the ILO's Conventions and Recommendations. To date, the United States has ratified only fourteen of the ILO's Conventions, not all of which remain in effect, even though many of them contain language that is similar to American law. Further, American courts have recognized the authority of ILO Conventions, including those that the federal government has not ratified. Perhaps most notably for the sake of this chapter and book is that among the ILO's provisions that the United States has not ratified are Convention 87, which acknowledges the right of workers to freedom of assembly, and Convention 98, which recognizes their right to organize and bargain collectively.

As with the Declaration on the Rights of the Child (Becker, 2002), American reluctance to ratify the ILO is grounded in fears that its provisions might conflict with federal and state law (Advisory Committee on Labor Diplomacy, Second Report to the Secretary of State and the President of the United States (Advisory Committee, 2001). In response to critics who might argue that the United States seeks to avoid international treaties while sitting in judgment of other countries, there can be no doubt that the combination of federal and state laws, whether on education or in other fields, affords workers at least as much, and even greater, protection than the ILO and other international instruments. Additionally, those who have reservations about the ILO can point out that American abstention from ratifying the document means that American employers would not be subject to various international tribunals that often lack the fundamental rights to substantive and procedural due process found in domestic law.

Reflection

Just as compulsory attendance laws did not emerge in the United States until the mid-nineteenth century and even later elsewhere, the rights of workers is a fairly recent phenomenon, having evolved out of struggles in the late nineteenth and early twentieth centuries, especially in Europe and the United States. A major impetus in this movement occurred in the United States after

World War I and the emergence of federal laws in response to unions. Post-World War II, the UDHR highlighted the international recognition of the rights of workers.

As crucial as the right to work is, conflicts have emerged as two camps have evolved over the rights of employees: those preferring unions and those supporting right-to-work laws that do not require unionization. Regardless of whether one is pro-union or pro–right to work, international standards recognize the right to organize and bargain collectively as a fundamental human right that is of particular significance in nations with developing economies.

In many developing countries, from "Poland to the Philippines and from Indonesia to South Africa" (Advisory Committee, 2001), unions have helped to promote democratic ideals dedicated to improving the quality of life for all workers, including teachers. Unions have played a key role in developing countries because, insofar as the legal systems in many of these nations have fully articulated the rights to due process that are widely accepted in countries such as Canada, various European nations, New Zealand, and the United States, unions have helped to heighten awareness of the need to provide such protection. As such, even in the absence of bargaining and unions, or in such nations as Malaysia where unions are not much of a force, it is imperative that educational leaders strive to ensure improved working conditions for educators on all levels in light of the valuable services that they provide for educating their nations' children for the future.

Conclusion

As the world continues to shrink and interdependence grows, one of the major challenges facing the global community is ensuring the educational rights of all children. As daunting and expansive as this crucial task may be, it is one that educational leaders, and all persons, should safeguard because, after all, children are the future.

Overview

In light of the uneven status of the employment rights of teachers in many places, this book includes essays by experts from thirteen nations to address commonalities in this important and timely issue. These experts, all of whom are accomplished academics and jurists, are from Belgium (Jan DeGroof); Brazil (Nina Beatriz Stocco Ranieri and Mônica Sifuentes); Canada (Greg M. Dickinson); China (Ran Zhang and Hongqi Chu); England and Wales (Anne

Ruff); France (Andre Legrand); Germany (Ingo Richter); Malaysia (Tie Fatt Hee); the Netherlands (Ben P. Vermeulen); New Zealand (Paul Rishworth and Sean Kinsler); Singapore (Mui Kim Teh and Kenneth Stott); South Africa (Marius Smit, J. P. Rossouw, and Rassie Malherbe); and the United States (Charles J. Russo).

Based on a common outline, these experts were asked to examine such issues as the nature of their national legal systems; the employment rights of teachers; the academic freedom, free speech, and religious rights of teachers; teachers' rights to due process on dismissal; and emerging issues. Acknowledging that issues vary from one nation to the next, especially in light of their cultural, religious, political, and practical differences, we asked authors to examine the topics as they saw appropriate and to present them from their own points of view.

By granting authors some latitude in addressing their topics, we could then draw conclusions in a final chapter that we hope will lead to future dialogue. Further, recognizing the importance of a representation as far-reaching as possible, we strove to ensure that we had at least one nation on each continent or region of the world represented. The first book of its kind and a companion volume to our earlier text on student rights, we hope that this collection of essays will enhance a common understanding of the rights of teachers throughout the world.

References

Advisory Committee on Labor Diplomacy, Second Report to the Secretary of State and the President of the United States, Dec. 31, 2001, at http://www.state.gov/g/drl/rls/10043.htm

Becker, J. (2002, May 4). "World Summit on Kids," *Newsday*, p. B 4.

Gregory, D.L. (1988) The Right to Unionize as a Fundamental Human and Civil Right. Mississippi College Law Review Vol. 9, 135–154.

International Labor Organization (ILO), http://www.ilo.org/ilolex/english/cvlist.htm (conventions); www.ilo.org/ilolex/english/reclist.htm (recommendations).

United Nations Universal Declaration on Human Rights (1948).

2

Belgium

Jan DeGroof

Constitutional Background

Intermittent political conflicts over the independence and public funding of (predominantly) non-governmental Catholic schooling during the nineteenth and twentieth centuries were finally laid to rest by the "School Pact" of 1958, an inter-party agreement that continues to serve as the framework for law and policy in the non-university sector. Secularists and Catholics put aside their struggles for hegemony and returned to the earlier emphasis on freedom of choice and democratisation of education, establishing the ensuing *schoolvrede*, or school peace. The focus was no longer on protecting the rights of the Church but, instead, on safeguarding the rights of parents to determine the philosophical basis on which their children would be educated.

The key term in the School Pact is *free choice.* Politicians realized that free choice in education was a dead letter without the necessary subsidies. Indeed, the financial situation was not tenable any longer, and the financially weak who wished to send their children to Catholic schools could not bear the costs. The School Pact introduced not only the principle of non-discrimination but also the democratisation of education through free admission to compulsory education.

The political agreement between the three big ideological groups (Catholics, socialists, and liberals) in Belgium was nevertheless a temporary compromise. Based on the assumption that one ideological group would no longer have the power, a majority in Parliament could change the consensus unilaterally. The permanent fear of this possibility seems to have been one of the most important reasons for amendment of the Constitution coupled with the federalization of the unitary State.[1]

Belgians are guaranteed the right to establish and operate non-state or "free" schools that meet quality standards set by public authorities and to choose such schools for their children. In order to ensure that the latter right may be exercised without limitations based on wealth, approved non-public schools receive public funding at quasi-parity with the schools operated by community, provincial, and municipal governments. Spread over the different educational networks, 68.8% of all pupils in Flanders are in subsidized private or "free" schools, 14.61% are in Flemish community schools, and 16.51% attend classes in municipal or provincial schools.

Article 24 of the revised Constitution (formerly Article 17) is the legal basis of educational freedom and justice in Belgium:

1.1. Education is free; any preventative measure is forbidden; the repression of offenses is governed only by law or decree.
1.2. The community offers free choice to parents.
1.3. The community organizes neutral education. Neutrality implies, notably, the respect of the philosophical, ideological, or religious conceptions of parents and pupils.
1.4. The schools organized by the public authorities offer, until the end of mandatory schooling, the choice between the teaching of one of the recognized religions and non-denominational moral teaching.
2. If a community, in its capacity as an organizing authority, wishes to delegate competence to one or several autonomous bodies, it can do so only by decree adopted by a two-thirds majority vote.
3.1. Everyone has the right to education with the respect of fundamental rights and freedoms. Access to education is free until the end of mandatory schooling.
3.2. All pupils of school age have the right to moral or religious education at the community's expense.
4. All pupils or students, parents, teaching staff, or institutions are equal before the law or decree. The law and decree take into account objective differences, notably the characteristics of each organizing authority, that justify appropriate treatment.
5. The organization, the recognition, and the subsidizing of education by the community are regulated by law or decree.

Not surprisingly, a question arises as to why these fundamental rights were taken up in the Constitution.[2] The first reason for this discussion is the wish to guarantee respect for fundamental rights in spite of the fragmentation of the competences. Communitarisation, the process of transferring competence from the national level to the community level, of education avoids the necessity of finding a political consensus at the national level. The political consensus in the past was always a balance between the Catholic majority of the north of the country against the non-Catholic majority of the southern part of the country. With the insertion of constitutional rights in education laws, each citizen now has recourse to a legal remedy to avoidance of a law or an order by the executive power of a community which is in conflict with the Constitution.

As a second reason, the School Pact was no longer workable in the framework of an educational policy with a view to full accomplishment of equality. In other words, social equality, meaning fully respected non-discrimination, could not have been reached when the School Pact and the Constitution were at a level of *status quo.* As a matter of fact, the mechanisms of consultation and pacification which had been installed by the School Pact—more properly, the "Commission" of the School Pact—no longer functioned. A good number of cases had to be treated under the continuous threat that the government would fall. It was clear that the ideological positions taken would not be abandoned by either the Dutch-speaking party or the French-speaking party. It was therefore necessary to find other, more reliable guarantees. For that purpose, an amendment of the Constitution became indispensable.

Article 24 contains obligatory neutrality of state education; freedom of choice for parents; free education during compulsory school time; the right to choose between religious and non-religious schools; and equality between all students, parents, teachers, and schools with reservation of certain objectives.

Except for the principle of freedom of education, which had been taken up in Article 24 in its previous draft, the right to education is now also a right guaranteed by the Constitution: freedom of education as an individual right, however, is void if the authorities do not realize at the same time the right to education (since long-standing Belgian legislation transformed this formal law into material law).

All of these principles are, as a matter of fact, enforceable, not only before an ordinary court, which can refuse to apply decrees and regulations that are in conflict with Article 24, and the Council of State, which can annul these decrees and regulations, but also before the Court of Arbitration, which can henceforth examine all decrees or laws for compatibility with Articles 10, 11, and 24 of the Constitution. If the occasion presents itself, the Court of Arbitration may annul these decrees or laws. This modification was a *conditio sine qua non* for the transfer of competence in educational matters to the communities in order to grant the ideological minorities true guarantees that they had drawn before from the School Pact.

Legal Framework: Recruitment, Salaries, Specific Duties

In order to provide education, the government arranges teaching at different levels, sets up establishments and departments for this purpose, and has the power to appoint (unlimited duration) or employ (limited duration) the necessary staff. The specifically ideological or philosophical character of the education arranged by the competent central authorities is usually determined directly or indirectly by the Constitution or by positive legislation; it can also respond to the general legal theory of the characteristics of public service. In order to guarantee the "neutral" character of state education, some national regulations contain specific provisions laying down the origin of the qualifications that teaching staff must fulfill. At the same time, the authorities subsidise or recognise educational establishments set up by private persons or decentralised authorities such as municipalities or counties and confer allowances.

These grants are often used to equip and run educational establishments or to pay part of the wages of staff working in these schools. As in most countries, legal security is mainly achieved when this right to salary "allowances" is a subjective right, meaning that it can be demanded before the courts once the statutory requirements have been fulfilled. In this way, the funding of educational establishments that are not directly dependent on the central authorities is not subject to parliamentary or governmental majorities. In these circumstances, officials are not concerned with an optional right but, rather, with a right acquired automatically if the statutory norms are observed. The mission of the State to found its own schools is balanced by its duty to support the types of education recognised as valid outside state education and to subsidise their staff.

Non-public schools must pay their lay teachers at least as much as equivalent public-school teachers. Teachers who fulfill the conditions to be subsidized receive their wages directly from the government. The organizing bodies are private legal persons, and relations with their personnel are governed by a private labor contract. The freedom of education and the freedom of contract guarantee that these bodies can demand ideological commitment on the part of their personnel.

Teachers must conform their teaching to the distinctive character of the schools that employ them, whether denominational or neutral. If school authorities demand commitments from their teachers with respect to specific educational projects, namely obligations and incompatibilities, which they are fully authorized to do and which has long been a condition for the effective achievement of the project, this is to be adequately clear in legality, meaning a contractual commitment declaration, and in reality. In this respect, school governors are obliged to give the required explanation of the pedagogical project, possibly on philosophical grounds as well, and to update it continually as the basis for such personnel decisions.

The educational legislation (*eindtermen*, duties of the teacher and statute of the pupils), along with the model curricula and the voluntarily accepted directives of the educational "umbrella organizations" (such as the Flemish Secretary of Catholic Education and the Secretariat), curtail the individual freedoms of teachers. Moreover, teachers are members of pedagogical teams that shape further their commitments. These teams work out a pedagogical project and pursue local school policies. In the rather restricted sphere of remaining discretion, teachers can act autonomously.

According to Article 24 of the Constitution, the organizing bodies or school boards of the free educational institutions have the right to recruit their personnel freely. In this regard, the Constitutional Court has pointed out that the freedom of education encompasses the freedom of the organizing power to choose the staff employed with a view to achieving its own educational objectives. The constitutional right to recruit on an ideological basis is reaffirmed in Article 15 of the decree of June 8, 1996, on the legal status of teachers of subsidized education and recognized by the Constitutional Court.[3]

The freedom of education is consistent with judgment no. 66/99 of the Constitutional Court, which repeats earlier orders[4] relating to the freedom of organizing bodies "to choose staff who are employed with a view to the fulfillment of the educational objectives particular to the organization."[5] Put another way, freedom of education requires a right to choose, which consequently influences the working relationship between such organizational powers and their staffs. The different legal position is consequently justified in contrast with official education, where the appointment or employment of staff is on a contractual basis. The term *justified*, then, refers to the terminology of the article of the Constitution itself for the purpose of indicating when a different treatment is justified according to the principle of equality.

The freedom of direction in its interrelationship with and influence on the freedom of establishment consequently hinders the integration of the public law status. The Constitutional Court thus recalls that the difference in legal position arises directly from §1 of Article 24 of the Constitution and appears to be an irrevocable consequence of this, with particular rights and freedoms that differ from official educational establishments by virtue of their very nature. Without this difference, freedom of education remains a hollow concept. It is, in other words, the very essence of freedom of education. The particular kind of education, the teaching plan, the curricula, and the methodology are disseminated, acquire from, and are realized by the staff who are chosen for this purpose. The credibility of a free school is at the same time critically examined from the perspective of the employment policy.[6] Moreover, interwoven with the freedom of association, which was mentioned earlier, is the fulfillment of the social goal of the legal person who is dependent on the freedom of appointment.[7]

The government statute is at odds with this aforementioned perspective. In an official school, the authorized management does not "choose" any staff but is to adopt the results of the stipulated procedures. The official management is not permitted to make appointments or promotions which are contrary to the statutory regulations regarding recruitment and promotion; candidates for positions as staff members have a subjective right to the positions if they have satisfied all of the stipulated standards and selection criteria.[8]

Equal access for Belgians to civil posts requires a procedure that enables relevant authorities to compare the titles and merits of the different candidates. An impressive piece of litigation regarding equal access to public office has, in the meantime, secured this obligation. However, free education can freely make use of the possibility of examining the files of candidates in question for their dedication to the particular ideological pedagogical plans and concepts that school officials have chosen.

Over the years the freedom of personnel recruitment of the free school boards has been limited by a variety of provisions of education legislation. The decree on the legal status of teachers of subsidized education provides some general conditions for the recruitment of new teachers. Subsidized schools must employ staff members who have the necessary qualifications equivalent to those possessed by public-school staff.[9]

The choice among applicants with the same qualifications is limited by a system of priority appointment: only if there are no teacher candidates with priority or existing teachers with a right in a position is a school board free to choose among equally qualified applicants. Those requirements being met, free school boards are totally free and do not have to explain why they have chosen candidates and may make decisions about employing and dismissing staff based on the religious or pedagogical character of the schools. Denominational schools may, of course, expect that their personnel profess the concerned religion. At the same time, specific regulations do exist and were approved by the Constitutional Court, explaining how church instances are entitled to sanction the authority of religious instruction.[10]

Rights, Freedoms, and Limits: The Far-Reaching Implications of Teaching

The Constitutional Court has made it clear what the consequences of freedom of education are: the organizing of education and having it provided (by teachers, whose role is to act as mediators) as well as in terms of both form and content of the curricula according to one's own outlook.[11] Pedagogical freedom defined at an institutional level is, despite all of its nuances and regulatory provisions, one of the very reasons for having pluralism in educational provisions.[12]

Judgment no. 76/96, December 18, 1996, examined whether the objectives of one's own ideological or methodological teaching plan can still be achieved after implementing developmental goals and final attainment levels by the government and whether it is possible to provide education inspired by particular pedagogical ideologies.[13] Teachers have the role of implementing particular pedagogical projects but also derive the right to have their own teaching styles directly from the position or office that they hold.

It should be recognised at the outset that academic freedom surpasses the freedom to express opinions and the freedom of conscience that forms the basis for this. More specifically, the freedom to teach in primary education, in secondary schools, and at the university level, with its own specific code of conduct, is different from providing vocational training, business courses, or political training.

When teaching young people to exercise their freedom, what is required is an individual viewpoint, the capacity to make personal judgments, and a fair amount of independence. It is difficult to imagine a more person-to-person-based context and one which demands greater responsibility. As a substitute parent, teachers act under the authority of their organising powers (or school boards in many other places) as educators in the school environment. This situation, to a large extent, sets the tone for the relationship between school management and teachers.

Teachers also have pedagogical freedom, since it does not have to be excluded from an undertaking in a subordinate context. Even this freedom has to be qualified. The first restriction to the freedom of education is contained in the special nature of the profession, which involves working for the cause of the personal development of the young. Teachers' own freedom, for example, the right to express opinions, is ruled out in the teaching profession.[14]

Teachers' demands may also conflict with the rights of school authorities or their representatives with regard to what is valid in the framework of the freedom of education and the freedom of religion.[15] The freedom of organising powers to determine their own educational programmes places restrictions on access to the teaching profession. For this, teachers freely accept restrictions of their rights, but this has to be unambiguous. To this end, the European Court of Human Rights has formulated specific criteria in such circumstances.

This development applies not only to the right of teachers to training and freedom of speech, because other basic rights can be placed on uncertain footing due to the freedom to establish educational programmes; such a discussion is beyond the scope of this chapter. Teachers' freedom to express opinions is limited by the pedagogical project which school communities set as their goal and the attendant commitments for teachers. This relativization of freedom in *forum externu* is the function of the freedom to establish a school, its denomination, and its organisation applies to the duty of school officials to involve teachers in specific areas of the freedom of education, where the material as well as the moral interest is important. The freedom to exercise their profession supposes that teachers are partly involved in bearing responsibility for their schools, a duty which they assume collectively.

How could a system of teaching aimed at instilling a sense of responsibility function without rules that promote this sense of responsibility within one's own community? This matter becomes increasingly important when, as is the case in several countries where government subsidies are provided, the statutory difference between teachers becomes blurred, despite the private or public status of schools. There is also another argument.

In academic schools, there is a tradition that teaching staff should be involved in a definite way and at various levels in school management and policy-making. There is an even greater need for this tradition to apply to those forms of education that deal with students who are less independent and therefore need more uniformity in teaching staffs and, in addition to that, greater pedagogical sensitivity. The exercise of this freedom is not an individualising postulate. Rather, it is seen as a collective right among the rights of teaching staffs. In this connection, reference may be made to the justified rights of the trade unions and their interest in education, teaching, and promotion of self-education.

There is thus an impressive range of regulations setting out the obligations of staff members in the various stages of their careers. The specific nature of schools or other educational establishments may set conditions regarding the staff that they employ. There have been debates in many countries concerning the extent to which activities in staff members' private lives can lead to sanctions or dismissal. The conclusion tends to be that legal procedures should be considered only if the activities or facts in question interfere with the relationship between the students and teachers. Under this approach, a staff member's private life may lead to sanctions only where it influences an educational relationship or a school.

Legislators seek to strike a balance between guaranteeing the nature of educational projects and the personal rights of staff members. The solutions provided by case law nonetheless diverge considerably, depending on the hierarchy of constitutional rights in each member state of the European Union.

Most European countries do not have specific liability for teachers. The general liability or tort system applies to them should they cause injury to one of their pupils. Some countries have a specific liability system for civil servants, an approach that also applies to teachers in the exercise of their jobs. Generally, this implies that only in the case of serious negligence or of intention are civil servants personally liable for damages.

In several reports, recent convictions have been reported that seemed to extend teachers' areas of liability. Extremely interesting is the discussion in England where a tendency might develop in the future to extend teachers' liability to the actual quality of teaching. A case was mentioned where a diagnosis of dyslexia was made too late and which led to the liability of the educational psychiatrist.

Boards of management in other countries are implicitly liable for the civil wrongs of their teachers during the course of their employment, and they generally include teacher indemnity in their insurance policies. This is also the case in Sweden, where employers are liable for the actions of employees in virtue of the general principles of tort law.

In some countries, there is a specific liability for teachers for acts committed by their pupils while they are under the teachers' care. In Italy this is called the *culpa in vigilando*, a concept also found in Belgium. The interesting aspect of the Belgian regulation is the presumption that an error of supervision has been made when a pupil causes damage or injury. Contrary to the general tort system, where an individual who seeks to impose liability on another has to prove the fault, in this case teachers must prove that they did not make errors of supervision. In general, this teacher liability does not constitute a large problem since schools and teachers are usually well insured against the risk.

Countries that do not have a *concours* (an examination competition with a ranking of candidates) usually select their teachers by private calls, interviews with selection boards, and the like. Vacancies are announced through advertisements in newspapers, teachers' magazines, and sometimes official publications. Several countries report the fact that priority arrangements have been made in order to favor teachers who have lost their jobs or who are receiving unemployment benefit. This is the case in Belgium. In such countries as Belgium and Germany, it is possible to have a permanent, or lifelong, appointment in private schools. This is remarkable since lifelong appointments are typical for the civil service and clearly originate from that sphere of employment.

A whole host of provisions in the regulations governing the terms of employment for staff can be enforced directly for individuals working in centrally run educational establishments as well as against staff requesting salary allowances in other establishments.

As with persons working in organic or functional public services, staff members must submit certificates stating that they have no convictions against them as well as a certificate of good character; they must, further, possess their civil and political rights and be sworn into office.

Staff members must possess the required qualifications that are deemed to be sufficient. To the extent that there is a wide range of desired qualifications available, there is a tendency to simplify the complicated web of regulations. Depending on the legal structure of a school or its ideological nature, officials may impose specific terms of recruitment.

Another area of concern is that the state of health of staff members is almost always subject to specific stipulations: individuals' conditions may not pose a danger to the health of students. This condition is, in most cases, checked regularly and effectively by administrative health services. Apart from checking the physical aptitude of teachers, there are also provisions regarding age limit, seniority, sickness and maternity leave, task description, and general holidays as well as regarding the definitive appointment of unlimited duration in the case of a contract, fixed tenure under the terms of public service employment.

In-service training for teachers is one of the main items of the European Union's actions in the field of education. Well-organised services have been reported from the United Kingdom and the Netherlands. In the Netherlands, the central government pays the authorities responsible for public and private schools an annual sum for in-service training per member of the staff establishment. In Spain, *Centros de Profesores* have been created to give impetus to the permanent training of teachers on the non-university level. Some countries mention bonuses for teachers for following an in-service training or take into account training when a promotion is in order. Sometimes, leaves of absence are also possible to follow courses.

Several countries recruit their teachers through a *concours*: an examination competition with a ranking of candidates. Passing the concours usually means that candidates are appointed to posts. The concours can be national, regional, or local. In addition, a concours is usually made public in an official publication and sometimes also through advertisements in newspapers and magazines. The concours, a way of recruiting civil servants in most countries, is organised for the selection of teachers where one is attached to the civil servant aspect of the teaching job. There are differences, however. In Belgium, even teachers who are civil servants are not recruited through a concours.[16]

Evaluation and Duties

In order to function as a fully fledged beginning teacher, each graduate has to display the relevant basic competences, meaning knowledge, skills, and attitudes. These basic competences enable teachers to progress to the professional profile of knowledge, skills, and attitudes of the teacher when practising their profession. Each profile consists at least of competences common to all teachers in terms of knowledge, skills, and attitudes as well as competences specific to a particular educational level.

The common core competences represent a study load of at least 45 credits. The decree of 1996 concerning teacher training and in-service training differentiates the following ten profiles: the teacher as a guide in learning and developmental processes, an educator, an expert in a particular field of study, an organizer, an innovator and researcher, a partner of parents or care suppliers, a member of the school team, a partner of people offering initiatives valuable for education, a member of the teaching community, and a culture participant. Each profile refers to specific competences teachers must master. Moreover, the decree mentions ten attitudes that should be inherent in future teachers: the capacity to make decisions, openness for relations with others, a critical attitude, eagerness to learn, the capacity to organize, openness for collaboration, a sense of responsibility, creativity, flexibility, and eagerness for correct language usage and communication.

Every staff member has to be evaluated at a minimum of once every three years. If the staff member has no office description, an evaluation is not possible. The governing body or the school cluster in subsidized education, or the board of directors in community education, negotiates on the general arrangements concerning evaluation with local committees.

The evaluation report describes carefully the complete performance of staff members compared to the official job descriptions agreed on, including the specific objectives and developmental objectives as agreed on for the relevant evaluation period. Evaluations must be carried out in the schools where the staff members teach. Each staff member has two evaluators, one of which is the headmaster or deputy headmaster. For religion teachers and non-confessional ethics (*niet-confessionele zedenleer*) teachers, the authorized authority of the religion or ideology concerned serves as evaluator for the content and technical aspects of the job. The normal evaluator is responsible for the other aspects.

Only in the case of an evaluation report that concludes with the final note "insufficient" may a staff member appeal to a college to challenge an evaluation. As long as a college of appeal does not function, evaluations with final notes of "insufficient" are not possible. If permanently appointed staff members or staff members appointed without specific termination dates receive evaluations with final notes of "insufficient," new evaluations have to be conducted. New evaluations must comprise a period of a minimum of eight and a maximum of twelve months of actual performance. Insufficiencies can lead to dismissals.

In secondary education, all members of personnel are evaluated, as of September 1, 2006. In continuing education, all members of personnel must be evaluated a first time starting September 1, 2006, up to and including June 30, 2009. For the pupil guidance centers, the starting date is September 1, 2007.

If evaluations are "insufficient," staff members may appeal these decisions to colleges of appeal for evaluations within a period of fifteen calendar days. "Insufficient" evaluations are definite if the period in which appeals are possible are over or after definite decisions have been taken in appeals. Regarding evaluations that are not "insufficient," staff members can respond in writing. These written reactions are added to the evaluation files of staff members.

Education personnel must look after the interests of education, the institution, and their pupils. Personnel must conscientiously fulfill the tasks allocated to them and behave correctly in their interactions with pupils, parents, and the public. Educators must avoid everything that can harm the trust of the public or the honor or dignity of their office. In addition, personnel are prohibited from accepting gifts, rewards, or other advantages. At the same time, educators cannot employ their authority for political or commercial ends and must keep to professional secrecy (such as after deliberating class committees). Further, educators cannot interrupt their offices without prior consent of the hierarchical authorities.

In subsidized education, the obligations that follow the specificities of pedagogical projects are to be observed and must be addressed before taking up one's duties such that governing bodies must communicate any incompatibilities in writing to competent authorities. The decree explicitly states that facts from teachers' private lives, which have no consequences for their relationships with pupils and other members of personnel in school life, cannot give cause to measures from governing bodies. In community education, members of personnel are to take impartiality into account and must give form to the pedagogical project of community education.

Conclusion

The legal qualification of the status of staff in subsidised establishments is not always clear. Exacting a statutory arrangement similar to that used in state education is more pertinent to the extent to which the support of the educational establishment through allowances is similar or equal to the funding applied to state education. This refers to rules laying down recruitment, appointment, selection, and promotion as well as the administrative ranks and transfers of the members of staff available, days off, the basic duties, and any incompatibilities with the post. A uniform system of qualifications is often introduced in this manner.

The status of state personnel employed in education protects the staff's private lives outside school against arbitrary decisions by school officials in more ways than one. This raises the question of whether legal relations between staff and private schools are subject to the same rules.

Another question arises as to whether an identical status jeopardises the founding of non-official educational establishments. In any case, there must be room for additional rules for the educational circles in question, if necessary, after consultation with the joint committees between employers and employees in conformity with social legislation that complement the common statutory provisions, regardless of the nature of the educational establishment. Specific provisions must hence be enforced between organising bodies and staff members concerning specific incompatibilities in the light of the characteristics of the pedagogical project. It is often countered that such a basic measure, which would be uniform for all members of staff in education, would not affect the private status of the educational establishments. It is thus an open question as to whether equality is the same as a uniform statutory legal position.

This problem needs to be placed in a wider context, especially as the borders between private and public law are becoming increasingly blurred. Authoritative voices argue in favor of abolishing the "national status" in education; in some countries the distinction between a statutory and a contractual legal position has become so small that the dismantling of the status of public civil servant as a possible strategy is being considered.

The so-called process of inclusion in public law of non-official educational establishments, stressing their contribution to the general interest, since they issue degrees with effects on civil law, provide compulsory education, and replace the organic public service, describes these establishments as a functional public service. Even non-official educational establishments have a public power entailing certain legal consequences such as the right to exercise particular occupations and access to higher education while the education they offer provides a public benefit. Some studies point out that the education provided here is cheaper than the education provided by the State.

Whatever the extent of the public nature of the staff status of non-official establishments, specific rights and duties are to be exercised differently according to the legal nature of the organising bodies. The duties intrinsic to public offices and their entailing rights such as to equal access to public office cannot yet be exacted in non-official education.

Bibliography

DEGROOF, J. (Ed.), *The Legal Status of Teachers in Europe*, Leuven: Acco, 1995, p. 324.

DEGROOF, J. (Ed.), *Personeelsbeleid aan de Vlaamse Universiteiten*, Antwerpen: Kluwer Rechtswetenschappen, 1995, p. 172.

DEGROOF, J., *De Schoolpactwet. Coördinatie en Annotatie*, Antwerpen: Kluwer Rechtswetenschappen, 1996, p. 192.

DEGROOF, J., *Education as a Social–Cultural Right*, Rome: Union Mondiale des Enseignants Catholiques, 1988, p.140.

Eurydice, *The Education System in Belgium–Flemish Community*, http://www.eurydice.org/portal/page/portal/Eurydice/EurContents?country=BN&lang=EN&expandMenu=False.

GLENN, C. and DEGROOF, J., *Finding the Right Balance. Freedom, Autonomy and Accountability in Education. Volume 1*, Utrecht: Lemma, 2002, p. 601.

HEYVAERT, J. and JANSSENS, G., *Onderwijszakboekje 2006–2007*, Antwerpen: Wolters Plantyn, 2006, p514.

Notes

1. As a side remark, education at universities followed another track. This is due to the historical equilibrium between two free universities, on the one hand, and between two state universities, a French-speaking one and a Dutch-speaking one, on the other hand. The two free universities had long been equally treated as far as finances go. Both also had the right to grant academic grades.

2. See DEGROOF, J., *De grondwetsherziening van 1988 en het onderwijs*, Story Scientia, Brussels, 1989, 233 blz. (and *La révision constitutionnelle de 1988 et l'enseignement*); *id.* The Belgian Model for Constitutional Rights on Education, in DEGROOF, J., *Subsidiarity and Education. Aspects of Comparative Educational Law. First Report of the European "Educational Law Association,"* Acco, Leuven, 1994.

3. Court of Arbitration, no. 34/98, April 1, 1998; Court of Arbitration, no. 18/93, March 4, 1993.

4. DEGROOF, J., "Slechts de contractuele lezing van de arbeidsverhoudingen in het vrij onderwijs is verstaanbaar met de grondwet: een nieuw dogma?" Nog over de juridische kwalificatie van de verhouding tussen de gesubsidieerd vrije onderwijsinstellingen en haar personeel, in *Tijdschrift voor Onderwijsrecht en Onderwijsbeleid*, 1999–2000, nr. 6, pp. 460–87.

5. Judgment of the Court of Arbitration, no. 76/96, December 18, 1996.

6. This applies to the modern interpretation of freedom of education in general: LEUNE, J. M. G., Vrijheid van onderwijs anno 2000 [Freedom of education in the year 2000], *Nederlands Tijdschrift voor Onderwijsrecht,* 2000, no. 2, p. 8:

A discrepancy can sometimes be discerned between the formal and actual identity of a free school as is, for example, evident from the policy of appointment and the policy regarding the establishment of the curriculum. Such a discrepancy undermines the legitimacy of the freedom of education. The ship should be sailing under the appropriate flag. Free schools that do not recognize the importance of this undermine the credibility of the freedom of education. It would be more credible if those schools would change their legal status.

See also "Regarding the Legal Position of Teachers in the Catholic Faith: A Statement about Freedom." *Nieuw Tijdschrift voor Politiek (New Journal for Politics),* 1989, no. 3, pp. 31–40.

7. An institution with a religious or ideological basis has the freedom to stipulate requirements regarding both the commencement of an employment relationship, the terms of employment and promotion. . . . Institutions for denominational education may stipulate more extensive requirements, particularly requirements which are necessary for the realization of their foundation in view of the goal of the institution.

OVERES, C. H. C., *Besturen en medezeggenschap in het bijzonder onderwijs. Een civielrechtelijke studie naar de besluitvorming in het bijzonder onderwijs (Management and participation in decision-making in denominational education. A civil law study of decision-making in denominational education),* Lelystad, 1994, p. 19.

8. This also applies to the autonomous body that has been assigned the power of organising community education. Recommendations of the Council of State, 1988–1989, no. 161/1.

9. In the same sense, this must ultimately allow significant scope for standards which the authorized authority of the school sets itself or which are voluntarily accepted in the social exchange with bodies other than the authority which provides the finance for maintenance. Both assume a private law form of organization for "special" (Dutch terminology for "denominational") education within which decision making primarily takes place in accordance with the principles (party autonomy, reciprocity) and rules of private law. Were it otherwise, there would be no workable framework within which to shape one's own direction according to one's own standards.

ZOONTJES, P. J. J., De smalle ruimte. Enige opmerkingen over privaatrecht en publiekrecht, bezien vanuit de positie van de bijzondere school [The narrow scope. Some comments regarding private law and public law as seen from the perspective of the special (denominational) school], *Nederlands Tijdschrift voor Onderwijsrecht,* 1999, no. 1, p. 32.

10. Court of Arbitration, no. 18/93, March 4, 1993.

11. Judgment of the Court of Arbitration, no. 18/93, March 4, 1993; Among others judgment of the Court of Arbitration, no. 76/96, December 18, 1996.

12. From the ruling of the Court of Arbitration and the recommendations of the Court of State, it appears that the communities must act "cautiously" with regard to this.

13. As laid down in the decree of February 22, 1995, relating to the validation of the developmental goals and the final attainment levels of ordinary pre-school and primary education.

14. MARCOU, G., La liberté d'enseignement et la liberté des enseignants, *Revue de droit public,* 1980, no. 1; LASALLE, J. P., La situation du personnel des établissements d'enseignement privé sous contrat, *Recueil Dalloz,* 1964, no. 1; IMBERT, T., Sur le statut particulier des enseignants (de 1800 à 1980), *Revue de droit public,* 1983, pp. 17 ff.

15. Cf. among others, GEORGEL, J., THOREL, A.-M., *L'enseignement privé en France du VIIIe au XXe siècle*, Dalloz, Paris, 1995, pp. 207 ff.; FONTAINE, N., *La liberté d'enseignement, De la loi DEBRE d la loi GUERNEUR*, Paris, 1975, pp. 139 ff.

16. In Germany, the *concours* is not a general examination but a *concours de mérite*, since examination results during teacher training are taken into consideration. Some countries, such as Spain and Italy, have both *concours* examinations and merit rewards.

3

Brazil

Nina Beatriz Stocco Ranieri and Mônica Sifuentes

Introduction

In Brazil over the last 100 years, five constitutions and at least six educational reforms have faced education challenges in the fields of equity, finance, access, and quality, all of which have affected the rights of teachers directly and indirectly. In a broad sense, this legislation is characterized by the absence of educational policies and planning, by the adoption of measures in response to immediate conditions, and by normative over-detailing. As a result, the more the federal government legislates, the less internally coherent the laws are, creating a gap between the legal country and the real country. All of this can be clearly seen in many aspects of education, including the rights of teachers.

Indeed, the rights of teachers in Brazil are provided for and guaranteed by the Federal Constitution; by the National Education Law, or NEL (Lei de Diretrizes e Bases da Educação); by labor laws; and by specific laws pertaining to each of the country's three educational systems (federal, state, and municipal) since Brazil is a federal republic. Within this legal context, the rights of teachers can be seen from different perspectives: the civil and political rights that all Brazilians are entitled to receive; the rights that all workers share; the rights that they are entitled to as teachers, specifically, and which can be referred to as academic rights; the rights that teachers are entitled to in the private education system; and the rights that they are entitled to as public school teachers, differing in some aspects according to the education systems within which they work.

Some of the rights of teachers overlap, especially between civil and academic rights, as a result of a complex legal network characteristic of the

Brazilian culture and its patchy democratic experience. Starting with the Portuguese colonization of Brazil in the sixteenth century, and except for some unsuccessful attempts, citizens never claimed their rights until recently. The government provided civil and political rights; labor and social rights were conceded, during the Vargas dictatorship in the 1930s, very often, as a political instrument to co-opt certain groups. As a result, people are not used to fighting for their rights in Brazil, and labor rights were seen as a privilege for certain categories, especially in the civil service.

Teachers' rights are no exception. Insofar as the status of teachers is essentially no different from that of other Brazilians, it is possible to understand why the numerous and specific legislative activities have occurred since the NEL became law in the late 1990s. In other words, the NEL attempted to eliminate discrepancies and privileges by establishing a national standard by which candidates enter and progress in the teaching profession.

The NEL is innovative and modernizing. In breaking off with many of the rigid provisions of earlier educational legislation, it allowed a revision of the State's position in relation to recurring issues in Brazilian schooling. Among the issues that needed to be addressed were decentralizing governmental control, financing public education, opening new career opportunities for teachers, and bringing about more active participation in organizing education. Sponsors of these changes expected that all of these measures, combined with a new fund for financing public basic education (FUNDEB), which obliges the government to allocate 60% of these resources on better salaries for teachers, would engender significant improvements in the educational system.

In Brazil, the term *basic education* refers to both preschool, which starts at the age of six, and primary education, which covers students between the ages of seven and fourteen. Primary education, also referred to as fundamental education, is compulsory, free to all and must be accessible to all, at any age. Secondary education must be available and accessible to all, by all suitable means. However, to date, there are no conclusive studies or research in the law describing the impact that these measures have had on the educational system.

At the same time, and in spite of the NEL, it is important to point out that there remains a significant difference between the rights of the teachers in private and public schools, a distinction which lies in the legal employment regime: in the private sector teachers are covered by the common labor laws, while in the public schools teachers are protected by specific statutory public laws which still maintain privileges established in the past and are difficult to abolish because of the power that unions continue to assert. The rest of this chapter, then, presents and comments on selected aspects of the complex legal structure of teachers' rights in Brazil.

Employment Rights of the Teachers: Civil, Political, and Social Rights

As Brazilian citizens, teachers are entitled to all liberal civil and political rights such as freedom of speech, freedom of belief, the right to participate in unions and political parties, and intellectual property rights. It is also worth keeping in mind that these rights are also still guaranteed in other articles of the Constitution and the NEL. Further, teachers are entitled to the guarantees of due process such as full defense and access to the judicial power. Moreover, the Brazilian Constitution broadly stipulates punishment for acts of discrimination by which officials or others may attempt to limit the fundamental rights and liberties of teachers, and it also prohibits the practice of racism, which Article 5 of the Constitution defines as a non-bailable crime.

Having mentioned freedom of belief, the NEL allows the existence of private schools of any religion or creed, maintained by religious entities; in this case, teachers are subject to the schools' religious orientations. In public schools, whether to provide religious education is not a decision ordinarily made by teachers and school officials. Rather, if religious instruction occurs in public schools, it usually does so based on demands made by students or their parents. This also applies to demands for multi-religious education.

Insofar as the State is secular, religious education must be offered with no extra cost in the public school system, but during the normal school period, teachers have to be prepared by churches or religious entities. In summary, in this area, students' rights prevail over the rights of the teachers. This is not new, as equivalent guarantees had already been provided for by former Brazilian constitutions in 1934, 1937, and 1946. However, the constitutions of 1967 and 1988 suppressed the free choice of religious education by students that was reinstated by the NEL.

Today it is possible to identify a certain consensus to accept that religious teaching must, first of all, be based on the principles of citizenship; religious education should not be used to convert people or impose dogmas, rites, or prayers but, rather, serve more as an educational tool to understand religions and human societies. The concept of religious teaching as an area of knowledge was established in Resolution no. 02/98 of the Chamber of Basic Education/National Education Council, which points to the necessity of having a qualified professional for the teaching of religion in primary and secondary education and not a volunteer or someone representing a religious denomination, as it was in the past.

In the field of social rights, teachers in both private and public schools are entitled to the employment rights guaranteed by Article 7 of the Constitution. The extension of these rights to public school teachers is recent, as a result of a broader reform of the civil servants statutory regime carried out in 1998.

In both sectors, these rights include a nationally unified minimum wage; a year-end, one-salary bonus; pensions; separate pay rates for night-shift work; family benefits in some circumstances; normal working hours not exceeding eight hours a day and forty-four hours a week; paid weekly leave, preferably on Sundays; annual vacations, with remuneration at least one-third higher than the normal salary; maternity leave without loss of job and of salary, for a period of 120 days; paternity leave; protection of the labor market for women through specific incentives; and prohibition of any discrimination with respect to wages and hiring criteria of handicapped workers. In addition, many of these rights were given by the law and not as a result of any specific demands or movements on the part of teachers.

Teachers in the private education sector must receive notice of dismissals in proportion to the length of service of at least thirty days, as provided by Article 7 of the Constitution. On the other hand, in the public sector, dismissals require a judicial sentence for tenured teachers and an administrative process for those who are yet to be tenured.

Rights Teachers Are Entitled to as Teachers

Freedom of teaching in Brazil has always been an educational principle except during the military dictatorship, when the Constitution of 1969 imposed restrictions on the practice of teaching under detailed and rigid education legislation (Law 4.024/62 and Law 5.540/68, which were revoked by the NEL in 1996).

In the Constitution, and with regard to the influence that governments and the private school boards exercise over the activity of teaching, Article 206 establishes some educational principles to protect and ensure teachers a certain autonomy in their activities such as the "freedom to teach, research and express thought, art and knowledge; pluralism of pedagogic ideas and conceptions and coexistence of public and private teaching institutions." Obviously, these rights are practiced within the legal framework of the National Education Plan (Law 10.172/01) and the NEL as also foreseen in the Constitution, which establishes the objectives and guidelines of this activity.

The NEL itself imposes a minimum standard to be upheld all over the country, which includes a national basis not only for syllabi at each level of education, whether primary, intermediate, or secondary, but also for teacher education, since the Constitution demands a "guarantee of standards of quality." Teacher education also varies according to the level of education: for lower education, a higher education degree is required; for higher education, a post-graduate degree is necessary.

A B.A. or post-graduate degree in pedagogy is required for administration, planning, inspection, supervision, and pedagogical counseling for primary education. Among the innovations introduced by the NEL education colleges (called *institutos superiores de educação*) is that they were created to prepare teachers for only primary and secondary education (Article 63). More specifically, the Brazilian legislation accepts the following degrees in the exercise of teaching: religious science, pedagogy, history, philosophy, social sciences, and psychology. Candidates who earn diplomas in education issued by the *institutos superiores de educação* can also enter the teaching profession.

A question that had been the subject of a great deal of controversy refers to the innovations introduced by the 1998 Brazilian Constitution concerning teachers who wished to serve native communities. This provision established that "the regular fundamental teaching shall be practiced in Portuguese language, still ensuring to the native communities the use of their maternal native language and to their proper learning processes" (Article 210). Bilingual education, appropriated to the cultural peculiarities of different groups, is better attended through indigenous teachers. In this point of view, the National Education Plan calls for the creation of specific programs in order to attend native schools as well as the creation of financing lines looking for an increase in education programs in native areas.

One of the goals in this National Education Plan is to professionalize and recognize, publicly, native teaching, giving preference to those teachers coming from their own communities and creating a specific teaching category. A second goal is increasing programs for a systematic native teacher education. The attempt to develop a special model native school represents a great novelty in Brazil's educational system, requiring a new vision of teacher training, apart from the regular official teaching system.

However, this change also requires responsible organizations and institutions to provide definitions about new dynamic actions, conceptions, and mechanisms, not only to incorporate these schools as part of the official teaching system but also to ensure that they are respected.

The challenge is that it is difficult to implement these requirements for teachers in the interior and poorer regions of the country, especially at the primary levels of education, while seeking to guarantee the quality of education that these schools will provide. The NEL tried to enforce these measures in the so-called Decade of Education (1997–2007), the purpose of which was to admit only teachers with higher education or with supervised teacher training (Article 87). This last requirement can substitute, in extraordinary circumstances and taking into consideration the enormous disparities that exist in a huge country like Brazil, the requirement of higher education for teaching in primary schools, as long as candidates have received the benefit of teacher education at the secondary school level (*Curso Normal*, as described in Article 62).

It must be observed that although these requirements aimed at improving and standardizing teaching and education, as far as possible, it also led to a race for postgraduate degrees from any institution as a means of improving careers without necessarily improving skills or qualifications. The fact that there is a lack of government control over the quality of these institutions and the specialization courses they offer has created a perverse phenomenon: although the law is observed, the result is a higher number of unqualified teachers.

At all levels of teaching, the NEL guarantees teachers the right to participate in the elaboration of pedagogic plans of their school. At the same time, the NEL demands commitment by teachers in the implementation of the plan and results, which include full dedication to planning, assessment, and continuous professional development as well as participation in the parents and teacher associations.

In addition, Article 206 of the Constitution highlights the "appreciation of the value of teaching professionals." In this way, Article 206 guarantees, in accordance with the law, career plans for public school teachers, with a professional minimum salary and admittance exclusively by means of public entrance examinations consisting of tests and presentation of academic and professional credentials.

Teacher Rights in Private Schools

Along with the rights identified previously, teachers in private schools are protected against arbitrary dismissal without just cause. Moreover, these teachers are entitled to unemployment benefits in the event of involuntary unemployment, to severance pay, to a minimum basic salary, to the maintenance of salaries when not under negotiations, and to receive notice of dismissal at least thirty days in advance.

Labor laws establish that the national minimum wage can be paid proportionally to the number of hours worked. Even so, teachers have a special working day that comprises four consecutive hours or six alternate hours (Article 318 of the Labor Law). Thus, private schools are not allowed to pay teachers proportionally to their working hours; teachers are entitled to receive the integral minimum wage.[1]

Teachers are also entitled to retirement pensions after 25 years of contributions to government pension funds for female teachers and 30 years for male teachers, at the ages of 60 and 65, respectively. Moreover, teachers are provided with occupational accident insurance paid by their employers, without excluding the employers' liability for indemnity in the event of malice or fault; with child benefits up to six years of age; with the right to be a member of a teachers' union, and with the right to receive the benefits agreed on with the unions.[2] Teachers who have disabilities are protected against discrimination with respect to wages and hiring criteria. Of course, equal rights are guaranteed for both tenured and non-tenured teachers.

It must be mentioned that the private education sector has grown stronger in comparison to the public education sector in terms of organization, infrastructure, and quality. From 1930 until 1988, it could be said that the State did not make education a priority as a public service. To the contrary, the State acted in favor of the private sector, even transferring public resources, to the detriment of the public sector (with some exceptions in the public primary and secondary schools and higher education, as in the state of São Paulo). This was a corollary of a public policy that the government adopted in the 1930s when the State assumed the role of the main actor in the promotion of economic development. This attitude on the part of the government also encouraged the proliferation of private schools, allowing the government to invest public resources in areas other than education. The military government maintained such an educational policy into the late 1960s and 1970s.

The Constitution of 1988 changed the picture considerably, especially in the public sector. By sharing responsibilities in public education through the allocation of specific incumbencies to each level of government and by creating new ways of funding education, the State reassumed its responsibilities for education. In fact, since Constitutional Amendment 14 was enacted in 1996, all three levels of government—federal, state, and municipal—are obliged to allocate 60% of their resources of two temporary funds (Fund for the Maintenance and Development of Fundamental Education (FUNDEF) and the recent Fund for the Maintenance and Development of Basic Education (FUNDEB), which extinguished the first; cf. Law 11.274/07) for better salaries for public school teachers.

The Constitution also abolished part of the former civil servant privileges in 1988 and again in 1998 and 2003 in Constitutional Amendments 19 and 41. However, Article 213 allowed public resources to continue to be transferred to private schools under specified conditions but limited this approach to not-for-profit and philanthropic schools. In Article 209 the Constitution reaffirmed that teaching is open to private enterprises, provided that the following conditions are met: compliance with the general rules of national education, authorization, and evaluation of quality by the Government.

Teacher Rights in Public Schools

Public school teachers come under the constitutional regime as civil servants in terms of employment rights with certain exceptions. This means that as a general rule, careers, salaries, professional statutes, and benefits are established by law, not by contract. As a consequence, this makes changes much slower and the whole system less flexible for public school teachers when compared with their counterparts in private schools.

On the other hand, benefits for public school teachers tend to be more ample, despite the administrative reforms of the Constitution of 1988 and the complex nature of the employment laws, especially where salaries are concerned. This complexity is due to the constant amendments to the law based on union pressure rather than on account of long-term career planning. Consequently, public school teachers are admitted to positions only through qualifying examinations, a rule stipulated by all former constitutions, with no exceptions, which entitles applicants to tenured positions after three years of teaching. During probationary periods, teacher dismissal is an administrative decision that calls for due process. Once teachers gain tenure, they can only be dismissed by a judicial decision, which represents a big legal advantage in terms of quality requirements in education when compared to the period prior to the 1988 Constitution, when teachers held lifelong tenure and permanence in their positions, making dismissals very difficult even when called for.

In terms of retirement, the situation is very different when compared to teachers in private schools since primary and secondary public school teachers can retire earlier, at 55 and 60 years of age for women and men, respectively, and after 20 and 25 years of contributing to government pension funds for female and male teachers, respectively; this is five years fewer than in the private schools. This benefit is extended to teachers who serve in administrative positions or in pedagogic activities such as supervision and coordination.

Public school teachers are also allowed a remunerated accumulation of two teaching offices or one teaching office with another technical or scientific office; the accumulation of public offices is forbidden by the Constitution as a general rule (Article 37, XVI). In this respect, the jurisprudence of Brazilian courts prevails today, allowing for this exception as long as there is a compatibility of working hours between the two jobs.[3]

Another aspect of the NEL which deserves some comment is the decentralization of the administration of public schools. This is an innovation in the Brazilian Administrative Law, especially in the public school system. Prior to the enactment of the NEL, administration was highly centralized in the hands of government entities such as state and municipal secretaries of education, a heritage of the legislation issued during the military dictatorship. Currently, Article

15 of the NEL allows educators in primary and secondary schools to practice a limited degree of autonomy in academic and administrative decision making. Together with this decentralization, Article 14 of the NEL demands that teachers participate in the elaboration of the pedagogic directives of their schools. Both of these measures—administrative decentralization and increased pedagogic participation—have greatly increased the rights of teachers.

Conclusion

According to the Brazilian Institute of Statistics and to the Ministry of Education, the Brazilian population was 188 million in 2006. Of that number, 25% were children enrolled in basic education—an average of 42 million students between the ages of 7 to 15 in fundamental education—and 9.8 million, between the ages of 15 to 18, were in secondary education. In higher education, the average is 3% of the population enrolled in undergraduate and postgraduate programs. In 40 years, the Brazilian population is expected to top 268 million. Thus, the roles of the State and of teachers are crucial in this educational scenario.

As can be seen, legislation concerning the rights of public school teachers in Brazil is much more complex than that in private schools. However, there is no guarantee of better quality in teaching for many reasons, such as the lack of adequate infrastructure, violence in the outskirts and centers of big cities, individuals holding more than one teaching job, mental and emotional stress from the job, and lack of teacher dedication. Unfortunately, years in service are seen merely as a means to retirement and not as a fulfilling working experience for many teachers.

In spite of the advances achieved by the Constitution of 1988 and the NEL, it is clearly necessary to face the difficult task of revising the career plans and structures for public school teachers, working schedules, and promotions and benefits in an attempt to de-bureaucratize and rationalize the system that is so full of inherited legal details and privileges that no longer serve a purpose. Some measures in this direction suggested by public school administrators are a combination of years of service, academic qualifications, and assessments based on learning results such as criteria for benefits and promotions to reduce absenteeism (one of the biggest problems in public schools), increased dedication, and motivation among teachers.

The general panorama of public education in Brazil is characterized by the lack of policies in human resources, with some exceptions. For example, leaders in some states, such as Rio Grande do Sul, Tocantins, and the capital Brasília, have taken steps toward drastic reforms in the public teaching careers.

Broadly speaking, the lack of administrative policies is due to negotiations between the government and the strongest teachers' unions, in which a variety of often-conflicting interests are at play. In circumstances such as these, the government usually reacts to the pressures and increases teacher privileges merely to maintain this public service without a clear reform plan in mind. Recently, the federal government announced a new education plan, trying to enforce some of the measures mentioned above, although such serious structural problems cannot be solved with a wave of a magic wand. Continuity of government policies in the field of education, once they have been set into motion, is fundamental.

These are some of the major problems that the rapidly expanding Brazilian educational system faces. If leaders fail to address these problems, then further difficulties in equity, finance, and access will only multiply. This is a phenomenon that is not limited to the area of education but is but one of the outcomes of the developmental conditions of the Brazilian State.

Bibliography

Azanha, J. M. (1995). *Educação:Temas Polêmicos.* São Paulo: Ed. Martins Fontes.

Boaventura, E. (1997). *A Educação Brasileira e o Direito.* Salvador: Ed. Ciências Jurídicas.

Bresser Pereira, L. C. (1997). *A Reforma do Estado dos Anos 90: Lógica e Mecanismos de Controle.* Cadernos MARE da Reforma do Estado. Brasília: Ministério da Administração e Reforma do Estado, v. 1.

Brzezinski, I. (1997). *LDB Interpretada: Diversos Olhares se Entrecruzam.* São Paulo: Cortez Editora.

Comparato, Fábio K. (1997). *Juízo de Constituição de Políticas Públicas. Estudos em Homenagem a Geraldo Ataliba.* São Paulo: Malheiros, pp. 343–59.

Coombs, P. H. (1985). *A Crise Mundial da Educação.* São Paulo: Ed. Perspectiva.

Fávero, O. (1996). *A Educação nas Constituintes Brasileiras (1823–1988).* Campinas: Ed. Autores Associados.

Goldemberg, J. (1993). *A Educação no Brasil.* São Paulo: Instituto de Estudos Avançados da Universidade de São Paulo, Série Educação para a Cidadania, no. 3.

Luzuriaga, L. (1959). *História da Educação Pública.* São Paulo: Cia. Editora Nacional.

Mello, G. (1990). *Social Democracia e Educação: Teses para Discussão.* São Paulo: Cortez Editora.

Moura Castro, C. (1994). *Educação Brasileira—Consertos e Remendos.* São Paulo, Rocco.

Ranieri, N. (2000). *Educação Superior, Direito e Estado.* São Paulo: Edusp.

Ranieri, N. (2003). *Federalismo Cooperativo e Garantia de Padrão de Qualidade do Ensino. O Caso Dos Estabelecimentos de Educação Infantil Jurisdicionados ao Sistema*

Escolar do Estado de São Paulo. São Paulo: Revista da Faculdade de Direito da Universidade de São Paulo, fascículo no. 98.

Sifuentes, M. (2000). *O Acesso ao Ensino Fundamental no Brasil: Um Direito ao Desenvolvimento.* Rio de Janeiro: América Jurídica.

Notes

1. Brazilian Superior Labor Court. *Tribunal Superior do Trabalho, Case 1438/2005-026-07-00.2,* Judge Barros Levenhagen. Published in the *Official Journal of Justice,* June 8, 2007.

2. Brazilian Superior Court of Justice. *Case No. 461.008/PB,* Judge Felix Fischer. Published in the *Official Journal of Justice,* April 16, 2007; p. 269.

3. Brazilian Superior Court of Justice. *Writ of Mandamus No. 11.566/DF,* Judge Arnaldo Esteves Lima. Published in the *Official Journal of Justice,* April 16, 2007; p. 165.

4

Canada

Greg M. Dickinson

Introduction[1]

Canada is a federation of ten provinces and three territories.[2] A sparse but highly pluralistic populace of approximately 33 million is spread across almost 10 million square kilometers. Its population tends to be concentrated in urban areas. Four Canadian cities have populations of approximately 1 million or more people.[3]

As a federation, Canada is governed by a federal constitution, an important feature of which is its distribution of legislative authority among the provincial and territorial legislative assemblies and the federal parliament. This distribution of powers has remained effectively intact since confederation in 1867 when the British North America Act, 1867 (renamed the Constitution Act, 1867 in 1982 when the Constitution was patriated from the United Kingdom) listed subject matter within the exclusive legislative jurisdiction of the provinces and the federal parliament.

For present purposes it is sufficient to know that education was such a centrally important issue in nineteenth-century Upper and Lower Canada (Ontario and Quebec) as to warrant a specific provision in the Constitution Act, 1867. Section 93 of the Act provides that the provinces have the exclusive right to legislate in matters of education, subject to the rights of denominational schools (now effectively Roman Catholic Separate Schools), which may not be negatively affected by provincial legislation or administrative action. Federal power in education is limited to a remedial or residual function.

There are, then, ten separate provincial systems of education (and three territorial ones)[4] in Canada and no national or federal ministry or even office of education. Education or school acts passed by the provincial legislatures, and regulations made by the executive branches of the provincial governments, are the central legal instruments of control. Other laws of general application, such as child welfare legislation, labor acts, employment rights legislation, and human rights codes, can have an important impact on education and schooling, especially in the area of teachers' rights.

Provincial education systems are typically arranged so that governance is shared between a central or provincial ministry of education and elected local school boards or districts. In some provinces local school or parent councils may play greater or lesser roles. The ministry of education typically issues various instruments of control in the nature of guidelines, memoranda, circulars, and the like. Its most powerful source of control is, of course, through its grip on the fiscal lever: in all provinces the lion's share of school funding flows from provincial coffers. School boards typically exercise administrative control at the local level through the bylaws, resolutions, policies, and directives they issue.

In any federated state of this sort, it becomes problematic to discuss legislative and administrative arrangements, which can vary widely across constituent jurisdictions. While there is a good deal of uniformity across the Canadian provinces' educational systems, for historical and other reasons, there are also some significant differences. Notably, Quebec's distinct cultural, social, and political experience has lent its institutions their own particular flavor. Further, while the rest of the country follows English common law, Quebec is governed by a Civil Code, a remnant of its Napoleonic heritage. In a chapter of this scope, it is impossible to do more than point out the general modes and some significant differences across the jurisdictions in relation to the issues discussed. Thankfully, Quebec aside, the congruencies greatly outnumber the differences.

This chapter emphasizes that educational governance in Canada is very much a provincial matter, and a significant event in 1982 strengthened the potential for a national legal influence on education. Even so, probably the most central, and certainly the best-known, feature of the Constitution Act, 1982 is the Canadian Charter of Rights and Freedoms, an entrenched bill of rights and freedoms that applies not only to the federal legislative and administrative spheres but also to provincial governments' laws and administrative actions. Hence, the Charter rights and freedoms as interpreted by the courts (ultimately the Supreme Court of Canada) can play a major role in lending education a national profile.

For the purposes of this chapter, it is important to note the Charter's guarantees of the traditional civil liberties of freedom of religion (s. 2(a)) and expression (s. 2(b)) as well as the right to equality without discrimination (s. 15). It is also noteworthy that the Charter does not protect economic rights per se, and thus its impact in matters involving financial interests (including employment matters) can be constrained. Nevertheless, the Charter is a formidable legal document: section 52 of the Constitution Act, 1982 provides that the Charter is the supreme law of Canada and any law (federal or provincial) that is inconsistent with it is of no force or effect to the extent of that inconsistency. Other federal acts that, due to their national application, impact school systems and teachers across Canada include the Criminal Code, the Youth Criminal Justice Act, and the Copyright Act.

Employment Rights of Teachers

Entry into the Profession

All Canadian provinces and territories place restrictions on who can teach in public schools by requiring individuals to have a teaching certificate, license, or other credential mandated usually by regulation by the government itself or by a self-governing professional body such as a college of teachers. In Ontario, for example, teacher accreditation is governed by a regulation made under the authority of the Ontario College of Teachers Act. Entry into the profession in Canada requires completion of a university degree or diploma program (whether consecutive or concurrent) in education at an accredited institution.

The majority of provinces also have provisions whereby temporary licenses may be granted on an exigency basis in cases where qualified teachers are unavailable. As well, the provinces have entered interprovincial accreditation agreements under which interim certificates or licenses will be granted to teachers trained in another province. Mobility rights under the Canadian Charter of Rights and Freedoms guarantee Canadians the right to move freely throughout the country and pursue a livelihood in any province, although the provinces retain the right to place reasonable restrictions on the entry into professions and other kinds of work.

Most, if not all, provinces require new entrants to the profession to complete a criminal record check to ensure that their backgrounds do not suggest any threat to the welfare of children. Canadian citizenship is no longer a precondition for membership in either a college of teachers or teachers' federation or for employment by a school board, although teachers who are not Canadian citizens must secure Canadian employment authorization from the federal government.[5]

The Hiring Process

Teachers are typically hired and employed by local school boards or districts or, in some provinces or posts, by the provincial government. Although they usually have individual contracts of employment, virtually all teachers in public schools are unionized. As such, the employment rights and obligations of teachers are almost exclusively governed by collective agreements between their unions and their employers, whether the provinces themselves or local school boards. Most collective agreements contain provisions regarding hiring protocols, including first-call rights for teachers who have been declared surplus or redundant, although much of the hiring process is outside the collective agreement insofar as applicants are generally not members of bargaining units until they have been hired.

Hiring policies and practices, including advertisements and interviews, must conform to provincial human rights codes that prohibit both direct and systemic discrimination based on sex, sexual orientation, race, ethnicity, disability, age, and other grounds. Many school boards have policies of affirmative action committing them to an attempt to have their teaching forces reflect the diversity of their students and communities. Under Canadian law, provincial human rights codes, and the Charter, such affirmative action or special programs put in place to remediate past exclusionary practices are exempt from claims of reverse discrimination.[6]

Conversely, human rights codes typically permit special interest organizations, such as private schools, to hire or give preferential treatment in advancement to employees who are representative of their clientele so long as such a distinction represents a bona fide occupational requirement as determined by Canadian case law. This generally means that a qualification must be honest and objectively reasonable in the sense of being reasonably required to carry out the aims and goals peculiar to an organization. Moreover, in some provinces Roman Catholic separate schools routinely have policies giving preference to Roman Catholics when it comes to hiring or promotion. The denominational rights conferred on such schools in some provinces under s. 93 of the Constitution Act, 1867 insulate them from claims of unlawful discrimination.[7]

Collective Bargaining

As mentioned, for all intents and purposes, all teachers in public schools in Canada belong to bargaining units certified under provincial labor legislation.[8] Teachers in private schools are far less apt to be unionized.[9] Public school teacher unions bargain either locally, with school boards,[10] or centrally, with the provinces,[11] or, in some provinces, bargaining takes place with both entities, depending on the issue, for example, working conditions as opposed to salary and benefits.[12]

Labor legislation typically provides for check-off fee payments which are authorized in virtually all collective agreements. Even though the right to freedom of association under the Canadian Charter of Rights and Freedoms guarantees the right to organize and belong to a labor union, the Supreme Court of Canada has held that this does not extend to guaranteeing a right to bargain collectively or a right to withdraw services via a work-to-rule or full strike.[13]

During a major reform of Ontario's education governance structure in the late 1990s, the government removed principals and vice-principals from the teacher bargaining units to which they had belonged. The reforming legislation left them outside their former unions and unable to form their own. A constitutional challenge failed: following the Supreme Court of Canada's jurisprudence mentioned above, the Ontario Court of Appeal found that the Charter guaranteed the principals' right to be voluntary members of the Ontario Teachers' Federation (OTF) but did not guarantee the right to have the OTF bargain on their behalf, and it did not grant them the right to form a union of their own with whom local boards were required to bargain under the Labour Relations Act.[14] Conversely, courts have also maintained that the Charter does not grant teachers the right to refuse to belong to a bargaining unit based on political or philosophical objection or to be exempt from a collective agreement's check-off provision.[15]

Evaluation and Promotion

Newly hired teachers are typically given probationary status, ranging usually from one (for example, in Ontario) to three (for example, in New Brunswick) years. Evaluation cycles and procedures are normally delineated in legislation or collective agreements or in both. In Ontario, for instance, Regulation 99/02, Teacher Performance Appraisal, provides detailed mandatory rules for conducting appraisals of new teachers during their probationary period. The rules, which may be augmented but not supplanted by local board policies and procedures, heed basic rules of procedural fairness and natural justice.

Performance appraisal must thus test the competencies set out in the regulation and board policies; include a classroom observation by the principal; be conducted according to the guidelines issued by the Minister of Education and the policies, methods, timelines, etc. established by the local board; include a meeting between the teacher and the principal in preparation for a classroom observation; include a meeting between the teacher and the principal after the observation to review the results (satisfactory, unsatisfactory, development needed) and to discuss other matters, including participation in the teacher induction program; and include preparation of a summative report setting out the principal's evaluation, overall performance rating, and the reasons therefore.

Based on Regulation 99/02, ss. 15–16, the teacher is entitled to a signed copy of the report within twenty days and may request a meeting with the principal to discuss the performance appraisal.

Continuing or permanent teachers may also be subject to periodic appraisal and mandatory continuing education requirements. Again, these requirements and the modes of carrying them out, depending on the province, are contained in statutes, regulations, and collective agreements. To continue with the Ontario example, the evaluation cycle for teachers other than new teachers is five consecutive years, and each teacher must have one evaluation year in each evaluation cycle pursuant to Regulation 99/02, s. 4. Principals must notify teachers within twenty days of the beginning of the school year if that year is to be an evaluation year.

Teachers must receive at least one performance appraisal, conducted by their principals, during each of their evaluation years. The general requirements for conducting the appraisals are virtually identical to those described above for new teachers and thus also conform to basic fairness principles, although the stipulated standards vary as noted in Regulation 99/02, ss. 5–8. It needs to be reiterated that the appraisal process can vary significantly by province and that collective agreements and local school board policies can also have considerable influence on the process.

Teachers' Freedoms and Privacy Rights

Freedom of Religion

Freedom of religion is guaranteed under s. 2(a) of the Canadian Charter of Rights and Freedoms. The issue of teachers' religious freedom in public non-Catholic education has arisen in a number of contexts, including, but not limited to, mandatory religious opening exercises;[16] mandatory religious instruction;[17] a board's refusal to grant paid leave to a Jewish teacher for Yom Kippur;[18] a demand that Muslim holy days be accommodated in a school calendar;[19] accommodation of the wearing of Sikh religious garb and symbols by pupils and teachers;[20] a teacher's voicing religious convictions about the immorality of homosexuality;[21] and teachers voicing their belief, partly based on religion, in an international Zionist conspiracy.[22] The chapter returns to three of these cases in its discussion of freedom of expression.

Freedom of Religion in Roman Catholic Schools

Roman Catholic schools, though part of the system of public schools in three provinces, enjoy special constitutional status and hence special religious or denominational rights that are not possessed by either public or private schools, except to the extent, as discussed above, that the latter can invoke bona fide occupational requirements as reasons for what otherwise would be discriminatory treatment of teachers and other staff. The denominational rights conferred on Roman Catholic Separate Schools in 1867 permit them to require not only that teachers be Roman Catholic but also that they conform to church doctrine both in and out of school.

As a matter of law at least, the privacy rights of teachers, especially insofar as they touch religious matters, are far more constrained than those of their colleagues who teach in non-Catholic public schools. For instance, in *Caldwell v. Stuart,*[23] the Supreme Court of Canada noted that insofar as it was a bona fide occupational requirement for a Catholic school board to demand its teachers follow Catholic doctrine regarding marriage and divorce, it was lawful for the board to dismiss a teacher who married a divorced person in a civil ceremony. Although this was a private Catholic school, the dicta apply to public Catholic schools.[24]

It should be noted, however, that s. 93 denominational rights, where they exist, are not equivalent to a blank check to discriminate. The courts have determined that each case must be investigated on its own facts to evaluate whether the matter in question was truly a guaranteed denominational right, one going to the heart of the school system's very existence, or whether it was just a non-denominational aspect of a denominational right, which would not be protected.[25] Consideration of when non-denominational aspects of a denominationally protected right are legally permissible involves examining whether they are bona fide occupational requirements.[26]

Freedom of Expression

Teachers' speech, or "expression," as it is constitutionally termed in Canada,[27] can occur either inside or outside school. The former, where it is contentious, implicates academic freedom, while the latter tends to speak more to teachers' privacy rights. However, it is not always clear, even when teachers are expressing themselves outside school (in a temporal and spatial sense) whether the law considers them to be speaking in a public or private capacity.[28]

Cases of alleged violations of academic freedom are relatively rare in Canada. It is generally assumed, but not universally so,[29] that academic freedom exists at colleges and universities but that teachers at the first two levels of schooling are expected to abide by the curriculum guidelines supplied and approved by the province and school board and to teach and model the values contained therein.[30]

A question thus arises if teachers choose to deliver the curriculum using a form of pedagogy or curricular materials that their superiors deem inappropriate. This issue came to the fore in *Morin v. Prince Edward Island,*[31] in which a second-year probationary teacher was effectively dismissed for showing the documentary film *Thy Kingdom Come, Thy Will Be Done* to his grade-nine language arts class contrary to the instructions of his vice-principal and principal. The film had generated parental complaints because it dealt with religious fundamentalism and was deemed inappropriate for grade-nine-age children. An internal appeal determined that the film was age appropriate but that the teacher could screen it only if his lesson preparation met the approval of the principal and school superintendent.

The ensuing controversy eventually resulted in the teacher's being granted a temporary leave of absence with pay until the end of the school year, but he was not rehired. The teacher brought an action against the school board for, among other things, breach of his freedom of expression rights under the Charter. Ultimately, the Prince Edward Island Court of Appeal accepted the argument that Morin's use of the film and his class preparation were both "expression" within the meaning of section 2(b) of the Charter[32] and the school's attempt to limit this freedom was not reasonable or justified.

The Court was of the opinion that the teacher was attempting to deal with religion as an important societal element and his teaching was consistent with the approved curriculum. Moreover, the Court asserted that the students had a right to hear and benefit from this expression. Although the teacher had claimed $350,000 in damages relating to his loss of employment and the ensuing breakdown of his marriage, the Court awarded him $15,000 for the violation of his freedom of expression rights.

Cases where teachers' contentious expression occurs "out of school" are more numerous and more problematic for a variety of reasons, two in particular. First, one would think that what teachers do or say in their out-of-school time should not be the business of either their professional governing bodies or their employers. Second, one might assume that the causal nexus between their words or actions and the school system's (and its constituents') well-being would be far more tenuous if they occurred at school. Nonetheless, three cases briefly disclose that, in the courts' view, the nature of teaching as a profession and a public occupation means that, in essence, when fundamental values and interests are at stake, teachers are never "off duty" but are subject to public and hence judicial scrutiny.

In *Ross v. New Brunswick School District No. 15,*[33] a high school mathematics teacher was notorious in the community for his anti-Semitic views even though he never voiced them at school. Nonetheless, the Supreme Court of Canada upheld the teacher's removal from the classroom because his views, though expressed out of school, poisoned the school environment and infringed on the equality rights of Jewish students.

The Supreme Court of Canada declared that the teacher's expression was protected under section 2(b) of the Charter. However, the Court interpreted the teacher's speech as so inimical to the fundamental egalitarian and multicultural values at the heart of the school system that limiting his right of expression was reasonable and justified under section 1 of the Charter, which provides that all rights and freedoms in the Charter are subject to such reasonable limits prescribed by law as can be demonstrably justified in a free and democratic society. The Court stopped short of condoning a gag order placed on the teacher by a human rights tribunal that would have led to his dismissal from his non-classroom teaching position if he continued to voice his anti-Semitism.

In a subsequent but slightly different case,[34] the British Columbia Court of Appeal upheld a teacher/counselor's suspension by the British Columbia College of Teachers for conduct unbecoming a member. The writings made it clear that the plaintiff considered homosexuality to be moral depravity that he, as a teacher and counselor, could not condone, let alone celebrate: "I refuse to be a false teacher saying that promiscuity is acceptable, perversion is normal, and immorality is simply 'cultural diversity' of which we should be proud."[35] The Court rejected the plaintiff's argument that the discipline he was subjected to infringed on his freedoms of religion and expression under the Charter.

While this was a complex case involving considerable Charter jurisprudence, the Court's reasoning can be reduced for present purposes to the following conclusion: while the plaintiff's freedom of expression was infringed, the infringement was reasonable and justified under section 1 of the Charter because he chose to express his views, albeit outside school, in his professional as opposed to personal capacity. In his writings the plaintiff clearly identified himself as a teacher and a counselor, thus tying his views to his profession and employment.

The Court drew heavily on the Supreme Court of Canada's dicta in *Ross*[36] to infer that the plaintiff's conduct harmed the environment for gay students as well as the reputations of his profession and school system. The Court explained that the State's interest in ensuring an equal, tolerant, and discrimination-free school environment; protecting students (especially those who are gay and lesbian) from such discriminatory speech; and upholding the integrity of and trust in the teaching profession and school system as nondiscriminatory institutions overrode the plaintiff's freedom of expression. The Court concluded that intolerant discriminatory speech was far from the core of expression protected under the Charter.

Finally, in a case that is perhaps the epitome of the extent of the State's interest in, if not outright intrusion into, the private lives of teachers, *Abbotsford School District 34 v. Shewan* (*Shewan*), a husband and wife who taught for the same board were disciplined after he sent pictures of his semi-nude wife to a "men's" magazine which published them in a section entitled "Girl Next Door Amateur Erotic Photo Contest."[37] After the pictures came to their board's attention, the teachers were suspended without pay for six weeks, sparking considerable controversy in the community. An appeal to a Board of Reference resulted in the overturning of the suspension. The school board appealed to the British Columbia Supreme Court, which reinstated the suspensions but reduced them to one month. The Court of Appeal dismissed a final appeal by the teachers.

It should be noted that *Shewan* was not about constitutional rights: it was dealt with as a matter of just cause for discipline, specifically whether there had been misconduct sufficient to warrant a sanction under labor law, and, if so, whether the sanction was fitting. First, the Court found that misconduct worthy of sanction can occur off the job as well as on the job because of the position of trust, confidence, and responsibility held by teachers. The Court pointed out that misconduct, even though it occurred out of school, could cause a loss in public confidence, both in the teachers in question and in their school systems; a loss of respect by students for these and all teachers; and controversy in the school and community that disrupts the ability of the education system to carry out its functions properly.[38] The Court was clear that teachers are exemplars who must maintain standards of behavior that most other citizens need not because they lack the same public responsibility and trust.

To summarize this section and the attitude of the courts on questions of teachers' off-duty conduct, one can do no better than quote Justice Gerard La Forest, whose words capture well the delicate balance involved:

> Teachers occupy positions of trust and confidence and exert considerable influence over their students. They are in a very real sense "role models" for their students. As a result, it is not enough for teachers to merely "teach" these values. We also expect them to uphold them, and this may involve their activities both inside and outside the classroom. Needless to say, however, teachers, like other citizens, enjoy rights of privacy, and to a considerable extent their off-duty activities should not be subject to external scrutiny. However, if teachers, by their extra-curricular conduct, displace the trust and confidence that their communities place in them and thereby disrupt the educational experience of their students, society has an interest in intervening.[39]

And intervene society will, and with the courts' support, as the cases show evidence.

Teacher Sanctions and Due Process

Teachers in Canada are subject to a broad array of sanctions for conduct associated with the practice of their profession. Some sanctions are peculiar to the teaching profession and employment, while others are of general application. The latter include criminal and civil sanctions that would be applicable to any person who committed certain acts, such as an assault charge for striking a person without consent and without lawful justification (Criminal Code, s. 265) or an action for damages for breaching a duty of care and thereby causing injury and loss. Of greater interest in the present context are those sanctions that are directed specifically at teachers *qua* teachers.

It is useful to first understand that in Canada teacher sanctions can be imposed by at least three or four different entities within the education system: teacher governing bodies (colleges or federations); teachers' employers (provincial governments or school boards); and teachers' unions.

First, teachers' governing bodies, whether colleges of teachers or teachers' federations,[40] can sanction their members for a variety of reasons, the most common of which are breaches of rules of ethical or professional conduct. In Ontario professional misconduct is governed by Regulation 437/97 made under the Ontario College of Teachers Act. The College receives about 1,500 expressions of concern annually from members, school boards, and the general public, but fewer than 20 percent result in formal complaints. When complaints are initiated, an Investigation Committee looks into the facts and decides whether to dismiss a complaint, resolve it by alternative means (including mediation), or refer it to the fitness to practice or discipline committee.[41]

Hearings that discipline committees conduct must conform to administrative law principles of natural justice and fairness[42] as well as the Canadian Charter of Rights and Freedoms. Hearings are oral, with the right to representation by a lawyer, to call and examine witnesses, and to make arguments.

Committees must be unbiased and weigh the evidence, determine on a balance of probability whether a case has been made out, and reach a decision. Committees must provide written reasons supporting their decisions. Committees may choose to issue reprimands, order counseling, impose fines or conditions, or suspend or permanently revoke members' certificates of qualification. Committees may also order that their decisions be published in the College's periodical *Professionally Speaking*.[43] The decisions of such disciplinary tribunals are generally reviewable by the courts for errors in jurisdiction and mistakes of law. In some provinces an appeal on the merits may be taken to court.

The most common types of sanctions are those imposed by teachers' employers, usually school boards. The imposition of such job-related discipline is typically governed by the just cause provisions of collective agreements, which usually provide for warnings and remediation, where appropriate, before harsher steps are taken. Of course, where serious misconduct or a culminating incident has occurred, drastic sanctions usually ensue, including dismissal, the so-called "capital punishment" of employment law. This is often the case where a teacher's conduct involves serious moral turpitude, especially involving inappropriate relationships with students. In such cases, criminal charges and professional discipline routinely precede dismissal, although teachers are first removed from classrooms and assigned administrative duties pending the outcome of criminal charges.

The spectrum of employers' sanctions, ranging from the least to the most serious, includes warnings and reprimands (oral and written), transfers, suspensions, and dismissal or termination of contracts. Collective agreements routinely provide rights- grievance protocols that tend to follow a typical pattern: in-house discussion and settlement via an informal resolution process (which may have more than one step and move from informal to formal mediation) and, failing settlement, formal arbitration by a one- or three-person board appointed by agreement of the parties or by a provincial authority.

Under Canadian law, labor arbitrators are restricted to deciding only arbitrable matters, namely, to interpreting and applying the collective agreement, although they may use human rights legislation, including the Charter, in doing so. Arbitrators may find that there was just cause for the discipline or that there was no just cause; in the former instance, they may find that the discipline was either justified or unjustified in light of the facts. Arbitrators may substitute alternative sanctions if deemed appropriate. Although judicial review of arbitration awards is possible, considerable judicial deference is shown to arbitrators, given their unique position in having heard the evidence and their expertise in labor matters. Usually a standard of reasonableness is applied; courts apply a more rigorous standard of review of correctness when mistakes of law or misinterpretation or misapplication of human rights legislation are involved.

Finally, as members of unions, teachers may also be sanctioned for failure to comply with their unions' bylaws and other policies. For example, teachers who fail to support and participate in collective bargaining action by failing to picket or even by crossing a picket line to go in to work during a strike may suffer formal sanctions that include, among other things, losing union support for any employer discipline they might face in the future; losing their entitlement to union-provided benefits, scholarships, or awards; and losing the entitlement to seek and hold union office. Needless to say, in professional communities the most significant sanctions are often informal: loss of the cooperation and collegiality of one's fellow teachers, if not outright ostracism.

Emerging Issues

A discussion of emerging issues in teachers' rights in Canada could constitute a chapter of its own, if not a book. Although this section examines two issues—(1) parental harassment, cyber-bullying, and cyber-libel, and (2) teacher safety in the classroom—there are many others, including (but not limited to) religious accommodation, class size and teaching loads (including attempts to make extracurricular participation mandatory), mandatory continuing professional education and periodic teacher testing, ever-increasing integration of pupils with special needs into regular classrooms with declining financial resources for teacher aides and other support, and teacher burnout and retention. Moreover, the substantial increase in the proportion of part-time teacher contracts in recent years has had a significant impact on teachers' rights insofar as part-time teachers typically have fewer rights and remedies than full-time teachers have.

Parental Harassment, Cyber-Bullying, and Cyber-Libel

Teachers have always had trouble with parents, and vice versa. This is unsurprising, given the intermediary position of students, whose best interests both parties claim to be serving. However, there has been a growing sense that the "trouble" of the past, sporadic and mostly benign in nature, has grown in both incidence and intensity.

In their book devoted to the topic, Keel and Tymochenko[44] point out that there are several reasons for this growth in parent–teacher friction: changing social and economic conditions; rapid educational reforms; expectations (often unrealistic) regarding special needs and gifted students; increasingly numerous and volatile child custody battles that usually, one way or another, end up visiting schools; and fewer specialized institutions and services for people with mental and emotional problems.[45] Consequently, more and more teachers face verbal, physical, telephone, written, and Internet harassment.

The seriousness of online harassment and defamation is exacerbated by the potential reach of the Internet[46] as well as the countless ways that technology can be used to manipulate and distort words and images and create false realities. Teachers and administrators have had to bring suits against parents to enjoin them from continuing to harass and defame them, either in person or on Websites.

Educators have also had to attempt to have Website providers shut down sites on which embarrassing and defamatory claims, statements, or pictures have been posted.[47] Where providers refuse to cooperate, the only recourse appears to be an application for an injunction to force sites to be shut down.

Even then, jurisdictional disputes can arise, as can claims of interference with free speech and expression. Further, the extent to which defamatory online communication can even be considered libel under Canadian law is far from settled,[48] although, as discussed below, some courts have awarded damages against the person posting libelous messages. Still, in large part, these are mostly uncharted legal waters, leaving teachers with little solace. Moreover, taking legal action against online assailants assumes the ability to identify perpetrators, something that is often difficult, if not impossible.

The most dramatic example to date of teachers invoking civil litigation to deal with defamatory material posted on the Internet is *Newman v. Halstead.*[49] *Newman* arose in British Columbia, where a mother sent emails that falsely accused nine teachers of violence toward students, unprofessional conduct, incompetence, bullying, and being the kind of people who associate with pedophiles. The mother also posted negative statements about the plaintiffs in chat rooms and on bulletin boards and a Website she created.

The British Columbia Supreme Court ruled the statements and pictures posted by the defendant were defamatory, after applying the test that they lowered the plaintiffs in the eyes of a reasonable observer. The Court awarded damages ranging from $15,000 to $150,000 and totaling more than $600,000 to the plaintiffs. The Court also awarded punitive damages of $50,000. Although it was unlikely that the defendant had the financial wherewithal to satisfy the awards, the issuing of an injunction preventing her from making further libelous statements provided a measure of relief for the plaintiffs, along with the publicity associated with their having won the case.

Where harassment is face to face or over the telephone, remedies appear somewhat more accessible and effective. For example, in one case of telephone harassment in which a parent was placing up to fifteen calls per day to a superintendent and school staff, a court granted an application for a restraining order.[50] Victims of telephone harassment can also contact the police, who can lay charges under section 372(3) of the Criminal Code of Canada.

Cases of harassment that have involved parents' physical attendance at school have been dealt with by the courts under criminal, education, and trespass legislation. For example, in *R. v. Day,*[51] discussed in Luft,[52] a parent was convicted under both the Criminal Code of Canada and the Newfoundland Schools Act with interfering with the use, operation, and enjoyment of school property and interrupting, obstructing, and interfering with a school by refusing to leave her child's class after being repeatedly asked to do so.

Recognizing that not only students pose increasing threats of violence and disruption at school, Ontario issued its Access to School Premises Regulation in 2000 as part of its safe schools reforms.[53] In *Martin v. Conseil des Ecoles Catholiques de Langue Francaise du Centre-Est,*[54] a court granted a school

principal considerable deference in using the regulation to ban a disruptive and abusive parent from the school premises, notwithstanding that the parent was the president of the school council. As noted elsewhere in commenting on this case, "if the court's admonition to [the parent] in this case [was] insufficient to deter parents who might be inclined to follow his aggressive and confrontational style of dealing with school personnel, perhaps its award of costs of $39,000 against him will be."[55]

This kind of case poses particularly difficult issues in light of the educational system's encouragement of parental involvement at school, the evidence that suggests its beneficial impact on the child's learning, and the sheer extent of parental presence at schools. It is obviously a question of degree and determining the point at which benefit becomes hindrance and then harassment.

Teacher Safety and Refusal to Work

Perhaps it is trite to say that Canada has not escaped the fallout of Columbine and subsequent school shootings in the United States. However, education law conferences; symposia; articles; and courses, pre-service, in-service, and graduate, in Canada have been preoccupied with the topic of safe schools, or at least one or more dimensions of it, for several years. What is more, public discourse, especially in the media, and hence political discourse have been equally and morbidly fascinated by the topic.

It is open to debate whether schools are safe, because safety is a relative term: reliable statistics are scarce, if not absent, and it is likely that schools are safer than most, if not all, other social places.[56] In fact, it is equally likely that more children are killed or injured within their own homes than they are at school. However, the issue here is not student safety at school but a spin-off of that topic: teacher safety.

In the wake of a multitude of school violence cases in the United States and Canada, some involving the deaths of teachers, it is understandable that teachers would add to their already long list of stressors that they might be subjected to violent students. In the minds of many teachers, they are increasingly being saddled with responsibility for the welfare and care of more and more difficult-to-serve students, while at the same time being exposed to more and more personal jeopardy, legally and physically, in their interactions with them.

The three major Ontario teacher federations[57] commissioned a survey in 2005 on the bullying of their members at school. The survey found that aggressive behavior by students was the most common form of bullying of teachers. Thirty-six percent of the 1,217 respondents reported they had been the victims of student bullying.[58] The bullying took the form of class disruptions or disrespectful behavior (82%); having personal property vandalized (41%); repeated physical assaults or threats (27%); persistent verbal abuse (16%); racial, sexual, or religious slurs (11%); and repeated attempts to intimidate (10%). Fewer than one per cent reported bullying via e-mail or the Internet.[59] As a result of the survey, the Elementary Teachers' Federation of Ontario sought an amendment to the provisions of Ontario's Employment Standards Act and Occupational Health and Safety Act to protect teachers against violence and psychological harassment.[60]

Some have argued that the Occupational Health and Safety Act already potentially permits teachers to refuse to work where their safety is in jeopardy. However, Nolan, Trépanier, and Elleker[61] point out that since teachers' rights under that legislation are subordinate to their duties under the Education Act, "a teacher cannot effect a work refusal if doing so would abdicate the teacher's responsibilities to ensure the health and safety, not only of the student who is acting violently, but also of the other students in the class."[62] In addition to seeking an amendment to the Act to buttress teachers' right to refuse to work, the teachers' union may attempt to negotiate collective agreement provisions that afford teacher refusal-to-work protections similar to those given other workers under the Act.[63]

Conclusion

The rights of teachers are constrained more than those of other professionals and employees because of the large degree of public responsibility and trust reposed in teachers. Even so, the rights of teachers are considerable under Canadian law. These rights are protected under provincial statutes and regulations, both specific to education and of general application, as well as under collective bargaining agreements between their unions and employers, whether a local school board or a province, and the common law. Moreover, the Canadian Charter of Rights and Freedoms, with its national application, provides all teachers in Canada with the same constitutional rights, except to the extent that denominational education rights exist in some provinces but not others.

Table of Legislation

Canadian Charter of Rights and Freedoms, Part 1 of the *Constitution Act, 1982*, being Schedule B to the *Canada Act 1982* (U.K.), 1982, c. 11.

Constitution Act, 1867 (U.K.), 30 & 31 Vict., c. 3.

Constitution Act, 1982, Schedule B to the *Canada Act 1982* (U.K.), 1982, c. 11.
Copyright Act, R.S.C. 1985, c. C-42.
Criminal Code, R.S.C. 1985, c. C-46.
Education Act (Ontario), R.S.O. 1990, c. E.2.
Employment Standards Act (Ontario), S.O. 2000, c. 41.
Human Rights Code (Ontario), R.S.O. 1990, c. H. 19.
Labour Relations Act (Ontario), S.O. 1995, c. 1, Sched. A.
Occupational Health and Safety Act (Ontario), R.S.O. 1990, c. O.1.
Ontario College of Teachers Act, S.O. 1996, c. 12.
O. Reg. 99/02, *Teacher Performance Appraisal.*
O. Reg. 437/97, *Professional Misconduct.*
Schools Act (Newfoundland and Labrador), S.N.L. 1997, c. S-12.2.
Youth Criminal Justice Act, S.C. 2002, c. 1.

Table of Cases

Abbotsford Sch. Dist. 34 v. Shewan (1986), 70 B.C.L.R. 40 (B.C.S.C.) *aff'd* (1987), 21 B.C.L.R. (2d) 93 (C.A.).

Andrews v. Law Society of British Columbia, [1989] 1 S.C.R. 284 (S.C.C.).

Caldwell v. Stuart, [1984] 2 S.C.R. 603 (S.C.C).

Canadian Civil Liberties Assn. v. Ontario (Minister of Education) (1990), 71 O.R. (2d) 341 (Ont. C.A.).

Casagrande v. Hinton Roman Catholic Separate Sch. Dist. No. 155 (1987), 51 Alta. L.R. (2d) 349 (Alta. Q.B.).

Chambly, Comm'n Scolaire v. Bergevin (1994), 115 D.L.R. (4th) 609 (S.C.C.).

Cromer v. British Columbia Teachers' Fed'n (1986), 29 D.L.R. (4th) 641 (B.C.C.A.).

Eggertson v. Alberta Teachers' Ass'n, [2002] A.J. No. 1358 (Alta. C.A.) [QL].

Irwin Toy Ltd. v. Quebec (Attorney General), [1989] 1 S.C.R. 927 (S.C.C.).

Islamic Schools Federation of Ontario v. Ottawa Bd. of Educ. (1997), 145 D.L.R. (4th) 659 (Ont. Div. Ct.).

Keegstra v. Lacombe Bd. of Educ. No. 14 (1983), 25 Alta. L.R. (2d) 370 (Alta. Bd. of Ref).

Kempling v. B.C.C.T. (2005), 255 D.L.R. (4th) 169 (B.C.C.A.).

Lavigne v.O.P.S.E.U., [1991] 81 D.L.R. (4th) 545 (S.C.C.).

Martin v. Conseil des Ecoles Catholiques de Langue Francaise du Centre-East, [2006] O.J. No. 5349 (Ont. S.C.J.) [QL].

Morin v. P.E.I. Regional Administrative Unit No. 3 Sch. Bd., [2002] P.E.I.J. No. 36 (P.E.I. C.A.) [QL].

Multani v. Commission Scolaire Marguerite-Bourgeoys, [2006] 1 S.C.R. 256 (SCC).

Newman v. Halstead, [2006] B.C.J. No. 59 (B.C.S.C.).

Nicholson v. Haldimand-Norfolk (Region) Police Comm'rs, [1981] 1 S.C.R. 92 (S.C.C.).

Ontario English Catholic Teachers' Assn. v. Dufferin-Peel Roman Catholic Separate Sch. Bd., [1999] O.J. No. 1382 (Ont. C.A.).

Ontario English Catholic Teachers' Assn. v. Ontario (Attorney General), [2001] 1 S.C.R. (SCC).

Ontario Teachers' Fed'n v. Ontario (Attorney General) (2000), 49 O.R. (3d) 257 (Ont. C.A.).

Pandori and The Ontario Human Rights Comm'n v. The Peel Bd. of Educ. (1990), 12 C.H.R.R. D/364.

Peel Dist. Sch. Bd. v. Taurozzi (1998). Unreported, Ont. Ct. Gen. Div., Campbell J.

P.S.A.C. v. Canada, [1987] 1 S.C.R. 424 (S.C.C.).

Public Service Employee Relations Act (Alta.), [1987] 1 S.C.R. 313 (S.C.C.).

R. v. Day, [2002] N.J. No. 353 (Nfld. Prov. Ct.) [QL].

Ross v. New Brunswick Sch. Dist. No. 15, [1996] 1 S.C.R. 825 (S.C.C.).

R.W.D.S.U. v. Saskatchewan, [1987] 1 S.C.R. 460 (S.C.C.).

Wasilifsky v. North Vancouver Teachers' Ass'n (1991), *Can. Labour L.R.* 1991, 16, 053: 14-520-14-547.

Zylberberg v. Sudbury Bd. of Educ. (1988), 65 O.R. (2d) 641 (Ont. C.A.).

Bibliography

Bezeau, L. M. (2006). Educational administration for Canadian teachers. Retrieved July 12, 2007 from www.unb.ca/education/bezeau/eact/eactcvp.html

Brown, D. (1998). *An educator's guide to independent schools*. Aurora, ON: Aurora Professional Press.

Cattani, D. (2007, June). Chair provides insights into discipline process. *Professionally Speaking*, p. 8.

Clarke, P. T. (1998–1999). Canadian public school teachers and free speech: Part II-A constitutional law analysis. *Education & Law Journal, 9*, 43–96.

Dickinson, G. (2005). The problem of heretic teachers: Kempling v. British Columbia College of Teachers. *McGill Journal of Education, 40*(3), 383–404.

Dickinson, G. (2007). Principal granted judicial deference in decision to ban disruptive student from school. *Education & Law Journal, 17*(1), 121–25.

Dolmage, W. R. (1999–2000). Lies, damned lies and statistics: The media's treatment of youth violence. *Education & Law Journal, 10*(1), 1–46.

Elementary Teachers' Federation of Ontario. (2007). Workplace harassment and bullying. Retrieved July 4, 2007 from www.etfo.ca/AdviceForMembers/PRS-MattersBulletins/Pages/Workplace%20Harassment%20and%20Bullying.aspx

Keel, R. G., & Tymochenko, N. (2004). *An educator's guide to parental harassment.* Aurora, ON: Canada Law Book.

La Forest, G. V. (1996–1998). Off-duty conduct and the fiduciary obligations of teachers. *Education & Law Journal, 8*, 119–137.

Luft, S. (2003–2004). Parents interrupting classroom activities may be subject to criminal charges. *Education & Law Journal, 13*, 327–29.

Matsui, J., and Lang Research. Bullying in the workplace. A survey of Ontario's elementary and secondary school teachers and education workers. Retrieved July 12, 2007 from www.oecta.on.ca/pdfs/bullying_execsum.pdf

Nolan, B. P., Trépanier, J. E., & Elleker, B. (2005). When special needs education and safety collide: Occupational health and safety implications of the education of special needs pupils in Ontario. *Education & Law Journal, 14*(3), 235–48.

Proudfoot, S. (2006, July 13). Unruly world of internet leads to rise in libel cases. *The StarPhoenix*. Retrieved July 10, 2007 from www.canada.com/saskatoonstarphoenix/news/story.html?id=44633f5a-6d26-422c-be8b-53a785a6d6dd&k=37041

Notes

1. I am grateful for the invaluable research assistance provided by David Young, a Ph.D. candidate in the Faculty of Education, The University of Western Ontario, and for the valuable suggestions offered by my colleague at the Faculty of Education, Dr. Derek Allison, who kindly reviewed the manuscript for this chapter.

2. The provinces are British Columbia, Alberta, Saskatchewan, Manitoba, Ontario, Quebec, New Brunswick, Nova Scotia, Prince Edward Island, and Newfoundland and Labrador. The three territories are the Yukon, the Northwest Territories, and Nunavut.

3. Toronto (4,750,000), Montreal (3,316,000), Vancouver (1,953,000), and Calgary (988,000).

4. There is an immense amount of diversity insofar as some of the provinces dominate statistically the educational landscape. For example, the four largest provinces (Ontario, Quebec, Alberta, and British Columbia) have 85% of the total student enrollment in elementary and secondary schools in Canada.

5. In *Andrews v. Law Society of British Columbia* (1989), the Supreme Court of Canada ruled that the British Columbia Law Society's regulation requiring members to be Canadian citizens violated the equality rights provisions of the Charter and constituted discrimination on the basis of national origin.

6. See, e.g., s. 15(2) of the Charter and s. 14 of the Human Rights Code (Ontario).

7. Alberta, Saskatchewan, and Ontario have maintained systems of section 93 Roman Catholic separate schools.

8. In all provinces except New Brunswick, Ontario, and British Columbia, the union and the teachers' professional organization are one and the same (Bezeau, 2006).

9. Brown, 1998, p. 112.

10. British Columbia, Alberta, Manitoba, and Ontario (Bezeau, 2006).

11. New Brunswick, Prince Edward Island, and Newfoundland and Labrador (Bezeau, 2006).

12. Quebec, Saskatchewan, and Nova Scotia (Bezeau, 2006).

13. *Re: Public Service Employees Relations Act*, 1987; *P.S.A.C. v. Canada*, 1987; *R.W.D.S.U. v. Saskatchewan*, 1987.

14. *Ontario Teachers' Federation v. Ontario*, 2000.

15. See, e.g., *Wasilifsky*, 1991, cited in Bezeau, 2006; and *Lavigne*, 1991.

16. See, e.g., *Zylberberg*, 1988.

17. See, e.g., *C.C.L.A.*, 1990.

18. See *Chambly*, 1994.

19. See *Islamic Schools Federation*, 1997.

20. See, e.g., *Pandori*, 1990; *Multani*, 2006.

21. See *Kempling*, 2005.

22. See, e.g., *Keegstra*, 1983, cited in Clarke, 1998–1999; *Ross*, 1996.

23. 1984.

24. See, e.g., *Casagrande*, 1987, where pre-marital sex provided grounds for dismissal.

25. See, e.g., *OECTA v. Ontario*, 2001.

26. See the discussion above and *OECTA v. Dufferin-Peel*, 1999, where a policy to promote only Catholic teachers was not automatically viewed as a guaranteed denominational right; it was necessary to ask whether "specific religious affiliation was necessary to maintain the denominational character [of the school system]" (p. 183).

27. Section 2(b) of the Charter guarantees freedom of thought, belief, opinion, and expression.

28. For example, in *Re Cromer and British Columbia Teachers' Federation* (1986), a teacher was disciplined for public criticism of a colleague in contravention of the Federation's Code of Ethics. A key issue was whether the teacher had been speaking in her professional or private capacity. The Court of Appeal rejected her claim to having been speaking qua private person:

> I don't think people are free to choose which hat they will wear on what occasion. Mrs. Cromer does not always speak as a teacher, nor does she always speak as a parent. But she always speaks as Mrs. Cromer. The perception of her by the audience will depend on their knowledge of her training, her skills, her experience, and her occupation, among other things. The impact of what she says will depend on the content of what she says and the occasion on which she says it. (p. 660)

The hat metaphor has been adopted by the Supreme Court of Canada in its jurisprudence on teachers' "off-duty" expression (see discussion below). But see also *Eggertson v. Alberta Teachers' Assn.* (2002), where the Court found such an ethical rule to be an unreasonable restriction on a teacher's right under the School Act to participate in her own child's education.

29. See, e.g., Clarke, 1998–1999.

30. See, e.g., *Keegstra*, 1983, cited in Clarke, 1998–1999, where a teacher who persisted in teaching Holocaust revisionist history, despite being ordered to conform to the approved history curriculum, was fired.

31. 2002.

32. In *Irwin Toy Ltd. v. Quebec (Attorney General)* (1989), the Supreme Court of Canada established that freedom of expression should be given a broad and generous construction and that "expression" should be considered any words or actions that "attempt to convey meaning."

33. 1996.

34. *Kempling*, 2005; see also Dickinson, 2005.

35. *Kempling*, 2005, p. 180.

36. 1996.

37. *Shewan and Shewan v. Board of School Trustees of School District No. 34* (*Shewan*), 1987.

38. *Shewan*, 1987, p. 110.

39. La Forest, 1996–1998, p. 120.

40. The potential for conflict of interest arises when complaints and sanctions are dealt with by federations that are also teacher unions: the hearing body is a federation committee, the prosecutor is an officer or employee of the federation, and the teacher's counsel is also provided by the federation.

41. Cattani, 2007.

42. The Supreme Court of Canada established basic rules of procedural fairness for statutory decision makers in *Nicholson v. Haldimand-Norfolk (Regional Municipality) Commissioners of Police* (1981). However, tribunals such as discipline committees are typically subject, whether by statute or at common law, to more extensive rules of natural justice, given the court-like nature of their proceedings.

43. Cattani, 2007.

44. 2004. This book thoroughly canvasses this topic and is recommended for those who wish to pursue the related issues in more depth.

45. p. 1.

46. Proudfoot, 2006.

47. Keel & Tymochenko, 2004, p. 48.

48. p. 48.

49. 2006.

50. *Peel District School Board*, 1998, cited in Keel & Tymochenko, 2004, pp. 99–100.

51. 2002.

52. 2003–2004.

53. Dickinson, 2007, p. 121.

54. 2006.

55. Dickinson, 2007, p. 125.

56. Dolmage (1999–2000) has examined in depth the influence of the media's misleading portrayal of youth and school violence on public perception and, ultimately, public policy.

57. Elementary Teachers' Federation of Ontario, Ontario Secondary School Teachers' Federation, and Ontario English Catholic Teachers' Association.
58. Elementary Teachers' Federation, 2007.
59. Elementary Teachers' Federation, 2007.
60. Elementary Teachers' Federation, 2007.
61. 2005.
62. p. 238.
63. p. 238.

5

China

Ran Zhang and Hongqi Chu

Introduction

China has the largest population of teachers in the world. In 2006, about 5.6 million fulltime teaches worked in primary education, and about 5.8 million fulltime teachers worked in secondary education. This chapter reviews the legal rights of teachers in the contemporary Chinese society. The chapter starts with a brief overview of the sources of law governing the rights of teachers in China and then elaborates on each major right. The chapter next explores emerging issues before rounding out with a short conclusion.

Sources of Education Law

Insofar as China is not a case law country, its sources of education law include the Constitution, statutes, regulations issued by the State Council, administrative rules issued by the Ministry of Education or other ministries, local legislation, legislation in the ethnic autonomous regions, and local administrative rules issued by provincial or some municipal governments.

The Constitution (1982) outlines the basic rights of Chinese citizens, including rights to equal protection under the law, freedom of speech and association, religious freedom, individual liberty, human dignity, and freedom and privacy of correspondence. However, although the Constitution is at the top of the hierarchy of the sources of law, judges and legal scholars usually believe that the Chinese Constitution cannot be directly cited in court opinions.[1] In fact, few cases in China have been decided solely based on the Constitution.[2]

The basic configuration of the rights of teachers is shaped by four major statutes. The Education Law (1995), the overarching statute concerning education in China, has a chapter devoted to "teachers and other education professionals."[3] The Teachers Law (1993) is the most elaborate statute on teachers' rights in China and covers teachers' qualifications, employment, responsibilities, and evaluation. The Compulsory Education Law (1986) has special provisions for teachers working in elementary and lower-secondary schools, where compulsory education is implemented.[4] The Law on Promotion of Privately Run Schools (2002) stipulates that teachers hired in private schools must be licensed and must be given the same rights as public school teachers in terms of professional development, professional titles, hiring, and calculation of seniority.[5]

Teacher Employment

Licensure

Teacher licensure is a prerequisite for teaching in Chinese schools.[6] Local educational agencies are responsible for the licensure of elementary and secondary school teachers. Teachers are licensed based on the level of the school where they teach rather than on their subject areas or grade levels. Teachers with higher-level licenses are automatically eligible to teach at lower-level schools.[7] For example, elementary school teachers usually get general elementary teacher licenses that do not allow recipients to teach in upper-secondary schools.[8] However, if upper-secondary teachers are transferred to elementary schools, they do not have to secure other licenses. Moreover, teacher licenses are valid nationwide.[9]

In order to obtain teacher licenses, applicants must meet four requirements:[10] hold Chinese citizenship; comply with the Constitution, applicable laws, and standards for professional ethics; demonstrate instructional capability, as indicated by basic quality and competency in teaching, basic proficiency in standardized spoken Chinese (Mandarin or *putonghua*),[11] and good health; and attain specified educational levels or pass a teacher qualification test.

The minimum education requirement for teachers varies with the level of license.[12] Elementary school teachers must, at a minimum, have degrees from secondary normal schools;[13] lower-secondary school teachers must have associate's degrees in teacher education or other disciplines; and upper-secondary school teachers must graduate from four-year teacher education programs or other four-year college programs.

If applicants cannot satisfy these requirements, they may still obtain licenses by passing teacher qualification tests.[14] The subjects and standards of such tests are prescribed by the Ministry of Education, while the tests are designed and administered by local educational agencies.[15] Thus, graduation from a teacher education program is not strictly necessary for licensure. However, local educational agencies may require those who have not graduated from teacher education programs or those who apply for teacher licensure based on teacher qualification tests to take courses in pedagogy and psychology. Such applicants for teaching positions must be interviewed and also deliver mock lessons if they apply for elementary licensure.[16]

Establishment of Teacher Employment

As part of the national personnel reform that aims to encourage competition in public employment, teacher employment is supposed to shift from the permanent placement of teachers in schools, an "iron bowl" practice that once guaranteed job security, to term employment established on the basis of contracts. In light of the ongoing nature of the personnel reform, neither the Education Law (1995)[17] nor the Teachers Law (1993)[18] goes beyond a general declaration that a system of employment contracts (*pinren*) and professional titles (*zhiwu*) is to be used. More detail is provided by administrative rules and policies issued by the Ministry of Education and the Ministry of Personnel. Insofar as public schools in China are defined as public service units (*shiye danwei*) and thus are distinct from government agencies (*xingzheng danwei*) and businesses (*qiye*), the general personnel policies applicable to public service units are applicable to teacher employment.

In principle, teacher employment is established by a valid contract to which a school and a potential teacher agree.[19] This contract must satisfy four requirements. First, employment contracts must be signed by the appropriate parties. Schools that possess charters, organization systems, teachers, facilities, equipment, and money are recognized as "legal persons" in the Chinese legal system.[20] Thus, contracts must be signed by the school principals or their agents on behalf of the school.[21] Individuals who sign contracts with schools must have or should expect to have teacher licenses.

Second, the parties must reach a mutual agreement on a voluntary and equal basis. No fraud or coercion can be involved. No severe imbalance of rights and duties between parties can exist. Third, employment contracts must contain specific, required components. The Ministry of Personnel requires that contracts should include teachers' length of service and descriptions of the teaching positions, along with job responsibilities, teachers' anticipated working conditions, salary and benefits, the conditions under which contract modification and termination can occur, and liability associated with contract violations.[22] However, general contractual theory suggests that a failure to include some of these provisions does not necessarily render employment contracts void. The parties can amend their contracts on further negotiation. If the parties are unable to reach further agreements, default legal requirements apply.[23] Fourth, contracts must be in a written form.[24]

In addition to these general requirements, contracts involving individuals who will be teaching for the first time must specify probationary periods.[25] Such probationary periods count toward the total amount of time covered by the contract and cannot be longer than one year.[26]

A System of Professional Titles

The professional title system is an important part of teacher employment in China. For schools, the system designates the categories and number of positions to be filled.[27] Further, for teachers, it is an important professional credential and has direct impact on their salaries and other interests.[28]

In elementary and secondary schools, teachers are classified into four categories: premier teachers, scale-one teachers, scale-two teachers, and scale-three teachers. The qualifications for each category of teacher differ in terms of education level, seniority, instructional and student management competence, and research capability.[29] The classification of teachers into categories is made by professional title evaluation committees organized by local educational agencies or by teacher evaluation teams formed at the school level. Evaluation decisions are made collectively through anonymous voting.[30]

These four categories are associated with three kinds of positions: premier teachers fill advanced positions, scale-one teachers fill intermediate positions, and scale-two and scale-three teachers fill basic positions. The ratio and number of these positions in schools are decided based on the number of teachers employed. Even so, the position allocation process is subject to external constraints imposed by local educational agencies.[31]

Evaluation

The results of teacher evaluations are important criteria that school officials and local educational agencies use when making decisions about teacher employment, salaries, awards, and sanctions.[32] School officials, who are responsible for teacher evaluations, are supervised and guided by local educational agencies.[33] In general, on completion of evaluations, teachers are rated as "excellent," "qualified," or "unqualified." Some schools and local educational agencies develop more carefully classified categories. Evaluation results are documented in teachers' records.

Teachers are usually evaluated based on their professional competencies, attitudes toward work, and job performance.[34] Job performance is the most important area.[35] Evaluations must be objective, fair, accurate, and attentive to teachers' own statements and to peer evaluations.[36] In addition, evaluations may account for feedback from community representatives and parents.[37]

Retirement

In China, when teachers retire is primarily determined by gender-differentiated cutoff ages. Those who have worked as teachers for at least 10 years can and must retire once they reach the legal retirement age, which is 60 for males and 55 for females.[38] Retired teachers receive a monthly pension for the rest of their lives. As in other nations, the amount of pensions is a percentage of individuals' prior salaries and depends on the person's years of service before retirement.[39] After retirement, teachers may be rehired and receive additional salary if school officials can demonstrate instructional need and teachers are both willing to and capable of continuing their service. Rehired teachers are not counted toward the maximum number of positions that schools can fill.[40] In recent years, the gender difference in retirement ages has been legally challenged as alleged gender discrimination.[41] However, arbitration committees or courts usually refuse to hear such disputes, and no formal policy changes regarding retirement ages have been made.

Unions

Teachers have the right to join or organize unions. According to the Trade Union Law of 1992, a union is a voluntary association of employees. A union's major responsibility is to safeguard the rights and interests of its members.[42]

In theory, when schools impinge on the legitimate interests of their employees, unions can investigate the infringements[43] and request that officials discontinue the offending actions.[44] If unions deem sanctions that school officials have levied on teachers to be inappropriate, they can raise objections. Unions should also organize employees to participate in democratic decision making in their schools;[45] voice employees' concerns regarding salaries, workplace safety, employee insurance, and other benefits;[46] and sponsor and organize training, entertainment, and sporting activities in collaboration with their employers.[47] In private schools, unions can negotiate with school officials and sign collective bargaining agreements on behalf of their members.[48] The law is not explicit regarding whether employees have the right to strike, and it imposes a duty on the union to negotiate with employers in the case of work stoppages or slowdowns.[49]

Although the Trade Union Law declares that unions are voluntary associations of employees, their actual role is, in fact, not very clear in China. There are three noteworthy points as to why the function of unions in China is unclear. First, specific institutional arrangements make typical unions relatively formal and hierarchical institutions. All school-level unions are supposed to be divisions of the All-China Federation of Trade Unions (ACFTU).[50]

In addition to membership dues and income from their own business, union revenues come from government subsidies and regular monetary contributions from members; the Trade Union Law requires employers to give the union the equivalent of two percent of the salaries of all school employees.[51]

Second, union members appear not to be the only beneficiaries of union activities. The word *employees* is used throughout the Trade Union Law when describing unions' goals and activities, while the word *members* is only associated with the internal structure of unions. As mentioned earlier, unions are supposed to protect the legitimate interests of school *employees*.[52] However, the law does not particularly highlight the interests of union members. Third, since union leaders are paid by their educational employers,[53] in practice, teacher unions are usually not powerful organizations in Chinese schools.

Teacher Rights

Article 7 of the Teachers Law (1993) specifies six major rights of teachers in China, each of which is discussed specifically. In addition to these rights, teachers have the fundamental rights the Constitution provides all citizens.

Right to Teach

"Teachers enjoy the right to conduct educational and instructional activities, reforms, and experiments."[54] Like teachers in many other countries, teachers in China have the right to select instructional methods but have no right to decide curricula. In the compulsory education sphere, which includes elementary and lower-secondary education, the Ministry of Education selects instructional content and curricula. Compulsory education schools and their teachers follow the prescribed instructional content and curricula.[55]

Right to Research

"Teachers enjoy the right to engage in scientific research and academic exchange, join professional academic societies, and fully express their views in academic activities."[56] This section of the Teachers Law highlights the rights to academic freedom, freedom of association, and expression that are relevant to the conduct of teachers as researchers. Moreover, the State Council has issued a regulation to encourage teachers to engage in research.[57]

Right to Student Management

"Teachers enjoy the right to guide students in their studies and evaluate and help develop students' conduct and academic achievements."[58] At the same time, the Teachers Law (1993) requires teachers to respect the dignity of students and to protect them from potential harm.[59] Accordingly, teachers are prohibited from discriminating against students and from using corporal punishment.[60]

Right to Receive Salaries, Benefits, and Summer and Winter Breaks with Pay

"Teachers enjoy the right to receive salaries and remunerations on schedule, to enjoy the welfare benefits prescribed by the State, and to take paid leave during the winter and summer vacations."[61] The salaries and benefits of public school teachers are a significant focus of educational laws in China. For example, laws require that teachers' salaries be higher than or at least equal to those of civil servants in the same region and that medical benefits available to teachers also must be equivalent to those of public servants.[62]

Right to Participate in School Management

"Teachers enjoy the rights to voice opinions and suggestions regarding teaching and learning, and the administration of schools and local educational agencies; and to participate in the democratic management of schools through congresses of teachers, staff and workers or through other forms."[63] In fact, the Constitution declares that Chinese citizens have a fundamental right to criticize government agencies and civil servants without being subject to retaliation.[64] However, in doing so, teachers are prohibited from fabricating or distorting facts.[65] The concept of being a "public figure" that is an element of the law of defamation in the United States is not established in Chinese law.

Right to Continuing Education

"Teachers enjoy the right to continuing education or other forms of training."[66] This right assigned by the Teachers Law is actually also a duty for teachers. In other words, the Regulation on the Continuing Education of Elementary and Secondary School Teachers (1999) mandates that teachers receive at least 120 hours of in-service training during their probationary period and at least 240 hours for every five years that they retain their jobs as teachers.

Other Constitutional Rights

Religious Freedom. Chinese citizens have the constitutional right to "believe in, or not to believe in, any religion."[67] Even so, religion and education are strictly separated in China, and organizations or individuals are prohibited from using religion to interfere with educational activities.[68] In China, organized religious activities are restricted to registered places of worship.[69] In light of this strict separation and regulation, it is unlikely that teachers can conduct visible private worship at school.

Privacy. Insofar as teachers are Chinese citizens, their homes and private correspondences cannot be searched without warrants.[70] However, the law is unclear on the standards governing the search of teachers' desks at work. Pursuant to the Temporary Regulation on Educational Administrative Punishment (1998), educational agencies can look for (*jiancha*) evidence in accordance with laws and administrative regulations and with two officials present.[71] The rule uses the weak word *jiancha* (look for) rather than the stronger term *soucha* (search). The scope and standard of *jiancha* and laws and administrative regulations that govern such situations are not clear in Chinese law. In addition to *jiancha*, applicants for teacher licensure are required to undergo medical examinations at designated hospitals and are supposed to be role models for their students.[72] These medical and lifestyle requirements have implications for teachers' right to privacy.

Equal Protection. All Chinese citizens are supposed to be equal before the law.[73] Chinese laws are particularly articulate on women's rights. Women have a fundamental constitutional right to get equal pay for equal work.[74] Employers are prohibited from dismissing female employees during pregnancy, maternal leave, and nursing periods.[75] Female employees can take maternity leave for at least 90 days.[76] When their maternity leave overlaps with summer or winter break, female teachers can take extended leave for the overlapped period.[77]

Teacher Sanctions and Dismissal

Article 37 of the Teachers Law of 1993 states,

> Teachers can be sanctioned or dismissed by schools, other educational institutions, or local educational agencies for: 1) intentional failure to accomplish job

assignments, resulting in losses to educational and instructional work; 2) use of corporal punishment in student discipline despite being warned not to do; and 3) engaging in improper conduct or insulting students, thus causing very harmful impacts.

Other provisions on teacher sanctions and dismissal are scattered throughout various sources of educational law but are often incomplete and unclear. This section of the chapter attempts to comb through the relevant laws and policies while sketching out the causes, procedural safeguards, and grievance procedures for major adverse personnel actions against teachers.

Teacher Sanctions

The Education Law of 1995 grants school officials the power to take disciplinary measures against their own teachers.[78] However, except in the three situations mentioned above, Chinese law does not provide a systematic account of what sanctions can be rendered, when, and with what procedures. As internal disciplinary actions, teacher sanctions may be governed by the categories and procedures used by government agencies to discipline civil servants. The Civil Servant Law of 2005 lists six kinds of sanctions applicable to civil servants: warnings, demerits placed on their records, severe demerits placed on their records, demotions, expulsions from administrative roles, and expulsions from their jobs or positions.[79] Under this law, employers must investigate the problematic activity carefully, inform the affected employees about the intended sanctions and their factual bases for acting, hear the employees' statements and defenses, render decisions within specified time periods, and notify employees of the decisions in writing.[80]

If disciplined teachers are dissatisfied with the sanctions that school officials have taken against them, they can file a complaint (*shensu*) with the local educational agency, which must then render a decision within 30 days after accepting the case.[81] If teachers still do not agree with the agency's decision, then they can file another complaint with the local government (*fuhe*).[82] However, teachers do not have the right to administrative review (*xingzheng fuyi*) or judicial review (*xingzheng susong*). The Administrative Review Law of 1999 and the Administrative Procedure Law of 1989 apply only to external administrative actions taken by government agencies and explicitly exclude internal disciplinary actions.[83] To the extent, as noted, that schools are defined as public service units rather than government agencies under Chinese law, teacher sanctions are internal disciplinary actions that are often exempted from administrative or judicial review.

Revocation of Teacher License

Local educational agencies can refuse to grant or can revoke already issued teaching licenses if applicants or holders are deprived of political rights or imprisoned for intentional crime; if they have obtained their certificates by fraud; or if they engage in improper conduct with or insult students, thus causing very harmful impacts.[84]

In the first situation, the bar against licensures is permanent. In the other two situations, applicants could reapply for teaching licenses five years after the revocations. Also, if individuals engage in dishonest conduct while taking teacher qualification tests, their scores are annulled and they are prohibited from retaking the tests for three years.[85]

If license applicants or holders are in danger of losing their licenses, the relevant educational agencies must inform them of the facts and rationale for their intended decision. Individuals have the right to present defenses and to request hearings within three days.[86] Once requested, hearings must be conducted. Persons who were not previously involved in the investigation of cases must preside at hearings. Certificate applicants or holders may bring one or two representatives to the hearings. During the hearings, investigators present the case, evidence, and the sanction that they intend to render, and the certificate applicants or holders and their representatives can defend and question evidence.[87]

If certificate applicants or holders are dissatisfied with hearing results, they can file a complaint (*shensu*)[88] or request an administrative review (*fuyi*)[89] from the local government or educational agencies in the higher level or can file administrative suits at local courts.[90] During administrative reviews or administrative litigation, local educational agencies are prohibited from collecting evidence from certificate applicants or holders or from witnesses.[91] In administrative litigation, local educational agencies bear the burden of proof.[92] Theoretically, if the proposed licensure refusal or revocation is ruled to be unfounded at this level, individuals can claim state compensation for the loss of property interest during the period of administrative sanction.[93] Still, the law is not clear on how to calculate the compensation in such situations, and the amounts that can be recovered are generally small.[94]

Termination of Employment

Besides the three circumstances for teacher dismissal cited earlier, the Ministry of Personnel specifies various situations in which employment can be terminated and ways in which employee dispute resolution can proceed. In general, employment contracts between teachers and schools can be renewed or terminated with the consent of both parties. The following discussion applies only to unilateral termination of employment in public schools by either party within the terms of contracts.

In a public service unit (*shiye danwei*) such as a public school, an employer may immediately terminate contracts if employees: are absent from work without permission for 10 consecutive days or for a total of 20 days in one year; visit another country without approval or stay in another country longer than the approved period; violate their duties and incur severe consequences; seriously interfere with the order of workplace, thus disrupting normal operations; or are imprisoned. In addition, probationary employees who cannot fulfill their job assignments but refuse to be transferred to other positions may be dismissed immediately.[95]

Public employers such as schools can terminate contracts with advance notice of 30 days when employees who return from medical leave are no longer competent in the functions of their prior positions or other jobs arranged by the employer, if they receive negative evaluations but refuse to be transferred to other positions, or receive poor evaluations in new positions. If employees are dismissed for one of these latter two reasons, employers must compensate them by an amount determined based on their years of service and prior salary level. Dismissal is prohibited if employees remain on medical leave in accordance with laws, regulations, or policies.[96]

Employees in a public service unit such as a school may also initiate employment termination. Employees can resign at any time during the probationary period or when they are admitted by regular higher education institutions, recruited by government agencies, or drafted into the military. If employees seek termination for other reasons and employers do not approve of their resignations, employees can unilaterally terminate their contracts after working an additional six months.[97] If employees' contracts require employers to pay training expenses, then the resigning employees must reimburse their employers for these funds; however, the amount to be reimbursed decreases 20 percent for every year employees have worked for the employers following the training.[98] Individuals who have received tuition waivers or special career scholarships to study to become teachers are obliged to work in the field of education for five years.[99]

If employers and employees have disputes regarding employment termination or about responsibilities specified in the employment contract, both parties can trigger a personnel arbitration process.[100] This process involves a personnel arbitration committee that is affiliated with government personnel agencies and is staffed by arbitrators from personnel and other government offices as well as by scholars and lawyers.[101] A mediation process is required at the beginning of arbitration, and a signed arbitration agreement is binding.[102] If the parties cannot reach an agreement, the arbitrators must render a decision based on the evidence presented by the parties and collected by the arbitrators when necessary.[103] Parties who are dissatisfied with the results of arbitration can file suits within 15 days of the delivery of arbitration decisions;[104] otherwise, arbitration decisions are enforceable. In addition, teachers can file a complaint (*shensu*) with local educational agencies if they believe that employment decisions made by school officials infringe on their legitimate interests.[105]

Emerging Issues

As discussed earlier, contractual relationships are supposed to replace permanent positions in teacher employment. This has to be understood in light of China's transition to a market economy and the reform of its former rigid personnel system. However, in spite of the fact that the Teachers Law of 1993 authorized the Ministry of Education to formulate policy on how this contractual system is to be implemented in schools, such a policy has not been developed over the past fifteen years.

General personnel policies on the employment establishment and termination in public service units could be applicable to public schools. Even so, little consideration has been paid to the special roles of teachers. Further, teachers are often in such a disadvantaged and powerless position that they have no choice but simply to accept whatever their schools say. In many instances, teacher employment resembles the past unilateral administrative order.[106] As a result, the new bottle of contractual employment still contains the old wine.

In light of the definition of their roles and the status of public schools in China, teachers are put into an awkward legal position. First, while they are characterized as "professionals" in the Education Law of 1995,[107] they lack the right to select curricular and instructional content. Further, since graduation from teacher education programs is not a prerequisite for licensure, the teaching profession hardly has a core body of knowledge. Second, teachers are considered to be professionals rather than civil servants in China.

The Teachers Law of 1993 requires the average salary of teachers to be no lower than that of civil servants. In practice, though, civil servants often have better benefits and much higher social status. To make matters worse, the payment of teacher salaries is sometimes delayed in areas where the local government faces financial difficulties. In order to attract excellent students to the teaching profession, it has been proposed to recognize teachers as civil servants.[108] Third, because public schools are public service units and the Administrative Review Law of 1999 and Administrative Procedure Law of 1989 exclude the internal disciplinary actions against employees in public service units from their review, teachers have limited recourse in these situations. To this end, future reform will have to address this legal vacuum in order to protect the rights of teachers.

In a manner similar to their peers in the other parts of the world, teachers in China are also faced with tremendous pressure of accountability. Insofar as the National College Entrance Exam is almost the single criterion for college admission, the pressure of performing well on this test trickles down in the educational system. In many schools, bonuses for teachers, which are a fairly large portion of their salaries, are contingent on their students' test scores, and the jobs of some teachers could be in jeopardy due to the persistently poor performance of their students.[109] In light of these award and sanction structures, some teachers assign much homework to students, extend students' in-school study time, and push students to memorize every point that might be included in upcoming tests.

While students have a heavy burden of study, teachers are also often overworked. In order to deal with these problems, the central government has repeatedly called for the transformation from an educational system that is oriented toward testing to a new one that aims at improving the quality (*suzhi*) of the Chinese population.[110] This new system stresses "all-round" development in the moral, intellectual, physical, and aesthetic aspects. However, to date, the implementation of these policies has not been very successful. In 2006, the revised Compulsory Education Law explicitly declared *suzhi* education as a general principle in compulsory education and promised to reform the testing system in China.[111] Unfortunately, it is unclear when the concrete changes in the testing system will take place and what their impact may be on the teacher evaluation system.

Conclusion

"Rule of law" is recapitulated by the Chinese government as a slogan that "there must be laws to rely on; where there are laws, they must be followed; laws must be strictly enforced; and violations of law must be corrected" (*youfa ke yi, youfa bi yi, zhifa bi yan, weifa bi jiu*).[112] In terms of teachers' rights, China has established a basic legal framework over the past thirty years. Even so, more delicate institutional designs of certain sub-areas of teachers' rights such as in employment have yet to be developed.

Laws regarding the rights of teachers sometimes have not been duly implemented, with the result that their rights have been violated. For instance, some teachers have not received their salaries on time, and officials have circumvented their actual participation in school management. Probably most fundamentally, as this recapitulation suggests, laws are often perceived as an instrument for social regulation in China. Therefore, in order to ensure the rights of teachers, a culture in which individual rights are truly respected and prioritized must be cultivated in China.

Acknowledgment

The authors would like to thank Xuemei Jiang from Beijing Normal University for her helpful suggestions regarding this chapter.

Notes

1. Supreme People's Court, 关于在刑事判决中不宜援引宪法作论罪科刑的依据的批复 [A Reply on the Inappropriateness in Citing the Constitution in Criminal Decisions] (1955) and 关于人民法院制作法律文书如何引用法律规范性文件的批复 [A Reply on How People's Courts Cite Laws in Issuing Their Legal Documents] (1986).

2. For a discussion on this issue, see Heidi Ross and Ran Zhang, *Guest Editors' Introduction: The Limits and Possibilities of Responsive Justice, Chinese Educ. & Soc'y*, vol. 39, no. 4, 3–10 (2006).

3. Art. 32–35.

4. In fact, the Compulsory Education Law was one of the first education laws enacted after the Cultural Revolution (1966–1976). In the 1980s and the early 1990s, it was the only national statute that governed teachers' rights. It was amended in 2006.

5. Art. 27, 28, 30.

6. Teachers Law, art. 10 (1993); State Council, 教师资格条例 [A Regulation on Teacher Licensure], art. 2 (1995).

7. *Id.*, art. 5.

8. 教师资格条例[A Regulation on Teacher Licensure], art. 4 (1995).

9. *Id.*, art. 16.

10. The Teachers Law, art. 10–11 (1993). Ministry of Education, 《教师资格条例》实施办法 [Implementation Methods for the Regulation on Teacher Licensure], art. 6–8 (2000).

11. Dialects vary greatly in different regions of China. Mandarin is the official language in schools. Law on the Nation-wide Commonly-used Languages and Characters, art. 10 (2000).

12. The Teachers Law, art. 11 (1993).

13. A secondary normal school is a specialized upper-secondary school devoted to teacher education.

14. 教师资格条例 [A Regulation on Teacher Licensure], art. 8 (1995).

15. *Id.*, art. 9.

16. *Id.*, art. 16.

17. Art. 34.

18. Art. 16–17.

19. The Teachers Law, art. 17 (1993).

20. Education Law, art. 26, 31 (1995).

21. The number of teachers a school can employ is subject to a limit established by a local educational agency and personnel agency.

22. 关于在事业单位试行人员聘用制度的意见 [Opinions on Experimenting Employment Contracts in Public Service Units] (2002).

23. See, e.g., Contract Law, art. 61–63 (1999).

24. 关于在事业单位试行人员聘用制度的意见[Opinions on Experimenting Employment Contracts in Public Service Units] (2002).

25. The Teachers Law, art. 13 (1993).

26. 关于在事业单位试行人员聘用制度的意见 [Opinions on Experimenting Employment Contracts in Public Service Units] (2002).

27. Commission of Education, 中学教师职务试行条例 [A Probationary Regulation on Professional Titles of Secondary School Teachers]; 小学教师职务试行条例 [A Probationary Regulation on Professional Titles of Elementary School Teachers], art. 2 (1986). Commission of Education was renamed Ministry of Education in 1998.

28. See, e.g., Commission of Education, 中小学教师职务工资标准方案 [Salary Standards for Elementary and Secondary School Teachers Based on Their Professional Titles] (1988). The plan was revised in 2007.

29. See 小学教师职务试行条例 [A Probationary Regulation on Professional Titles of Elementary School Teachers], art. 8–13 (1986); 中学教师职务试行条例 [A Probationary Regulation on Professional Titles of Secondary School Teachers], art. 8–15 (1986).

30. Commission of Education, 关于中、小学教师职务试行条例的实施意见 [Opinions on the Implementation of the Probationary Regulations on the Professional Titles of Elementary and Secondary School Teachers] (1986).

31. 中学教师职务试行条例 [A Probationary Regulation on Professional Titles of Secondary School Teachers], art. 2 (1986). 关于制定中小学教职工编制的意见 [Opinions on Calculating the Positions of Teachers and Supporting Staff in Elementary and Secondary Schools] (2001).

32. The Teachers Law, art. 24 (1993).

33. *Id.*, art. 22.

34. *Id.*

35. Commission of Education, 关于《中华人民共和国教师法》若干问题的实施意见 [Opinions on Several Issues in the Implementation of Teachers Law of the People's Republic of China] (1995).

36. *Id.*, art. 23.

37. Ministry of Personnel and Ministry of Education, 关于深化中小学人事制度改革的实施意见 [Opinions on Furthering the Reform of the Personnel System in Elementary and Secondary Schools] (2003).

38. State Council, 国务院关于安置老弱病残干部的暂行办法 [Probationary Methods on the Placement of Old, Physically Weak, Sick, and Disable Cadres], art. 4

(1978).

39. *Id.*; the Teachers Law, art. 30 (1993).

40. Commission of Education, 关于中、小学教师职务试行条例的实施意见 [Opinions on the Implementation of the Probationary Regulation on Professional Titles in Elementary and Secondary Schools] (1986).

41. See, e.g., 退休年龄为何女不如男 55岁退休优待还是歧视 [Special Protection or Discrimination: Why is Retirement Age for Females Lower than That for Males?], 中国新闻周刊 [*China News Weekly Update*] (Nov. 10, 2005). http://news.xinhuanet.com/fortune/2005-11/10/content_3760031.htm (last visited August 20, 2008).

42. Art. 2, 6.

43. *Id.*, art. 25.

44. *Id.*, art. 22.

45. *Id.*, art. 5, 6, 19.

46. *Id.*, art. 30, 38.

47. *Id.*, art. 31.

48. *Id.*, art. 20. All China Federation of Trade Union and Ministry of Education, 在社会力量举办的学校建立工会组织的意见 [Opinions on Establishing Trade Union Branches in Private Schools], 2002. In contrast, the "base" teacher salary in public schools is set by standard government policies.

49. The Trade Union Law, art. 27 (1992).

50. *Id.*, art. 2.

51. *Id.*, art. 42.

52. *Id.*, art. 2.

53. *Id.*, art. 40, 41.

54. The Teachers Law, art. 7, sec. 1 (1993).

55. Compulsory Education Law, art. 35 (1986). The law was substantively revised in 2006.

56. The Teachers Law, art. 7, sec. 2 (1993).

57. 教学成果奖励条例 [A Regulation on Incentives for Teaching Accomplishment] (1994).

58. The Teachers Law, art. 7, sec. 3 (1993).

59. *Id.*, art. 8.

60. Compulsory Education Law, art. 29 (2006).

61. The Teachers Law, art. 7, sec. 4 (1993).

62. *Id.*, art. 25, 29, 28.

63. *Id.*, art. 7, sec. 5.

64. Constitution, art. 41 (1982). See also The Teachers Law, art. 36 (1993).

65. Constitution, art. 41 (1982); General Principles of the Civil Law, art. 101 (1986).

66. The Teachers Law, art. 7, sec. 6 (1993).

67. Constitution, art. 36 (1982).

68. Education Law, art. 8 (1995).

69. State Council, 宗教事务条例 [A Regulation on Religious Affairs] (2004).

70. Constitution, art. 39, 40 (1982).

71. 教育行政处罚暂行实施办法 [Probationary Implementation Methods for Administration Punishment in Education], art. 24 (1998).

72. The Teachers Law, art. 8 (1993). Compulsory Education Law, art. 28 (1986).

73. Constitution, art. 33 (1982).

74. *Id.*, art. 48.

75. Ministry of Personnel, 关于在事业单位试行人员聘用制度的通知 [A Notice on Experimenting Employment Contract System in Public Service Units] (2002). Labor Law, art. 29 (1994).

76. Labor Law, art. 62 (1994).

77. Education Commission, 关于女教师产假有关问题的复函 [A Reply on Maternal Leaves for Female Teachers] (1992).

78. Art. 28, sec. 6.

79. Art. 56.

80. The Civil Servant Law, art. 57 (2005).

81. The Teachers Law, art. 39 (1993).

82. Commission of Education, 关于《中华人民共和国教师法》若干问题的实施意见 [Opinions on Several Issues in the Implementation of the Teachers Law of the People's Republic of China] (1995).

83. Administrative Review Law, art. 6, 8 (1999); Administrative Litigation Law, art. 11, 12 (1999).

84. The Teachers Law, art. 14 (1993); State Council, 教师资格条例 [A Regulation on Teacher Licensure], art. 19, 20 (1995); Commission of Education, 教育行政处罚暂行实施办法 [Probationary Implementation Methods for Administration Punishment in Education], art. 18 (1998).

85. Commission of Education, 教育行政处罚暂行实施办法 [Probationary Implementation Methods for Administration Punishment in Education], art. 19 (1998).

86. *Id.*, art. 25, 27.

87. *Id.*, art. 27. Administrative Punishment Law, art. 42 (1996).

88. The Teachers Law, art. 39 (1993).

89. Commission of Education, 教育行政处罚暂行实施办法 [Probationary Implementation Methods for Administration Punishment in Education], art. 31 (1998). Administrative Review Law, art. 6 (1999).

90. Commission of Education, 教育行政处罚暂行实施办法 [Probationary Implementation Methods for Administration Punishment in Education], art. 31 (1998). Administrative Procedure Law, art. 11 (1989).

91. Administrative Review Law, art. 24 (1999). Administrative Procedure Law, art. 33 (1989).

92. Administrative Procedure Law, art. 32 (1989).

93. Administrative Compensation Law, art. 4 (1994); Commission of Education, 教育行政处罚暂行实施办法 [Probationary Implementation Methods for Administration Punishment in Education], art. 33 (1998).

94. The Administrative Compensation Law (1994) limits the amount of compensation for unlawful revocation of a license to "necessary operating costs during the period" (art. 28, sec. 6). Since operating costs are primarily a concern for business or organizations, it is questionable whether individual teachers can claim such costs. The general rule of compensation for property loss is compensation for direct damages (art. 28, sec. 7). However, even for false imprisonment, the calculation is based on

the national average employee wage in the prior year, not the wage of the particular individual in question (art. 26).

95. Ministry of Personnel, 关于在事业单位试行人员聘用制度的意见 [A Notice on Experimenting Employment Contract System in Public Service Units] (2002).

96. *Id.*

97. *Id.*

98. Ministry of Personnel, 事业单位试行人员聘用制度有关问题的解释 [Interpretations on Several Issues Related to the Experimentation of Employment Contract System in Public Service Units] (2003).

99. Commission of Education, 关于《中华人民共和国教师法》若干问题的实施意见 [Opinions on Several Issues in the Implementation of the Teachers Law of the People's Republic of China] (1995).

100. Ministry of Personnel, 人事争议处理暂行规定 [Probationary Regulation on Dealing with Personnel Disputes], art. 2 (1997).

101. *Id.*, art. 5, 6, 7, 9.

102. *Id.*, art. 14, 15.

103. *Id.*, art. 18.

104. Supreme People's Court, 关于人民法院审理事业单位人事争议案件若干问题的决定 [A Decision on the Hearing of Personnel Disputes in Public Service Units by People's Courts] (2003).

105. The Teachers Law, art. 39 (1993).

106. Mingguang Huang and Jinshun Zhang, 论《教师法》对教师管理的滞后性及修改建议 [The Outdatedness of the Teachers Law and Several Revision Suggestions], 《九江学院学报(社会科学版)》[Journal of the Jiujiang Institute (Social Sciences)], March 2006.

107. Art. 3.

108. 全国人大代表王斌泰：应将教师纳入公务员序列管理 [Wang Bintai, A Delegate to the National People's Congress, Proposes the Application of Civil Servant System to Teachers],《中国教育报》[China Education Daily], (March 13, 2007), p. 2; Li Yin,《教师法》实施10年：守望与期待 [The Implementation of the Teachers Law over the Past 10 Years: Waiting and Longing], 《教 育 理 论 与 实 践》 [Educational Theories and Practice], 2005, iss. 2, pp. 13–17.

109. 《教师法》为何难以保障教师合法权益 [Why the Teachers Law Can Hardly Protect Teachers' Legitimate Interests?], www.teacherblog.com.cn/blog/8030/archives/2006/69783.shtml (last visited June 26, 2007).

110. See, e.g., 中共中央关于教育体制改革的决定 [The Central Committee of the Chinese Communist Party, Decisions on Reforming the Educational System] (May 27, 1985); 中共中央国务院关于深化教育改革，全面推进素质教育的决定 [The Central Committee of the Chinese Communist Party, On Furthering the Educational Reform and Fully Implementing Quality Education] (June 13, 1999).

111. Art. 1, 3, 34, 35.

112. This was originally from a speech given by Xiaoping Deng in 1976. See《邓小平文选》[Selected Works of Deng Xiaoping], vol. 2, p. 147.

6

England and Wales

Anne Ruff

Introduction

In England and Wales, the rights of teachers are similar for the most part to those of other employees. Where the rights of teachers differ reflects the organisational structure in which they are employed and the fact that their working lives involve contact with children and young people. The concept of "rights" is not often used in English law, which has traditionally been phrased in terms of duties and powers. Nevertheless, such duties and powers can give rise to corresponding rights.

This chapter is primarily concerned with the situation in England and Wales. It does not include Northern Ireland.[1] Insofar as the legal position of teachers in Scotland is governed by different legislation than their counterparts in England and Wales,[2] the situation there is not considered in this chapter.

Education in Wales has been the responsibility of the Welsh Assembly since 2006.[3] In practice before 2006, the Welsh legislation was normally similar, if not identical, to the legislation for England; this continues to be the position for the moment.

In England and Wales, the legal rights of teachers are contained in ordinary legislation and in case law. The rights and duties of teachers differ according to whether they are employed in the maintained sector, that is, publicly funded state schools, or in "independent" schools, where parents pay school fees.

This chapter concentrates on the legal rights of teachers in maintained schools in England and Wales. The legal issues of particular interest relate to the tripartite relation between central government, local government, and teaching staff; the professional status of teachers; the desirability of having a single set of terms and conditions of employment; and the impact of religion on employment in schools.

Employment Rights of Teachers

The terms and conditions of teacher employment have been regulated by statute since 1987. The employment rights of teachers are also governed by their contracts of employment and hence by the ordinary rules of English contract and employment law.

The introduction of statutory terms and conditions of teacher employment in 1987[4] was controversial at the time. The controversy arose because it replaced the traditional idea of employment contracts based on negotiation and agreement between trade unions and employers. Instead, this schema was replaced with the imposition by the central government, after consultation, of terms and conditions of employment on a large public sector workforce.

The relevant primary statutory provisions are found in the Education Act 2002.[5] In the autumn of each year, the School Teachers' Review Body, which was established by the School Teachers Pay and Conditions Act of 1991, receives submissions from teachers' organisations, local education authorities (LEAs), organisations of governing bodies, and the Secretary of State on teachers' pay levels and structure as well as conditions of employment relating to their professional duties or working time.[6] The Secretary of State implements the recommendations with implementation by way of statutory orders. Teachers must be paid only in accordance with such orders, and nothing in a teacher contract that is prohibited by or inconsistent with orders is effective.[7]

The statutory provisions are supplemented by a document entitled "Conditions of Service for School Teachers in England and Wales" and known as "The Burgundy Book," which was first published in 1979 and reflected the outcomes of collective bargaining over many years. The Burgundy Book remains the foundation of many important terms and conditions of employment for teachers in the maintained sector of education.[8] To this end, there are a number of special characteristics of the teacher–employer relationship in England and Wales that are worth noting in some detail.

Tripartite Relationship

This is made up of the central government department; the Department for Children, Schools and Families (DCSF);[9] LEAs; and teachers. The DCSF has overall responsibility for schools. It is headed by a government minister, the Secretary of State. The legal responsibility for schools rests mainly on LEAs and governing bodies. Until the late 1980s, the central government had a supervisory role over schools, with little involvement in their management and operation.

Education in schools remains the legal responsibility of LEAs in England and Wales, although the government wishes to change their role from "provider" to "commissioner" of education for their area. This change is reflected in the establishment of two new types of school, academies and trust schools, which are not subject to the LEA supervision applicable to the schools mentioned below. The LEAs correspond to local government boundaries such as counties or London boroughs.

In the maintained sector, teachers are employed by LEAs, where they are employed to work in community or voluntary controlled schools, community special schools, or maintained nursery schools.[10] LEAs have the power to move teachers from one school to another school in their areas.

The governing bodies of such schools, while not employers, have specific statutory powers in relation to appointment, suspension, discipline, and dismissal of their teaching staff, but the precise scope of their powers can be unclear. This is illustrated by a number of recent court cases.[11] In addition, LEAs are entitled to attend and offer advice at all proceedings relating to the selection or dismissal of any teacher.[12]

Where teachers are employed by voluntary aided schools, foundation schools, foundation special schools, or other forms of maintained schools, they are employed by the schools' governing bodies.[13] LEAs are entitled to advise governing bodies in relation to the exercise of any of the governing body's functions of appointments, engagements, and dismissals of teachers.[14]

Qualifications, Fitness, and Suitability—Elements of Status

There are detailed regulations relating to health and criminal record checks as well as ensuring that prospective teachers are not barred from working with young children. For example, when teachers are being appointed, LEAs are required to ensure that the persons proposed meet staff qualification requirements. These include requirements as to: qualifications, registration, health and physical capacity, or fitness on educational grounds or in any other respect. Moreover, since 2004 first-time head teachers of maintained schools in England are required to hold the National Professional Qualification for Headship (NPQH) or its equivalent in Wales, Scotland, or Northern Ireland.[15]

Teachers[16] are classified as either qualified or unqualified in certain, specified circumstances. The latter category includes overseas-trained teachers, instructors, and those following the Graduate or Registered Teacher Programme routes. "Qualified teacher" status is defined and explained in legislation.[17] The Secretary of State, or the National Assembly for Wales, has the power to require that specified activities may be carried out only by qualified teachers[18] who possess full registration with the General Teaching Council for England (or Wales).[19] In addition, provisional registration may be required of unqualified teachers undertaking specified work in schools.[20]

The Education Act 2002 reinforced the requirements relating to the fitness and suitability of teachers. Certain identified activities may be carried out only by persons who satisfy specified conditions as to health or physical capacity.[21] The Secretary of State in England and the National Assembly in Wales have the power to give directions prohibiting named persons from carrying out specified works on grounds of unsuitability, past records of misconduct, or health problems.[22]

In recent years much greater emphasis has been placed on the suitability of persons appointed or recommended for appointment. Concern over child abuse cases, the new focus on the legal status of the child, and the implementation of the Human Rights Act 1998 have led to the replacement of relatively informal monitoring undertaken by central government with a more extensive, centralised scheme for the maintenance and checking of criminal convictions of persons seeking posts to work with children by the Criminal Records Bureau (CRB). The murder of two primary school pupils by the school caretaker who lived next to the school, the Soham murder, and the Bichard report reinforced the need for an improved system of checks.

In January 2006, following concern relating to the employment of a small number of teachers who had been cautioned or convicted of sexual offences in relation to children or persons under 16, the Secretary of State introduced new legislation which establishes a new vetting and barring scheme to be phased in from 2008.[23] Also in 2006, regulations were introduced that tightened up existing procedures.[24] These additions included requiring enhanced criminal record certificates to be obtained where supply staffs are used.[25] The Court of Appeal has held, in relation to an enhanced criminal record certificate for a midday assistant who worked at a secondary school supervising pupils in the lunchtime break, that the police were entitled to disclose all relevant information, including child protection matters and not just information about a person's actual or potential criminal activities.[26]

The Secretary of State has the power to bar or restrict a person's employment.[27] Individuals whom the Secretary of State bars from employment as teachers may appeal to the Care Standards Tribunal.

Single Set of Terms and Conditions

The original aim was that the School Teachers' Review Body would provide a reliable and comprehensive pay structure for all teachers in maintained schools in England and Wales. However, this has not proved to be the case. In practice, a significant number of teachers are employed in other ways, in particular through teacher supply agencies. Such teachers do not come within the statutory definition of *school teacher* because the statutory definition applies only to teachers who have contracts of employment or for services with governing bodies of maintained schools or LEAs.[28]

At the same time, the Education Act 2002 does envisage that teachers may be employed in schools other than under contracts of employment and enables staff to be engaged to work in these schools other than under contracts of employment.[29] Since 1991 many employment agencies have found a lucrative market in the supply of teachers, particularly for short-term cover. There is little consistency in these contractual arrangements, and often the agencies do not pay teachers so employed the statutory pay rates because they are considered to be employees of the agencies rather than the governing bodies or the LEAs.

This situation is also the source of an anomaly in relation to teachers' pension rights as well as equal pay issues, given that supply teachers are predominantly female. The European Court of Justice rejected the argument that this is unlawful discrimination in pay,[30] giving rise to an equal pay claim in *Allonby v Accrington and Rossendale College.*[31] The Court decided that as far as ordinary salary is concerned, comparisons can be made only between women and men who are employed by the same employers and cannot be made between men and women who perform the same jobs or jobs of equal value in the same employment sector.

An alternative approach to challenging discrepancies in pay and other terms and conditions between agency teachers and teachers employed by LEAs or governing bodies is illustrated by the ruling of the Court of Appeal in *Dacas v Brook Street Bureau (UK) Ltd.*[32] The Court indicated that in certain circumstances agency employees may have contracts of employment with their ultimate employers rather than the agencies. In particular, the Court explained that this may be the case when someone recruited from an employment agency effectively comes under the direction of the management of an agency's customer, and an employment contract relationship may well be established between that customer and the worker.

The current position of agency workers remains unsatisfactory. In 2007 the DTI undertook a consultation[33] exercise on proposals to introduce various amendments to the Conduct of Employment Agencies and Employment

Businesses Regulations 2003 in order to protect vulnerable temporary agency workers. The European Commission published a draft directive on the Working Conditions of Temporary (Agency) Workers which was supported in principle by the majority of European Union (EU) Employment Ministers Council in December 2007. In May 2008 the U.K. government agreed to implement the directive so that agency workers who have been employed for 12 weeks or more will receive equal treatment to permanent workers.

In addition to teachers who are employed through teacher supply agencies, teachers may be appointed under the statutory terms and conditions by LEAs or governing bodies on a part-time basis or to provide short-term cover for a fixed period. The latter are colloquially known as "supply teachers." Both groups may be employed full-time or part-time and may be requested to work on very short notice. Recent legislation has provided that employees on part-time or fixed-term contracts should normally not be treated differently from full-time colleagues on permanent contracts.[34]

Arguments have arisen over whether teachers on a succession of fixed-term contracts with LEAs should be regarded as continuously employed for the purpose of establishing rights under employment legislation. In *Cornwall County Council v Prater,*[35] the Court of Appeal held that since a teacher who was employed on a variety of fixed-term contracts, varying from a few months to several years, over a ten-year period was continuously employed, the gaps between the contracts were temporary cessations of work.

Appraisal and Pay

The Education Act 2002 enabled the Secretary of State, and the National Assembly for Wales, to make regulations requiring the appraisal of the performance of teachers and allowing schools to use the information obtained when making decisions on a teacher's pay.[36]

The government had also been concerned that career progression for teachers meant moving out of the classroom and into management. In September 1998 "advanced skills teachers" (ASTs) were introduced into the statutory pay and conditions framework. It was the government's intention to encourage particularly able teachers to remain in the direct teaching of pupils and students, rather than move into school management. In 2004 such teachers could be assessed as "excellent" by external assessors and advance to higher pay levels. The National Union of Teachers opposed its introduction. In particular, there were concerns that trade union activists would suffer discrimination in the assessment process. Further, there is ongoing debate over whether awards of such payments by one employer confer a status on teachers that is binding on subsequent employers.

Non-Pay Conditions

In 1987 the government decided that it was necessary to define what the job of teaching entailed. The current provisions are found in the Education Act 2002 and provide that teachers' contracts may not contain provisions on duties and working time other than those contained in an order made under the Act.[37] The effect of the order is that if a particular duty is not in an order, teachers cannot be required to undertake the work.

Teachers' working hours are now divided into directed and non-directed time. Teachers' directed working year is limited to a maximum of 1,265 hours over a maximum of 195 days, of which 190 shall be days of pupil attendance at school. The specified hours and days are the maximum. However, the 195 days and 1,265 hours do not define the totality of teachers' working time. There is, in addition, an obligation that teachers work such additional hours as may be necessary to complete whole jobs; this is known as non-directed time.

Concerns have been expressed about the increasing bureaucracy imposed mainly by central government on teachers that have resulted in increasing levels of stress. In 1999, the European Working Time Directive came into force, but teacher stress related personal injury claims increased, as illustrated by an important House of Lords' decision in 2004.[38]

Ideological and Academic Freedom

In the school sector in England and Wales, unlike the further and higher education sectors,[39] there is no express right to academic freedom for individual teachers in either the maintained or the independent sector. In the maintained sector, teachers by implication are free to express their views within certain constraints. In particular, there is a requirement that the school curriculum should be "balanced and broadly based."[40] In addition, LEAs, the governing bodies, and the head teachers are required to forbid "the promotion of partisan political views in the teaching of any subject in the school"[41] and to take reasonable steps to ensure that "where political issues are brought to the attention of pupils they are offered a balanced presentation of opposing views."[42]

In May 2007, for example, the Secretary of State sent a copy of the Al Gore film *An Inconvenient Truth* to every state secondary school in the U.K. as part of a pack containing four other short films and a cross-reference to a government Website, which contained a guidance note. The High Court reasoned that the Secretary of State's action was unlawful because, insofar as the film was partisan, his having sent it out breached ss 406 and 407 of the Education Act 1996.[43]

Schools do address controversial topics such as religious education, sex and relationship education in secondary schools, and collective worship as part of their curriculum. Teachers at maintained schools, which are non-denominational or do not have a religious character, have the legal right to opt out of teaching religious education based on their religious opinions. In particular, teachers are not disqualified from employment at such schools on account of their religious opinions, their attendance or non-attendance at religious worship, or their refusal to provide religious education.[44]

On the other hand, teachers at schools with a "religious character" are not similarly protected, despite the recent legislation on religious discrimination. However, where schools have a religious character, there are three exceptions to this principle. First, in connection with the appointment of persons as head teachers of foundation schools with a religious character, or voluntary controlled schools, regard may be had to their ability and fitness to preserve and develop the religious character of the school.[45]

Second, teachers employed to work in voluntary aided schools supported by the Anglican, Roman Catholic, or other churches or religions will normally find an obligation to avoid conduct that offends the religious faith or doctrine to which the school is linked expressly written into their contract of employment. The SSFA 1998 s 60 expressly authorises the inclusion of such terms. The law also provides that where schools are voluntary aided, preference may be given, in connection with appointments, remuneration, or promotion of teachers at the school, to persons who are believers, worshippers, or willing to teach the school's religion or religious denomination. Further, regard may be had, in connection with the termination of the employment of teachers at such schools, to any conduct on their part that is incompatible with the precepts, or with the upholding of the tenets, of the religion or religious denomination so specified.[46]

In *Board of Governors of St Matthias Church of England School v Crizzle* (1993) ICR 401, the applicant, the school's deputy head teacher, was a non-practising Roman Catholic of Asian origin who applied unsuccessfully for the post of head teacher. The Employment Appeals Tribunal (EAT) held that the Board of Governors of a Church of England voluntary aided school was justified in making it a condition for the post of head teacher that the applicant was a committed, practising Christian and that such a condition was not a breach of the Race Relations Act 1976.

Third, special rules apply to the appointment and dismissal of teachers of religious education in such schools. These teachers are described as "reserved teachers." The majority of the provisions apply to foundation and voluntary controlled schools with a religious character rather than voluntary aided schools. In particular, a number of teachers may be selected for their fitness and competence to provide religious education. The number of reserved teachers in such a school shall not exceed one-fifth of the teaching staff, including the head teacher.[47]

The Employment Equality (Religion or Belief) Regulations 2003 have implemented EU legislation that makes it unlawful to discriminate against people at work on the basis of their religion or belief. This may, for example, protect teachers who do not wish to teach aspects of sex education with which they disagree such as sex before marriage or homosexuality. The EU agreed that the provisions contained in the School Standards and Framework Act 1998, which permit religious schools to give preference to teachers who practise the schools' faith, will continue to be lawful.

The U.K. regulations provide that it is not unlawful to discriminate against job applicants or employees, where being of a particular religion or belief is a genuine and determining occupational requirement.[48] In a recent case from Scotland, this provision was interpreted restrictively by the EAT, which found in relation to Scottish legislation that being a Roman Catholic was not necessarily a genuine occupational requirement for a post in a Roman Catholic school.[49]

Arguably, the domestic statutory provisions are in conflict with the Human Rights Act 1998 and Article 9 of the European Convention on Human Rights (ECHR), which provides for freedom of thought, conscience, and religion, including the freedom to manifest one's religion or belief in worship, teaching, practice, and observance. Even so, this freedom is subject to limitations, including the protection of the rights of others. This suggests that even if statutory provisions do breach Article 9.1, the limitations in Article 9.2 may protect the position of schools with a religious character and allow them to give preference to teachers who are sympathetic to the religious denomination or religion of such schools.

Another issue that has arisen recently is whether teaching assistants and, by analogy, teachers, are entitled to wear full face veils when teaching. In *Azmi v Kirklees Metropolitan Council* the EAT held that an LEA, in suspending a Muslim teaching assistant for refusing to remove her veil when working directly with children, had not discriminated against her in breach of U.K. or EU law.[50] Similarly, health and safety issues may arise where Muslim teachers wish to wear full-length loose *jilbabs*.

As a consequence of EU legislation, it is normally unlawful to discriminate against homosexual applicants or employees based on their sexual orientation. However, there is an important exception in the U.K. regulations that applies to schools with a religious character. Where employment is for purposes of an organised religion and employers can argue that being of a particular sexual orientation is a genuine and determining occupational requirement in order to comply with the doctrines of the religion or to avoid conflicting with the strongly held religious convictions of a significant number of the religion's followers,[51] they are free to act in accord with their beliefs.

These provisions were thought to possibly breach the Human Rights Act 1998 and Articles 8 and 14 of the ECHR. Article 8 provides for the right to respect for private and family life. Article 14 prohibits discrimination in the exercise of conventional rights. However, the decision of the House of Lords in *Pearce v Governing Body of Mayfield School*[52] was not encouraging. The claimant was a teacher who was subjected to abuse by pupils because she was a lesbian.

The House of Lords rejected the teacher's claim that she was discriminated against due to her sex. At the time of the discrimination, the Human Rights Act was not in force. Their Lordships added that the school was not vicariously liable for the actions of its pupils. Subsequently, in *R (ota) Amicus—MSF Section and 6 Others v Secretary of State for Trade and Industry and (1) Christian Action Research Education; (2) Evangelical Alliance; (3) Christian Schools Alliance (Interveners)*,[53] the High Court held that this genuine occupational requirement exception was compatible with the EC Council Directive 2000/78 and with the ECHR 1950 Articles 8 and 14.

Teacher Sanctions, Due Process, and Dismissal

The Employment Act 2002[54] now requires employers to operate disciplinary and grievance procedures that satisfy statutory procedural requirements. These measures are broadly consistent with those that have long been applicable to school staff members with the aim of achieving fairness in dismissals and to resolve grievances. There are two significant consequences of these changes for teaching staff. First, there is no longer any statutory requirement that governors must be involved in the dismissal of staff members. Second, dismissals may take effect before appeals have been concluded on the basis that the dismissed staff member may be reinstated on successful appeals. However, these provisions describe only minimum statutory requirements.

The Education Act 2002 and its regulations[55] contain additional provisions on how governing bodies and LEAs should deal with staff conduct, discipline, and grievances; serious concerns about the performance of the head teacher; and suspension and dismissal of staff. Governing bodies must establish disciplinary and grievance procedures for school staff as well as procedures for dealing with lack of capability.[56]

Teachers' contracts are unusual in that normally they can only be terminated on three days in the year: December 31, April 30 (or the last day of the school's Easter holiday if it is earlier and the teacher is moving to a new teaching job in the summer term), and August 31. Notice of resignation or termination for teachers other than heads is two months to terminate on December 31 or April 30 and three months to terminate on August 31. One month longer is required in the case of the head teacher. The reason for this is to protect schools and pupils from the obviously disruptive effects of midterm changes.

As is the position with the appointment of teachers, the provisions for suspension and dismissal of staff vary according to whether schools are community or voluntary controlled, where LEAs are the employers,[57] as opposed to voluntary aided or foundation schools, where governing bodies are the employers.[58] Different provisions may apply to academies and trust schools.

In the case of community and voluntary controlled schools, both governing bodies and head teachers have the power to suspend teachers for good cause but must immediately inform LEAs and head teachers or (as the case may be) governing bodies.[59]

Governing bodies do not have the power to dismiss teachers but may decide that any persons whom they employ or engage to work at schools should cease to work there; in such circumstances, they must notify authorities in writing of their determination and the reasons for so deciding.[60] LEAs as employers are required to terminate contracts of employment.

As indicated above, the respective roles of LEAs and governing bodies are not always clear in practice. In *Green v Governing Body of Victoria Road Primary School and Kent County Council*,[61] the Court of Appeal ruled that the governing body was the correct respondent for a constructive dismissal claim notwithstanding the fact that the applicant teacher had a contract of employment with the local authority. In relation to a claim brought by a teacher under the Disability Discrimination Act 1995, the Court of Appeal found that the liability of a governing body of a school as an employer only existed when the claim related to its exercise of employment powers vested in it by statute.[62] In *Northamptonshire County Council and Abington Vale Middles School v Gilkes*,[63] the EAT asserted that a school's failure to follow a protocol devised by an LEA and to which the school subscribed did not render the LEA liable for a teacher's claim for unfair dismissal. The Court concluded that any liability lay with the school.

In the case of voluntary aided and foundation schools, both governing bodies and head teachers have power to suspend teachers for good cause where, in the opinion of the governing bodies or head teachers, suspension from schools is required. Only governing bodies may end suspensions under this regulation.[64] The governing bodies of voluntary aided and foundation schools are employers in their own right and have the power to dismiss in accordance with normal employment law principles.

In addition, where teachers are dismissed for misconduct or incompetence or resign in circumstances in which they would have been dismissed or considered for dismissal, employers must notify the relevant General Teaching Council (GTC).[65] The appropriate GTC then considers a case to decide whether a teacher's GTC registration should be withdrawn or qualified. No one may be employed as a qualified teacher without a GTC registration, and a person may only be employed as a qualified teacher subject to such conditions as the relevant GTC may have specified. There is a right of appeal to the High Court. The GTC for England does not consider cases which the Secretary of State reserves for his own consideration and action under the Education (Prohibition from Teaching or Working with Children) Regulations 2003.[66]

Emerging Issues

A major issue not yet resolved is whether teaching has the status of a profession. The concept of a profession was of importance up to the twentieth century, but its importance has diminished and may continue to diminish in the twentieth-first century as specialist knowledge becomes available to all and professional skills are less valued than they once were.

Nevertheless, the establishment of the GTCs in 1998 addressed what had long been an aspiration of teachers: that they should be seen as a profession with a self-governing body in the same way as doctors and lawyers.[67] However, the creation of the GTCs at a time when self-regulation has been criticised for being ineffective from the perspective of the consumer has perhaps led to their being initially uncertain about their role. Even so, the GTCs have become an effective regulatory role for professional standards and have established an effective professional disciplinary function. The GTCs also exist to promote high professional standards in teaching and perhaps need to develop a higher profile by commenting on the issues of debate and controversy in education.

A teacher must normally have the status of a "qualified teacher" in order to be a teacher, but it is arguable that once a governing body has awarded the status of, for example, an Advanced Skills Teacher, teachers should retain this status when they move to a new employer. This has not been the approach adopted by most LEAs in England and Wales, although it does influence teacher employment relationships in other countries. This analysis involves affording teachers a status which they earn and which, provided they give no cause to the relevant professional bodies to take it away, they then retain in their "ownership" throughout their careers.

At the same time as the recognition of professional status, there has been a move to de-skilling. The government has introduced a new workforce of "higher level teaching assistants" to help reduce the burden on teachers.[68] The provisions are controversial because the government was thought to be trying to dilute teacher professionalism and expertise while reducing its value by the use of these assistants to undertake certain "specified work" that could previously only be undertaken by qualified teachers. The government denies that this was its intention, but the wording of the regulations remains ambiguous.

Meanwhile, the role of teachers' trade unions appears to have been weakened. In particular, the largest teaching union, the National Union of Teachers (NUT), refused in 2003 to accept a national agreement reforming teachers' workloads because of its concerns about teaching assistants and performance-related pay. As a consequence, the Secretary of State has refused to consult the NUT about teachers' conditions of employment. This reflects a more general trend in the U.K. which has seen the development of individual employment rights, the declining influence of trade unions in the workplace, and a shift from collective bargaining toward dispute resolution through the legal system.[69]

Current issues of particular importance for individual teachers include the call for a right for teachers accused of physical or sexual abuse against pupils to remain anonymous until allegations have been upheld by courts. This is because teachers have virtually no means of redress where unsubstantiated allegations damage or even destroy their health or career.

Another matter of concern to teachers is the change in the age at which they can retire and claim their pensions. Teachers who were employed before January 1, 2007, may retire on full pension when they reach the age of 60 but may continue to work until they are 65 years of age. New entrants to the profession will normally only be able to claim their pension when they reach the age of 65. The legality of requiring teachers to retire at a specific age may be in breach of the age discrimination legislation. Even so, the teaching profession has an aging profile, and the evidence indicates that there will be a shortage of qualified teachers in key subjects, which may enable those teachers who wish to continue working to do so.

Conclusion

The formal recognition of teaching as a profession has come at a time when the school workforce has become more casualised and diverse. Moreover, the traditional tripartite relationship continues to blur the lines of responsibility. The introduction of new types of schools such as academies and trust schools potentially undermines the community role of LEAs.

The employment rights of teachers have become more individualised and less collective. However, the professional role of teachers has diminished as the central government has reduced their autonomy by, for instance, imposing detailed curricular requirements on teachers and regulating their terms and conditions of employment through legislation. Respect for teachers has diminished as part of a broader change in society as a whole, while a significant number of parents and pupils no longer consider it inappropriate to abuse teachers, both verbally and physically. Perhaps the right to respect should be a new legal right for teachers.

Cases

Allonby v Accrington and Rossendale College, European Court of Justice Case C-256/01 decision 13 January 2004

Azmi v Kirklees Metropolitan Council [2007] IRLR 484

Barber v Somerset County Council [2004] 1 WLR 1089; [2004] 2 All ER 385

Cornwall County Council v Prater, [2006] EWCA Crv. 102.

Dacas v Brook Street Bureau (UK) Ltd [2004] IRLR 358

Dimmock v Secretary of State for Children, Schools and Families [2007] EWHC 2288 (Admin), [2007] NLJR 1462.

Elsner-Lakeberg v Land Nordrhein-Westfalen (C-285/02) (2004) 2 CMLR 36

Enderby v Frenchay Health Authority and Secretary of State for Health [1993] IRLR 591, ECJ Case No C–127/92

Glasgow City Council v McNab [2007] IRLR 476

Governing Body of Victoria Road Primary School and Kent County Council v Green [2004] 2 All ER 763(CA)

James v Greenwich London Borough Council [2008] EWCA Civ 35; [2008] IRLR 302

Murphy v Slough Borough Council and Another [2005] EWCA Civ 122, [2005] IRLR 382

Northamptonshire County Council and Abington Vale Middle School v Gilkes (unreported) UKEAT/0579/05/CK

Pearce v Governing Body of Mayfield School [2004] 1 All ER 339; [2003] IRLR 512; [2003] ELR 655

R (ota) Amicus—MSF Section and 6 Others v Secretary of State for Trade and Industry and (1) Christian Action Research Education; (2) Evangelical Alliance; (3) Christian Schools Alliance (Interveners) [2004] 2 All ER 763; [2004] ELR 75

R v Secretary of State for Employment, ex p Equal Opportunities Commission [1993] 1 All ER 1022, [1993] 1 WLR 872, [1993] 1 CMLR 915, CA, [1993] ICR 251, [1993] IRLR 10

Smith v Kent County Council [2004] EWHC 412 (QB)

*Whitehead v The Governing Body of Corley School and Coventry City Council (*2007) (UKEAT/0438/06/DM)

Notes

1. Education legislation in Northern Ireland has been affected by the political and religious difficulties of the province. Northern Ireland was under direct rule by London from 1974, which meant that much education legislation was formulated in London and reflected legislation in England and Wales. Sometimes it was adapted to local circumstances. Under the Northern Ireland Act 1998, direct rule ended and the Northern Ireland Department of Education was headed by a Minister for Education responsible to the Northern Ireland Assembly. However, the Assembly was suspended in 2000 and was only revived in 2007.

2. E.g., Education (Scotland) Act 1980, Standards in Scotland's Schools, etc. Act 2000; The Requirements for Teachers (Scotland) Regulations 2005 SSI 2005/355.

3. Government of Wales Act 2006.

4. The Teachers Pay and Conditions Act 1987, which was replaced by the School Teachers Pay and Conditions Act of 1991.

5. Education Act 2002 (EdA 2002) ss 119–130, as amended.

6. EdA 2002 s 120.

7. EdA 2002 s 122.

8. In *Smith v Kent County Council* [2004] EWHC 412 (QB), the High Court held that the Burgundy Book had been incorporated into the claimant's contract of employment, and its provisions as to the amount of a deduction for strike action (1/365 of the annual salary) should be deducted rather than the amount (1/195) argued for by her employer, based on provisions in the School Teachers' Pay and Conditions Document.

9. Until June 2007 it was known as the Department for Education and Skills.

10. EdA 2002 s 35; School Staffing (England) Regulations 2003, SI 2003/1963 Part 2 as amended by School Staffing (England) (Amendment) Regulations 2003, SI 2003/2725, by the School Staffing (England) (Amendment) Regulations 2006, SI 2006/1067 and by the School Staffing (England) (Amendment) (No 2) Regulations 2006, SI 2006/3197. For the position in Wales, see, e.g., the Education (Modification of Enactments Relating to Employment)(Wales) Order 2006 SI 2006/1073; the Staffing of Maintained Schools (Wales) Regulations 2006 SI 2006/873 (W.181) as amended by SI 2007/944 (W.80) and SI 2007/1069 (W.109).

11. *Governing Body of Victoria Road Primary School and Kent County Council v Green* [2004] 2 All ER 763(CA) and *Murphy v Slough Borough Council and Another* [2005] EWCA Civ 122; *Northamptonshire County Council and Abington Vale Middle School v Gilkes* (unreported) UKEAT/0579/05/CK.

12. School Staffing (England) Regulations 2003, SI 2003/1963 reg 12.

13. EdA 2002 s 36; School Staffing (England) Regulations 2003, SI 2003/1963 Part 3 as amended by School Staffing (England) (Amendment) Regulations 2003, SI 2003/2725, by the School Staffing (England) (Amendment) Regulations 2006, SI

2006/1067 and by the School Staffing (England) (Amendment) (No 2) Regulations 2006, SI 2006/3197.

14. School Staffing (England) Regulations 2003, SI 2003/1963 regs 21, 22.

15. EdA 2002 s 135; Education (Head Teachers' Qualifications) (England) Regulations 2003 SI 2003/3111.

16. EdA 2002 s 122.

17. EdA 2002 s132; Education (School Teachers' Qualifications) (England) Regulations 2003, SI2003/1662 as amended by EdA 2005 s 74

18. EdA 2002 s133; Education (School Teachers' Qualifications) (England) Regulations 2003, SI 2003/1662 as amended by EdA 2005 s 74; Education (Specified Work and Registration) (England) Regulations 2003 SI 2003/1663. For the position in Wales, see, e.g., Education (School Teachers' Qualifications) (Wales) Regulations 2004 SI 2004/1729 (W. 173) as amended by SI 2008/215 (W. 26) and the Education (Specified Work and Registration) (Wales) Regulations 2004 SI 2004/1774 (W.183).

19. EdA 2002 s 134. Education (School Teachers' Qualifications) (England) Regulations 2003, SI2003/1662 as amended by EdA 2005 s 74; Education (Specified Work and Registration) (England) Regulations 2003 SI 2003/1663.

20. Education (School Teachers' Prescribed Qualifications, etc.) Order 2003 SI 2003/1709 as amended by EdA 2005 s 74.

21. EdA 2002 s 141.

22. EdA 2002 s 141–145; the Education (Health Standards) (England) Regulations 2003, SI 2003/3139; the Education (Health Standards) (Wales) Regulations 2004, SI 2004/2733 (W 240).

23. Safeguarding Vulnerable Groups Act 2006.

24. School Staffing (England) (Amendment) Regulations 2006 (SI 2006/1067).

25. School Staffing (England) (Amendment) (No 2) Regulations 2006, SI 2006/3197; new statutory guidance (Safeguarding Children and Safer Recruitment in Education (04217-2006BKT-EN) also came into force on January 1, 2007.

26. *R (ota L) v Commissioner of Police for the Metropolis and Secretary of State for the Home Department* [2007] EWCA Civ 168.

27. EdA 2002 s 142; the Education (Prohibition from Teaching or Working with Children) Regulations 2003 (SI 2003/1184), as amended in 2004 (SI 2004/1493) and 2007(SI 2007/195).

28. EdA 2002 s 122.

29. Ss 35, 36.

30. See in particular, Case No C-127/92 *Enderby v Frenchay Health Authority and Secretary of State for Health* [1993] IRLR 591, *ECJ and R v Secretary of State for Employment, ex p Equal Opportunities Commission* [1993] 1 All ER 1022, [1993] 1 WLR 872, [1993] 1 CMLR 915, CA, [1993] ICR 251, [1993] IRLR 10; *Elsner-Lakeberg v Land Nordrhein-Westfalen* (C-285/02) (2004) 2 CMLR 36; *Part-time workers: The effect of Elsner*, Chris Walter, Emp LJ (2005) February, pp. 12–13.

31. European Court of Justice Case C-256/01 decision January 13, 2004.

32. *Dacas v Brook Street Bureau (UK) Ltd* [2004] IRLR 358; see *James v Greenwich London Borough Council* [2008] EWCA Civ 35; [2008] IRLR 302.

33. Success at Work: Consultation on Measures to Protect Vulnerable Agency Workers (February 2007).

34. Fixed-Term Employees (Prevention of Less Favourable Treatment) Regulations 2002 SI 2002; Part-Time Workers (Prevention of Less Favourable Treatment) Regulations 2000, SI 2000/1551.

35. [2006] 2 All ER 1013; [2006] IRLR 362. See also *Casual Workers and Continuity of Employment*, ACL Davies, ILJ (2006), Vol. 35, pp. 196–201.

36. EdA 2002 s 131; Education (School Teacher Performance Management) (England) Regulations 2006, SI 2006/2661, and the Education (School Teacher Appraisal) (Wales) Regulations 2002, SI 2002/1394. See also DfES Guidance 3984/2006: "Teachers' and Head Teachers' Performance Management Guidance" (October 2006).

37. EdA 2002 s 122(2) (c).

38. *Barber v Somerset County Council* [2004] 1 WLR 1089; [2004] 2 All ER 385.

39. Education (No 2) Act 1986 s 43.

40. Education Act 1996 s 351 as amended by the Education Act 2002 s 78.

41. Education Act 1996 s 406.

42. Education Act 1996 s 407.

43. *Dimmock v Secretary of State for Children, Schools and Families* [2007] EWHC 2288 (Admin), [2007] NLJR 1462. A parent governor at a school applied for judicial review of the Secretary of State's decision to send out the pack. The Court considered that the Secretary of State should have made it clear that the views expressed in the film were not promoted by him and that there was a contrary view, which should be explored. The guidance should have been incorporated into the pack and should have identified a number of serious errors in the film. The Secretary of State agreed to amend the guidance and did so in October 2007 (*The climate change film pack. Guidance for teaching staff* [amended October 2007].)

44. SSFA 1998 s 59.

45. SSFA s 60(2).

46. SSFA 1998 s 60(5).

47. SSFA 1998 s 58. The Education and Inspections Act 2006 s 37 provides that the head teacher of a foundation school with a religious character is no longer prohibited from being a reserved teacher.

48. Employment Equality (Religion or Belief) Regulations 2003 SI 2003/1660, as amended by SI 2007/2269, reg 7.

49. *Glasgow City Council v McNab* (2007) IRLR 476.

50. [2007] IRLR 484.

51. Employment Equality (Sexual Orientation) Regulations 2003 SI 2003/166, as amended by SI 2007/2269, reg 7.

52. [2004] 1 All ER 339; [2003] IRLR 512; [2003] ELR 655.

53. [2004] IRLR 430; [2004] ELR 311.

54. S 29(1).

55. For example, the School Staffing (England) Regulations 2003, SI 2003/1963; Government of Maintained Schools (Wales) 2005 SI 2005/2914 (W 211); Staffing of Maintained Schools (Wales) Regulations 2006, SI 2006/873 (W 81). Guidance is provided in "Staffing Guidance under sections 35(8) and 36(8) of the Education Act 2002."

56. School Staffing (England) Regulations 2003, SI 2003/1963 regs 6 and 7.

57. EdA 2002 s 35.

58. EdA 2002 s 36.

59. School Staffing (England) Regulations 2003, SI 2003/1963 reg 16.

60. School Staffing (England) Regulations 2003, SI 2003/1963 reg 17. In *Whitehead v The Governing Body of Corley School and Coventry City Council* (2007) (UKEAT/0438/06/DM), the EAT considered that paragraph 17.1 of the School (Staffing) (England) Regulations 2003 did not require school governors to notify the local education authority before the appeal was determined of a decision to dismiss a teacher, whose contract provided that notification should only be given after determination of an appeal. Notification prior to the determination of the appeal amounted to a breach of contract.

61. [2004] 2 All ER 763; [2004] ELR 75.

62. *Murphy v Slough Borough Council and the Governing Body of Langleywood School* [2005] IRLR 382.

63. (Unreported) UKEATR/0579/05/CK.

64. School Staffing (England) Regulations 2003, SI 2003/1963 reg 25.

65. The Teaching and Higher Education Act 1998 Part 1 and Schedules 1 and 2 as amended by the EdA 2002; General Teaching Council for England (Disciplinary Functions) Regulations 2001, SI 2001/1268; General Teaching Council for Wales (Disciplinary Functions) Regulations 2001, SI 2001/1424.

66. SI 2003/1184.

67. All qualified teachers are eligible for registration, but registration with a GTC is only now compulsory for teachers working in schools.

68. Education (Specified Work and Registration) (England) Regulations 2003 SI 2003/ with parallel regulations in Wales. See also Education Act 2005 Part 3.

69. *What space for unions on the floor of rights? Trade unions and the enforcement of statutory individual employment rights*, Trevor Colling, *ILJ* (2006) 35 pp. 140–60.

7

France

Andre Legrand, translated by Margot Hervey

Introduction

The status of teachers in France derives essentially from legislative and statutory rules. The main distinction is between the teaching staffs of public schools and those of private schools.

The first category of teachers consists of civil servants or other public agents of the State. They are therefore bound by the public law rules. Established public servants, who form the greater part of the workforce, are subject to the clauses of the two laws that govern the general status of the civil service (laws of July 13, 1983, and January 11, 1984). However, the special demands of teaching justify the existence of many exceptions to the laws. Some of these requirements result from legislative clauses and are brought together in Title IX of the Education Code.

The others are created by the special statuses established by decrees, applied to the different teaching professions amongst which teachers are divided, according to the level of teaching. Non-established teachers are subject to public law rules, which are mainly the result of both statutory provisions and rules set by precedents.

There are two sorts of private establishments. In the schools that are totally independent from the State, teachers are entirely subject to normal labour law. However, many private establishments, for the most part described as Catholic, have, in accordance with the provisions of the Debré law of December 31, 1959, agreed to a contract of partnership with the State that associates them with the public service. This partnership has one important consequence: the salaries of the later establishments' teachers are paid by the State.

Teachers in private establishments under partnership contracts are therefore generally linked to the State contractually. These teachers thus have a hybrid status: one of private law concerning their relationship with the teaching establishment, in the sense that heads of school have an important power of control and decision on the teachers' activities. On the other hand, the January 5, 2005, law (Loi Censi) specifies that public law applies to the carrying out of the teaching functions "for which the teachers are employed and paid by the State." In their relationship with the State, then, these teachers are in public law situations.

Teachers' Employment Rights

Teachers in Public Establishments

Established teachers form the most important category among civil servants. In fact, there are 750,000 established teachers in primary and secondary education. The status of teachers in nursery and primary schools, called schoolteachers ("professeurs des écoles") is the result of the August 1, 1990, decree. Teachers in secondary education are divided into three distinct bodies. "Agrégés" and "certifiés" teachers, whose status is set by the July 4, 1972, decrees, teach in general and specialised education establishments. Teachers in secondary schools prepare pupils for specified professions. Staff members in higher education are divided into professors and lecturers, in accordance with the June 6, 1984, decree.

The established teachers are recruited by competitive examinations. These examinations consist of tests in which candidates' results are evaluated by an independent jury, made up mostly of practising teachers and who list, in order of merit, a number of candidates equal to the maximum number of seats offered by the competitive exam. Appointing authorities are bound by this ranking.

In order to qualify for admission, applicants must conform to specified general rules to be accepted as civil servants; these include being citizens of the European Union, being in full possession of their civic rights, being of good character, being healthy, and possessing educational qualifications appropriate to the jobs they seek. Teachers in primary and secondary education must have a bachelor's degree, while professors and lecturers in higher education must possess a doctorate.

Successful teacher candidates then become trainees. For primary and secondary education, candidates undergo a year of training at the University

Institute of Teachers Training (IUFM). On successful completion of training, teacher candidates become established civil servants. From then on, teachers benefit from a "career" status that guarantees regular promotions. Civil servants' salaries are fixed by a scale depending on their grade and step. Likewise, established teachers within the same profession are bound by identical service obligations that are determined by the amount of time they actually spend teaching.

Non-established public teachers are far less numerous. Most of these teachers are recruited by contract, for set periods of time. In some cases, the very specific requirements of the subjects being taught or the particular skills of a professional call for a personalised recruitment of what are described as associated teachers. In other cases, such as the nature of the subject, mostly educational guidance for young students, young doctoral candidates can obtain positions that allow them to gain experience for their subsequent careers.

Teachers in Private Establishments under Partnership Contract

There are 150,000 teachers in contract private education. About a third of these teachers are delegated as assistants who are recruited for a year at the beginning of each academic year: they are in unsettled situations. The other two-thirds of the teachers are linked to the State by contract. The recruitment conditions, namely age and character, of this latter set of teachers are the same as in public education. In reality, the way these teachers are recruited is getting closer to the way in which civil servants are employed. For example, in 1993, competitive examinations were organised for private school teachers.

Similarly, young teachers' training is organised in accordance with rules that are very much like those applicable to teachers in public education. More specifically, these teachers now require one year of preparation in a teacher training establishment organised by agreement between the State and representatives of private establishments.

Two main distinctions characterize the situation of public establishments' teachers and contractual teachers from the private education system. On the one hand, the State cannot impose the appointments of teachers to private establishments. Indeed, such appointments depend on prior approval by the heads of the establishments. On the other hand, teachers from private education benefit neither from security of employment, even though they have a degree of protection as soon as they are engaged by permanent contracts, nor from the civil servants' pension regime.

As to career structures, the November 25, 1977, Guermeur law imposes the principle of parity. This law implies that contractual teachers of private establishments under partnership contracts benefit from the same rules as established public education teachers who have the same level of education and training. This law applies regardless of whether the issues concern the rules related to work conditions or suspension of duty, social benefits, or training opportunities.

Trade Union Rights and Career Management

All teachers, whether in public or private establishments, may belong to trade unions. In a country where a small percentage of the workforce belongs to trade unions, the membership of teachers is relatively high. Although they share a common basis, the situations of teachers in public and private establishments have certain differences.

In labour law, as it applies to teachers in private establishments, collective bargaining agreements are an important basis of law. Accordingly, many agreements have been settled between teachers' trade unions and Catholic teaching establishments, for example, regarding teachers' professional training conditions.

In the public law system that characterizes the situation of teachers in public establishments, teachers are in a legal and statutory situation; normally, laws and statutes are the only legal authority. However, in reality there exist many agreements between the State and trade union movements that directly influence the practices adopted in schools. Moreover, there exists a technical joint committee at the Ministry of Education that includes, in equal numbers, representatives designated by represented trade union movements and representatives of school administrations. This committee must, in particular, be consulted on every text of a statutory nature.

Personal issues, such as transfers or promotions and, for private education, appointments or dismissals, are examined by joint administrative committees or by joint advisory committees, who include in equal numbers trade union representatives elected by the staff and representatives of the administration. The advice given by these committees is, in theory, purely advisory and, indeed, in reality the administration usually does not take their advice into account.

Ideological/Academic Freedom, Free Speech, and Religious Rights

The situations of public school teachers are determined by the general rules of the civil service. The situations of teachers are based on essential distinctions between freedom of opinion and freedom of speech. Insofar as the first is a hard and fast rule, the State cannot de-bar or sanction teacher candidates on the basis of their political, trade union, philosophical, or religious views. In the 1930s and 1940s, the highest administrative court (hereafter, the *Conseil d'Etat*) overruled a refusal by the State to a candidate to a primary education teacher post on the sole ground that she had spent her education in a private establishment and likewise a refusal to nominate based on the fact that she was part of a religious group in her free time. The Conseil d'Etat also forbade the distribution of application forms to an IUFM that could have indirectly revealed the candidates' political, trade union, or religious membership.

An essential question concerns freedom of speech. Like all civil servants, teachers have a moral obligation. Still, this obligation is very strong when it comes to teachers in light of the importance of the principle of secularity in public education and respect of children's integrity.

When teaching, educators must be completely neutral in their views. Any biased or proselytising attitudes that affect the content of educational activities justify disciplinary sanctions and can constitute offences for which teachers are personally liable. A conflict tribunal (*Tribunal des conflits*) decided this in 1908 when a teacher made violently anti-religious remarks in his classroom. Administrative courts have recently reached similar judgements against teachers who have expressed racist points of view in their classrooms. This kind of lapse in behaviour can also attract sanctions against teachers in private establishments who are working under partnership contracts.

Another important question is how secularity applies to dress. The matter has arisen concerning clergymen. A law of 1886, which appears in Article L.141-4 of the Education Code, forbids the recruitment of clergymen in public primary schools. No provision exists concerning secondary education. Further, in a 1912 judgement, the Conseil d'Etat agreed with the refusal to accept the application by a clergyman to sit at a competitive entry teaching examination, ruling that the priesthood, evidenced at the time by the wearing of the cassock, demonstrated the public expression of an opinion that could cast doubts on his neutrality. However, it is generally accepted that this precedent is no longer applicable and, in 1970, an administrative court allowed a priest to sit in on the competitive examination for recruitment of secondary education English teachers. Of course, a priest or members of religious order teaching in a public secondary education establishment would be obliged to respect its secularity. In higher education, there are no restrictions.

The question of wearing the Islamic veil has arisen concerning female teachers. By established precedence, this is incompatible with the secularity principle. The wearing of the veil in a teaching establishment and refusal to remove it therefore justify not only the rejection of an application to an IUFM but also permit disciplinary actions that can include dismissal.

As far as private teachers are concerned, a distinction must be made between the establishments that have a partnership with the State and those lacking such agreements. The latter are at liberty to specify the conditions of recruitment and service as long as they do not violate the law. The former are associated with the public service. The new version of Article L. 442-5 of the Education Code, which dates from 2005, reiterates an essential principle: establishments must respect teachers' freedom of conscience, but in return teachers must take into account the specificity of the establishments in question.

In 1978, after many judicial disagreements, a "Cour de cassation" judgement led to much debate. The Court upheld as legal the action of officials in an establishment operating under a partnership contract when they dismissed a teacher who was divorced and remarried. Even so, most authors refuse to place any precedential value on that decision. This outcome seems incompatible with the position taken by the Constitutional Court, and now repeated by the law, which reaffirms the teachers' freedom of conscience. The moral obligation is essentially negative. As a senior magistrate has written, a philosophy teacher of a Catholic school could not declare his atheism in front of his pupils. Still, this does not mean that the philosopher would have to teach in a set way or that he has to be a model of the Catholic faith in his personal life.

Teacher Sanctions, Due Process, and Dismissal

Whether from public or private establishments, teachers may be liable on civil, penal, or disciplinary grounds, each having its own specificities. The law of tort contains specific references to teachers. This is less true for responsibility and disciplinary liability.

Law of Tort

The question of teachers' tort liability is contained in the April 5, 1937, law, whose main provision is now included in the Education Code. Improperly named "law modifying the evidence rules concerning primary education teachers' liability," in reality, the law applies to all educational staff who may have supervisory duties. Precedence also extended this liability to include teachers in private establishments under partnership.

When injuries are caused by or to pupils under teachers' supervision and they are attributable to a lack of teacher supervision, the law substitutes the State's liability for the teachers' in forbidding direct action against teachers before the courts. There is therefore a very important derogation to the usual rules set by the Civil Code, whereby all individuals are responsible for the damages resulting from their own actions or from the actions of others depending on them such that this confers a special protection on teachers.

In theory, when the State is liable in such circumstances, it may take action against the teachers or civil servants who are at fault. However, in reality, such actions are rare and are mainly to be seen in cases involving vice. The State's liability is heard in judicial courts; actions taken against teachers are judged by administrative courts.

Responsibility

The issues that derive from responsibility and the rules that apply to it are not specific to teachers. For about fifteen years, the number of prosecutions taken against several categories of people, namely politicians, business managers, and civil servants, concerning actions committed during the exercise of their electoral or professional functions has risen. Teachers can be found guilty of ordinary offences. This is the case when teachers make remarks that constitute offences, such as racist remarks. However, the commission of some offences in schools or in the exercise of educational duties can constitute aggravating circumstances—harassment, for example—and can incur heavier sentences.

The important question that has arisen lately in France concerns recklessness. The development of litigation of this kind of offence can be explained by several factors. The reason for this development is the changing attitudes coupled with the fact that users of public services or other citizens no longer accept some forms of waivers of liability concerning representatives of the authorities or their agents. A modification to the Penal Code extended liability to include unintended offences. The application of this law has raised so many issues that it has had to be rewritten twice. Although not very numerous, cases in this category have concerned dramatic events such as an accident that received extensive media coverage in which, on a school day-out, several children visiting a river bed drowned after a river dam gave way.

Following the enactment of the July 10, 2000, law, when identified recklessness or negligence has constituted the direct cause of injury, teachers' responsibility can be involved. On the other hand, if teachers have only indirectly contributed to injuries by creating situations that led to the occurrence, the question of their responsibility arises only if they committed offences exposing others, typically pupils, to very high risks of which they could not have been unaware. In reality, this distinction is not always clear, and the question is still subject to debate even though ordinary criminal legislation and proceedings give teachers basic guarantees. For example, a recent case in which a teacher was found guilty of manslaughter of a girl in his class who had fallen from a window while he was filling a box with school equipment caused much disquiet in the teaching world.

Disciplinary Liability

Civil servants or state employees who fail to meet their obligations are liable for disciplinary action. The rules of the various established public teaching bodies therefore both provide that the competent authorities may decide on punishments and list the possible sanctions.

Case law lays down the requirements of disciplinary procedures. It is now highly codified and very juridical in character, covering description of grievances, defence entitlements, and consultation of disciplinary committees, which include staff representatives, along with administrative and juridical appeals. Rules applying to established public teachers are those relating to the public sector in general. The only specificity concerns teachers in higher education against whom judgements are made by true judiciary bodies.

The disciplinary regime to which teachers in partnership contract establishments are subject to is similar to that of teachers in public education. The relevant texts designate the authority with competence for disciplinary matters, which is normally the appointing body. Disciplinary powers may be exercised either for duly noted professional inadequacy or for behaviour incompatible with teaching.

Disciplinary actions generally begin at the initiative of the heads of the establishments. In serious cases, these disciplinary actions can result in the Minister for Education's decision to withdraw academic qualifications or dismiss teachers. In the case of a teacher who was dismissed for writing racist remarks in the school's newspaper, the European Court of Human Rights judged in 2004 that this interference in his freedom of speech by public authorities was justified.

Rules of procedure require the communication of grievances, the right to defence, and access to the competent consultative committee, which includes staff representatives. Its decisions are subject to juridical appeal.

Matters Arising and Conclusion

One outstanding issue is the evaluation of teaching and teachers' educational freedom. The traditional independence of teachers in higher education who have academic freedom is the reason why they are not subject to inspections. Evaluation of the work of teachers in higher education is only made by their colleagues. In particular, regulations that allow for an evaluation of teaching by students specify that this cannot result in an evaluation of teachers. On the other hand, concerning primary and secondary education, the State has created a body of inspectors, part of whose responsibilities is to evaluate the individual capabilities of teachers. These inspectors cover both public and private establishments.

Inspections raise two issues. Individual evaluations play a non-negligible part in teachers' careers. These evaluations decide, in particular, their teaching marks, which account for 60% of the overall mark taken into account when considering promotions. However, in reality, this system is inadequate in two ways: the frequency of inspections varies widely between disciplines, while differences between individuals in geographic areas and specific inspectors can frequently lead to unfair treatment of teachers.

At certain times in the recent past, the inspection system was severely criticised by vociferous minorities among the teaching body on the left of the political spectrum who saw this as a way of imposing uniformity and an encroachment on their freedom to teach. This concept has today been adopted by conservative elements in the teaching world who would like to see a return to traditional teaching methods and have found recent education ministers to be sympathetic to their cause. The traditional division of responsibilities within the educational system was based on a simple principle: objectives and programmes were decided centrally and the choice of methods was left to individual teaching establishments. Changing collective and social demands, the rise in a new attitude that had no place in the traditional duality, and an emphasis on results are factors that are leading to a crisis in the traditional way of working. It all but goes without saying that these concerns are bound to have an effect on the status of teachers.

References

Code Soleil : Système éducatif : carrières et statut, éd. SUDEL, Paris, 62ème éd., 2005.

DARCY (Gilles), *La responsabilité de l'Etat du fait des accidents scolaires. Eléments pour une réforme de la loi du 5 avril 1937.* Paris, II, 2 volumes, dactylographiée, 1976.

FIALAIRE (Jacques), *Responsabilité en matière d'enseignement,* Jurisclasseur administratif, éd. LITEC, Paris, fascicule 966.

MONIOLLE (Carole), *Indépendance et liberté d'expression des enseignants-chercheurs,* Actualité juridique, Droit administratif, 2001, 226.

OBIN (Jean Pierre), *Les enseignants,* in Bernard TOULEMONDE (dir.), *Le système éducatif,* La Documentation Française, Paris, 2ème éd., 2006.

TAILLEFAIT (Anthony), *Les maîtres des établissements d'enseignement privés sous contrat d'association après la loi Censi: une publicisation « achevée »?*, Actualité juridique, Fonction Publique, juillet 2005, 478.

TOULEMONDE (Bernard), *Les maîtres des établissements d'enseignement privés entre droit public et droit privé: une hybridation législative*, Actualité juridique, Droit administratif, 2005, 478.

8

Germany

Ingo Richter

Introduction

The Basic Law of the Federal Republic of Germany contains no explicit provisions on teacher rights. Even so, one or the other of the constitutions of Germany's 16 federal states contains such provisions, and the federal constitution contains provisions applicable to teachers that are relevant to their rights.

Rules Governing Legislative Competence

While the federation has legislative competence for what is known as the status rights of civil servants, including teachers, provided they have civil servant status, it has no such competence when it comes to the careers, salaries, and pensions of civil servants. In other words, the body of law relevant for teachers is, in essence, state law. This goes for teacher training as well, federal legislative competence being restricted to university admissions and university degrees. The legal circumstances of teachers with public sector employee status instead of civil service status are regulated by state-level collective bargaining agreements.

Rules Governing the Status of Teachers

Art. 33 IV of the Basic Law stipulates that the exercise of sovereign authority must, as a rule, be restricted to civil servants. Unlike European Union (EU) law, German law is predicated on the assumption that since instruction and education are, as a matter of principle, sovereign tasks, teachers must generally have the status of civil servant, a state of affairs that has done little to prevent states from hiring teachers as public-sector employees. The issue, a highly contentious one, has yet to be settled. There is some reason to believe that in the future teachers will generally be public-sector employees, no longer civil servants. This is already largely the case in the new German states that once constituted the German Democratic Republic (GRD). The Federal Labor Court has ruled (BAGE 70, 309) that teachers stemming from the GDR must be taken over en bloc as state public-sector employees, even in the case that they should have been Party members or have worked for the GDR State Security Service.

Basic Rights

According to the Basic Law, all German citizens are equally eligible for any public office, including the teaching profession, based on their aptitude, qualifications, and professional achievements (Art. 33 II GG). The Basic Law contains no specific fundamental teacher rights such that there is, for example, no basic right of pedagogic freedom. To this end, the basic right of freedom of science and inquiry applies only for university teachers, not for school teachers.

School instruction and education are tasks entrusted to teachers by the State; they are not teacher rights. Still, at school teachers can invoke their basic personal rights and, in particular, their rights of religion, free speech, assembly, and association. While teachers with civil service status have no right to strike, teachers with the status of public-sector employees do. The principle of equality enshrined in the Basic Law prohibits any discrimination on racial, religious, gender, or political grounds. Indeed, the Basic Law explicitly stipulates that the State is obliged to "promote the actual implementation of equal rights for women and men" (Art. 3 II; this is also discussed below).

Employment Rights of Teachers

Teacher Recruitment

In Germany, eligibility for teaching positions is restricted to candidates who have completed an education course of studies at a university or institution of higher education. This course of studies takes between four and six years, depending on the school type in question. All teacher trainees are required to study education as well as at least one subject offered in schools. Once teacher trainees have completed their studies, they are admitted to the first state teachers' examination. This is followed by a two-year phase of post-graduate practical training, the so-called *Referendarzeit*, which concludes with a second state teachers' examination.

The traditional German course of teacher training is being converted, in connection with the so-called Bologna Process, discussed below, into a bachelor's/master's system, the details of which have not yet been finalized. While private schools are permitted to employ teachers who have not completed the two state examinations, the Basic Law does mandate that the professional training of private school teachers may in no way be inferior to that of teachers in public schools. In exceptional cases, and in particular as far as technical, artistic, and athletic subjects are concerned, public schools are also permitted to hire teachers who have not completed the required course of university studies.

Once they have completed the second state examinations, candidates are allowed to apply for positions in the civil service as teachers. There is no right to positions at a public school or in the civil service. All positions must be advertised publicly. Hiring decisions are made by the competent public administration on the basis of procedures involving the schools themselves as well as teaching staff councils.

All candidates must be accorded equal treatment. In particular, preferences and discrimination on political or religious grounds are prohibited. To cite an example, the hiring policies of schools attended by a majority of Catholic students are not permitted to give preference to Catholic teachers, and a government or municipal administration is not allowed to accord preference to candidates "of their own political stamp." The two state examinations, which also test for teaching skills, serve to determine candidate professional qualification. These may be examinations taken in another EU member state, for there is an EU directive (Directive 89/48/EEC, December 21, 1988) in effect that stipulates that diplomas awarded in one EU member country must be recognized in all other EU countries.

As a rule, it is presumed that teacher candidates are personally qualified to teach unless there is evidence to the contrary. Applicants have the right to a judicial review of hiring decisions concerning them such that unsuccessful applicants are entitled to take legal actions in their capacity as competitors for jobs. Here, though, the courts very rarely review the judgments actually made of applicants' qualifications, and the best that can be expected of successful legal actions is that hiring decisions may be set aside, not that courts will rule that specific applicants must actually be hired.

In view of the fact that vacant teaching positions are applied for by practicing teachers as well as by new entrants to the profession, the selection procedures and criteria in effect apply for the former as well. Both the examinations and the teaching experience of these applicants from the teaching profession are accorded consideration as an element of their qualification. Performance evaluations compiled in connection with official visits to their classes are generally used to assess the professional experience of these teachers.

Only in exceptional cases are political considerations allowed to be taken into account in the hiring procedure, such as where applicants fall under the so-called Extremist Decree (1972), where there are doubts as to their loyalty to the Basic Law. Such doubts are seen as given if applicants were or had been members of the (banned) former Communist Party of Germany, the subsequently founded German Communist Party, or a National Socialist or other radical right-wing party or grouping.

Applicants are permitted to dispel doubts by convincing recruiting authorities of their loyalty to the Basic Law. However, reference to the fact that no objections have been made to their teaching practices is not sufficient in this case. While these rules pertain not only to teachers but for all civil servants and public sector employees, they have been applied particularly often in the hiring of teachers. On the one hand, parents in particular have again and again publicly demanded that the provision on loyalty to the Constitution be upheld. On the other hand, parents and students have repeatedly publicly come out in favor of teachers who provide good instruction.

The German Federal Constitutional Court long ago, in a case involving a teacher, approved this application of the Radical Decree (BVerfGE 39, 334). However, the European Court of Human Rights, likewise in a case involving a teacher, saw in this practice an infringement of the freedom of speech and the freedom of association and assembly enshrined in the European Convention on Human Rights (ECHR, *Vogt v. Germany*, judgment of September 26, 1995, case number 7/1994/454/535, Series A No. 323).

Since reunification, the German courts have taken a different approach in cases involving teachers from the GDR, ruling that mere membership in the GDR's Communist Party or activity in the GDR's State Security Service was not a sufficient ground on which to deny applicants access to the teaching profession. The Court also noted that any marked identification with the aims of the Party or proved offenses against the rule of law or against humanity were a sufficient basis to turn applicants down (see both above and BverfGE 92, 140; 96, 171). More recently, only a limited number of cases have become known in which teachers were denied employment on such political grounds.

Another highly significant issue, though, and one that has not yet been resolved, is equal rights for women in the teaching profession. All told, more women than men are employed in the teaching profession in Germany, the reason being that discrimination in hiring is prohibited, and due heed is paid to this provision. Still, when it comes to promotions and, in particular, selection of school principals and board of education members, who are not only in charge of higher-level tasks but are also paid appreciably higher salaries than normal teachers, claims of discrimination are voiced repeatedly, stressing that there are far fewer women active in these positions.

A review of hiring and promotion practices with a view to the aspect of gender equity is heavily influenced by the decisions handed down by the European Court of Justice, which watches over the prohibition on discrimination laid down on the EU Treaty. In deciding the *Kalanke* case in 1995 (*Kalanke*, European Court Reports 1995, pp. 1–3051), the European Court of Justice ruled that the rigid quota rules in place in Germany were in violation of European law because they discriminate against men. In other words, assuming that all applicants are equally qualified, it is not permissible to give women preference for a given category of positions until women account for the same percentage as men such as in senior positions.

The Court explained that all such decisions must be made on a case-by-case basis, giving consideration to the facts and circumstances concerned, with men also having a real chance of being hired (*Marschall*, ECJ, November 1997, European Court Reports 1997, pp. 1–06363). These cases notwithstanding, it is permissible, and perhaps even required by the principle of equal opportunity, to define targets bearing on gender equity, and the new equal opportunity laws adopted by the German federal and state governments provide for arrangements of this kind.

Teacher Employment

It is essential to distinguish between civil servants and public-sector employees. While the terms and conditions of employment are defined by law for teachers with civil service status, the terms and conditions applicable for teachers working as public-sector employees are defined in collective bargaining agreements. Moreover, while teachers may, in parliamentary hearings attended by members of their representative bodies, seek to influence the shape of the relevant legislation, in the end the legislative, and more specifically the political, majority in a given state decides the issues. Collective bargaining agreements, on the other hand, are worked out in negotiations between the state governments and the labor unions or professional associations while such talks are conducted under the threat of strike and require the approval of the relevant union organs.

To be more precise, the terms and conditions of teacher employment, and in particular salaries and hours required to be taught, are defined on the basis of laws or collective bargaining agreements. In Germany, teachers are required to provide between 18 and 28 hours of lessons per week, depending on the school type.

Teachers' workloads are reduced if they take on any of a great variety of additional tasks, meaning that teachers actually teach far less than they are required to. Currently, there are plans to replace the present system based on mandatory hours to be taught with a new system based on a realistic calculation of the hours teachers, in fact, work. The process of adopting a new system of this kind is proving extremely protracted due to the difficulties involved in calculating teacher working hours.

Starting salaries for teachers in Germany range between 2,500 and 4,500 Euros per month. This means that German teachers are among the world's best paid, second only to their Swiss colleagues. Teachers' salaries rise in keeping with the principle of seniority. In addition, there are pay supplements that serve to raise teachers' salaries. In Germany, the discussion on the adoption of performance-based salaries is still in its first stages; having already been introduced in the higher education sector, it is safe to assume that performance-linked salaries will not be long in coming to the school sector as well.

Teachers can, even against their wills, be transferred from one school to another, although they do have legal means to contest such transfers. In Germany, teachers' tenure ends when they reach retirement age—as a rule, 65 years—although teachers often opt for early retirement for reasons of illness or the so-called burnout syndrome. Retired teachers receive 75% of their last salaries as permanent pensions; their widows or widowers are entitled to 60% of the pensions. In recent years, high life expectancy has caused the pension burdens of the German states to skyrocket. It therefore now appears that there is no alternative to an urgent reform of teacher salaries and pensions, particularly in view of the fact that teachers pay no contributions of any kind toward their own retirement benefits.

While the terms and conditions for teachers referred to above are, for purely legal reasons, not applicable for private schools, where the legal modalities are defined in private service contracts, Art. 7 IV GG provides for the possibility of revoking the licenses of private schools if they are unable to provide sufficient protection of the legal and economic needs of their teaching staffs. What this means, de facto, is that private schools are obliged to provide their teachers terms and conditions of employment equivalent to those found in public-sector schools.

In Germany, there are no legal regulations defining the educational duties of teachers. The legislature preferred instead to provide for certain sanctions that are to be imposed in cases of neglect of duty (discussed below), but without describing the duties concerned. In other words, these duties derive from a professional approach to teaching that is instilled in the course of training and constantly developed by school inspection authorities.

Teachers have a large measure of freedom in day-to-day school activities; neither parents nor school principals are in a position to tell teachers how they are to approach their task. Parents can complain to principals who can issue instructions to teachers, but ultimately administrative measures of this kind have no real control quality of their own. Principals or school inspectors—as a rule, themselves former teachers—are responsible for teacher supervision. Beyond that, in Germany there has traditionally been no other systematic internal or external evaluation. This situation is now changing, with schools obliged to conduct both regular internal and external evaluations. Regular in-service teacher training is becoming mandatory. Most of the German states have recently adopted so-called school inspections patterned on models from other countries.

Art. 9 III GG guarantees teachers freedom of association to represent their professional interests. In Germany there are both teachers' associations and teachers' unions. For teachers with civil servant status, these rights are restricted to efforts to safeguard professional teacher interests because the avenue of collective bargaining, including the right to strike, is not open to civil servants. While teachers with the status of public-sector employees have the right to collective bargaining, including the right to strike, the position of the relevant labor unions is so weak that they make very little use of this right.

Basic Rights

Pedagogic Freedom

As mentioned above, teachers in Germany have no basic right to "academic freedom" that they might invoke when school principals or school inspectors issue them instructions bearing on educational matters. While the German school laws provide for what is referred to as pedagogic freedom, this freedom is not a basic right. One might say that if this pedagogic freedom is not a basic right, it is a functional principle of schools, one protected by the traditional principles of the professional civil service and anchored in Art. 33 V of the Basic Law. However, since these rights are very broad in nature, they need to be concretized by the legislature, which has substantial leeway in doing so.

The number of hours teachers are required to teach in class is defined by law or set down in collective bargaining agreements. Classes, and hours, are assigned to teachers on the basis of a schedule prepared by principals. What is taught in schools is determined by school curricula, which, in turn, are set by the State in the form of an administrative order, meaning that it is a regulation with legal quality.

Teachers do not have a free hand in the selection of textbooks; this is a matter on which a conference of specialist teachers decides, and in coming to a decision, it is bound by a list of books approved by the competent ministry. So what is left of the teacher's pedagogic freedom? What is left is individual teachers' methodological freedom, their freedom to select particular methods of instruction. In other words, teachers are free to select what methods they use and how to organize the instruction they provide, even though this, too, of course, is only within the framework defined by a given set of curricula and textbooks.

Criticism has long been voiced of this integration of teachers into a close mesh of bureaucratic regulations. This is thought to be one reason for the performance deficits noted for German schools. In recent years the German state legislatures have, for this reason, granted schools a certain measure of autonomy in this regard, with the schools themselves, and not school administrations, now permitted to come to decisions on educational issues, including the use of the personnel and financial resources involved. However, granting schools more educational autonomy does not necessarily serve to strengthen the individual teachers' pedagogic freedom; quite to the contrary, many teachers are of the opinion that school autonomy does more to restrict individual teachers' pedagogic freedom than the "faraway school inspector" ever did.

Such restrictions on teachers' basic rights do not apply to private schools because the institutions that operate these schools are bound to have full respect for the basic rights of the teachers that they employ. However, freedom of contract has precedence here, meaning that the contracts offered by private schools may restrict the basic rights of their teachers, and this is, for functional reasons, an inescapable fact of life for those employed at private schools.

Basic Rights

In public schools teachers can invoke their universal basic rights, even in the context of the instruction they provide. These basic rights are not automatically restricted by the fact that public school teachers are civil servants or public sector employees working in public institutions. In earlier times basic rights were generally regarded as restricted in such public institutions, but the Basic Law set this restriction aside. It is only the legislature that has the power to restrict the basic rights of teachers, and to do so, it needs good educational or institutional grounds. Teachers can contest any such restrictions of their basic rights by instituting legal proceedings and ultimately by appealing to the German Federal Constitutional Court.

Religious Freedom

The basic right of religious freedom and freedom to profess a religious creed enshrined in Art. 4 GG applies for teachers as well, both as a positive and as a negative basic right; that is, while teachers are allowed to belong to religious communities, they are not required to. The freedom to profess a philosophical–ideological creed likewise enshrined in Art. 4 GG ensures that atheists are eligible for the teaching profession.

As noted above, religious affiliation is not a material factor in selecting applicants for the teaching profession. Additionally, teachers have the right to profess their religions actively; that is, they are allowed to practice their beliefs openly both in their religious communities and in public. Here, too, it is important to emphasize that this applies in the reverse toward abstention from the practice of religion, meaning that teachers are not required to go to church or otherwise worship.

Teachers are allowed to address their creeds openly in class and to profess their religious beliefs, although they are required to show restraint in doing so; that is to say, all forms of missionary behavior are prohibited in class. Teachers are not allowed to disparage or to slight other religions. Indeed, teachers are required to treat other religions with tolerance. This goes both for the Christian churches and for the relations between Christians and other religions, in particular, Islam. It is not always easy for teachers to find the right balance between the exercise of their own religions and their task of teaching all students, with their own various religious and philosophical orientations.

For years now, Germany, like other countries, has been faced with disputes over religious symbols in school and, in particular, over the issue of whether female Muslim teachers should be allowed to wear headscarves in school. One effect of this dispute has been to draw other religious symbols like the crucifix or the kippa or particular items of clothing like the nun's habit into the discussion. The Koran instructs all devout Muslim women to cover their hair in public that, in any case, is a widespread interpretation, the justification of which is beyond the scope of this chapter and cannot be discussed in the present context. This largely means wearing headscarves, and some female teachers wish to wear them in school, even when they are teaching class.

While girls are largely allowed to wear headscarves in school in Germany, with the decision generally being left to local school administrations or even individual schools, all German school administrations have prohibited female teachers from wearing headscarves in class. The justification provided is that the headscarf is at once a religious symbol and the profession of a political creed that violates the duty of civil servants to exercise restraint in political matters, as discussed below.

In a dispute over the appointment of a woman to the position of teacher with civil servant status in the German state of Baden-Württemberg who refused to remove her headscarf in class, the German Federal Constitutional Court ruled that requiring her to remove her headscarf in class constituted an intervention into her religious freedom, that legislation was required as a basis for any such intervention and that the State lacked such legislation (BverfGE, September 24, 2003, in: *Neue Juristische Wochenschrift* 2003, 3111). In other words, the Federal Constitutional Court avoided reaching a judgment on the matter at hand by calling on the legislature to create a legal basis to deal with the issue. The German state legislatures have now acted.

Some states, such as Baden-Württemberg, have banned only the Muslim headscarf but not other religious symbols such as the kippa or the crucifix, while other states, such as Berlin, have banned all religious symbols. Other states, such as Lower Saxony, looking to the French model, have banned only the demonstrative wearing of religious symbols, which means that it is now possible to wear a discrete crucifix, while the more visible headscarf is banned. In other words, the German courts have yet to decide finally on the issue. However, it is important to note that in Germany there are limits to the religious freedom of teachers and that these limits need to be defined by the legislative in addition to being justified on educational grounds.

Freedom of Speech

Teachers enjoy not only basic religious rights but also basic political rights guaranteed by the Constitution. Teachers are allowed to be members of political parties. In elections, teachers are allowed to run for political offices and become members of parliaments and governments. In fact, a fairly large number of teachers serve as members of parliaments. Some commentators have even referred to the German state parliaments as teacher parliaments. Such teachers are granted leaves from their teaching duties during their terms in office; that is, as long as they are serving as members of Parliament or government officials, they are not required to teach and their rights as civil servants are suspended. As soon as their term in office comes to an end, their full rights as teachers and civil servants are reinstated.

Teachers also enjoy the right of association; that is, they are permitted to become members of associations and assume high-ranking positions in these organizations. This goes for political associations as well, including labor unions or nonprofit organizations such as Greenpeace or Amnesty International. Germany's present associational landscape would be inconceivable without teachers. It is also safe to say that teachers' educational work benefits from their activities in parties and associations; it brings an element of political practice to schools. Finally, teachers are allowed to participate in political demonstrations outside their schools.

The actual problem posed by the basic political rights of teachers is not their involvement in nonschool political life. Rather, it is their exercise of their political rights at school. The freedom of speech and expression that Art. 5 GG guarantees also applies for teachers, including the instruction they provide at school. In other words, when it comes, for example, to political education, teachers not only can and must communicate political facts, analyzing them in scientific and educational terms, but they are also expected to make their own contributions to shaping public political opinion and public policy.

What does this mean in concrete terms? Are teachers allowed to indicate the party for which they intend to vote? Are they allowed to come out in favor of one party or the other or at least to warn against voting for certain parties? When elections are set to be held, are teachers permitted to address and analyze party programs in class? Are they allowed to state their own opinions on these programs? What goes for elections goes for politics in general. There are a limited number of legal principles with bearing on teachers' rights to free speech and expression in class.

First, teachers are obliged to exercise restraint in political matters; according to §35 of the German Framework Civil Service Law, "as far as political activities are concerned, the civil servant has the duty to show moderation and restraint commensurate with his or her position with regard to the overall polity and to remain fully mindful of the duties of his or her office."

Second, teachers must remain neutral as far as partisan political issues are concerned, meaning that they are not allowed to come out openly in favor of any one political party; pursuant to §35 of the German Framework Civil Service Law, "The civil servant serves all of the people, not one political party."

Third, at the same time, teachers are required to stand up for the basic principles of democracy under §35 of the German Framework Civil Service Law: "The civil servant is obliged, in the whole of his or her behavior, to embrace, and to stand up for, the free and democratic constitutional order laid down in the Basic Law."

These principles, rooted as they are in civil service law, stand in a certain tension to teachers' educational tasks, which are likewise safeguarded by the functional principle of pedagogic freedom. In this sense, the obligation of civil servants to exercise political restraint constitutes a problem in that teachers have no choice but to reveal their own identity, a good part of which is, of course, political.

Teachers must show that they are committed, that far from being indifferent to the world in general and their students in particular, they are a matter of importance to them. Even though one of the tasks of teachers is to shed scientific light on all aspects of a given problem, even though they are not permitted to take sides from the outset, the fact that teachers are forced to tread very warily between positions is a terrible one; the principle of impartiality very often means that opinions of immediate educational relevance are simply not discussed. Finally, loyalty to the Constitution itself poses a problem: democracy and instruction in politics are not well served by mere lip service to the Basic Law.

The problem is even greater in that while all too many teachers accept the Basic Law as such, they do not impart to their students the actual meaning and spirit of the Constitution. In other words, the overall concern involved in the basic political rights of teachers is that the latter are able to communicate their own political opinions in ways credible enough for them to be effective in educational terms, but without infringing the constitutional framework, yet the framework set by a free, democratic constitution is a broad one.

Personality Rights and Privacy Rights

At school teachers can invoke the same rights of personality they enjoy outside school. The days are long gone when teachers were expected to evince "irreproachable behavior" even in their nonschool lives as this was construed to mean, for example, practicing such virtues as marital fidelity, moderation in alcohol consumption, and commitment to the common good. All these things are no longer among the duties of teachers. Still, at school teachers are expected to exercise their personality rights is such a way that they do not conflict with their educational tasks.

What is at stake here today? Teachers are no longer expected to adapt their dress and hairstyles to standards regarded as socially normal. Today teachers teach their students wearing jeans and T-shirts, and one would be hard pressed to specify any sound educational reasons why male teachers should have to wear suits and ties or why female teachers should have to wear dresses instead of trousers when they teach. Here, too, there are limits: part of what teachers teach is the way in which they exercise their personal rights; that is, their demeanor and their views on just about everything must be personally credible in nature, and as long as they are, they are permitted to deviate from the norm.

Sanctions

When teachers have neglected their duties, the questions arise as to what sanctions can be imposed and what rights, in turn, teachers have available.

Administrative Proceedings

If teachers neglect their duties, principals and administrative officials are usually informed by students or their parents. If informal procedures fail to remedy situations, students or their parents are entitled to lodge official objections over such matters as concerning examination or test results—objections that may ultimately lead to formal legal actions as noted below. When matters in question concern informal decisions such as cases of alleged discrimination, students or their parents are entitled to file formal disciplinary complaints, also referred to as "wastepaper-basket complaints" because these kinds of complaints are thought not to be particularly effective. Still, since teachers are bound by guidelines and directives issued by their superiors, the latter may, and do, issue such directives on the basis of guidelines.

Once internal administrative procedures have reached a certain level of formality, teachers must be given personal hearings. The proceedings must then be brought to a certain formal conclusion, which finds its way into the teachers' personnel files. Teachers are allowed access to their personnel files at any time and are also permitted to put their own views of the matters in official record. This protocol, too, is then added to the teacher's personnel file.

German schools have personnel councils to which teachers may turn in such cases; they, in turn, are entitled to bring conflicts in need of clarification to the attention of principals or a school's administration. Schools also have mediation boards entrusted with the task of resolving conflicts between teachers and students or their parents. Art. 103 I GG, the basic right to a hearing, applies for these administrative procedures. What this principle means today is that all of the authorities concerned are obliged to provide for due process of law.

Disciplinary Proceedings

In cases in which teachers with civil service status are accused of neglect of duty, the competent oversight authorities may initiate disciplinary proceedings. Proceedings of this kind are based on the disciplinary codes of the individual German states. Disciplinary proceedings are patterned on criminal proceedings. The disciplinary penalties provided include reprimands, fines, salary reductions, and revocations of pension entitlements. Normal disciplinary proceedings are conducted by accused teachers' immediate supervisors and normally end with disciplinary rulings which may call only for reprimands or fines.

All other proceedings are formal disciplinary proceedings that are conducted by disciplinary tribunals. Such cases include disciplinary attorneys and attorneys representing the civil servants with a disciplinary tribunal made up of professional judges and civil servants. Such proceedings are bound to the same due-process rules that apply in other courts of law, including a right of appeal. In actual practice, disciplinary proceedings play a very small role. There are no such proceedings for teachers with public service employee status; normal labor law applies in such cases, meaning that in situations involving breaches of discipline, salaried teachers may be warned and then dismissed.

Other Legal Proceedings

If breaches of duty committed by teachers constitute criminal offenses, normal criminal proceedings are initiated. If such criminal offenses are committed against students, the matters generally generate considerable publicity, particularly in the media. Such criminal offenses often involve violence toward and sexual abuse of students. Corporal punishment of students has been banned in Germany since the 1950s, and such cases are prosecuted as bodily injury committed by a person in public office. Sexual offenses committed by teachers against students are punished severely as cases of sexual abuse of dependent minors.

One issue of particular interest for day-to-day school life is liability for damage or injury caused to students by teachers. This, for the most part, has to do with accidents that take place at school and, in particular, on school excursions. In Germany, the law that generally applies for teachers, as well as for all other persons, in such cases is the civil damages law; that is to say, if teachers culpably cause damage or injury, they can be held liable for damages, and in cases of doubt this can be enforced through legal actions in civil courts.

Teachers can be liable only within the framework of their duties as teachers to exercise proper care; however, the standards for teachers' supervisory duties are set high. If teachers cause damage or injuries in exercising their official duties, in the usual case, their employer, the State, pays compensation for the damages incurred, and only in cases of willful or gross negligence does the State have recourse to the teachers. Otherwise, for some time now, all German school students have been insured, on a mandatory and cost-free basis, against accidents at school; in other words, today this accident insurance pays for damages or injuries, with insurance companies having recourse to teachers only in cases of willful or gross negligence. Even though teachers are protected by insurance and by public liability against consequences stemming from their liability in cases of "normal neglect of duty"—those involving minor negligence—many teachers are concerned about the alleged risk implied by their liability for damages or injuries.

If school authorities make decisions that infringe upon the rights of teachers, the latter are entitled by Art. 19 IV GG to turn to the courts, since this article guarantees everyone, including teachers, access to courts of law. The only question here is the type of dispute concerned.

If the decisions of school authorities affect teachers' conditions of employment, the crucial issue is whether they have the status of civil servants or public-sector employees. While administrative courts are responsible for civil servants, teachers with the status of public-sector employees can turn to labor courts.

The labor courts are always responsible for teachers who work in private schools. If the issue at stake is teacher task fulfillment, and if teachers wish to take legal action against decisions taken by school authorities, teachers, pointing to their rights, must first refuse to follow instructions. In such cases, responsibility devolves to the instance in which the instruction was given.

Teachers also have the option of taking legal action in administrative courts; in these instances, teachers are first required to lodge protests on which their superior authorities are required to decide. All of these actions fall under procedural law which provides for extensive safeguards for the rights of the parties. These safeguards include the right to legal counsel and to a hearing, examination of witnesses, and documentation in the form of records. There is every reason to believe that the rights of teachers are properly safeguarded in such proceedings, although they are, as a rule, not conductive to the ongoing educational process at school.

Reforms

A number of reforms of teacher training and employment, but also educational reforms, are set to be launched in the coming years. These reforms, which will have immediate effects on teachers, will sharply alter the legal status they enjoy.

The So-Called Bologna Process

In the 1920s the first steps were taken to academize teacher training in Germany, and in the 1950s teacher training was transferred to universities in nearly all of the German states, where it was organized separately for each school type. The Bologna Process—namely, the decisions taken by European education ministers in connection with the 1999 Bologna Declaration—is designed to create what is known as a European Higher Education Area (EHEA); this means, among other things, that teacher training is set to be harmonized throughout the EU.

Traditional teacher-training courses are to be replaced by courses of study leading to the acquisition of bachelor's and master's degrees. These new courses of study will be modularized or made up of smaller units that can be combined variably. Trainee performance will be assessed on the basis of the European Credit Transfer System, which likewise permits different credits to be combined variably. In Germany, the bachelor's degree course of studies is currently being introduced for basic teacher training in both education and relevant major subjects. There is still some debate in Germany as to whether the bachelor's degree should be followed by a one- or two-year course of study for a master's degree and what qualifications, both in education and other major subjects, should be required of students for the different school types in Germany.

Reform of the German School Structure

The German school system has traditionally consisted of kindergarten, which is not operated by teachers; primary school; and then a four-tier secondary school system made up of the *Hauptschule* (a kind of lower secondary school), the *Realschule* (an intermediate secondary school), the *Gymnasium*, and the special, or special-needs, school. In stage II of secondary education, a system of dual vocational training consisting of in-company and school training is offered in parallel to the higher grades of the *Gymnasium*.

Put another way, Germany has primary school teachers, *Hauptschule* teachers, *Gymnasium* teachers, special-needs school teachers, and vocational school teachers. However, as far as professional pride and the awareness of the general public are concerned, there are only two categories, namely the primary and *Hauptschule* teachers on the one side and *Gymnasium* teachers on the other, while the other groups seek to carve out a place for themselves within the coordinates defined by these two categories. This is why teacher training and teacher rights are closely interrelated with school structure.

The school structure is currently undergoing different changes. Because the 1960s attempts to create a comprehensive school in Germany failed, Germany is faced with a good number of "reform construction sites." First, kindergarten is being redefined as an education institution, which means that it will now employ teachers. Second, primary school, which takes four years to complete in most German states, may be extended by two years, which would mean that primary school teachers would have to teach for two extra years.

Third, the *Hauptschule* is set to vanish, which will give rise in Germany, on top of the special school, to a two- or three-tier school system in which teachers may no longer be recruited on the basis of training. Fourth, there are strong currents in Germany that advocate that special school students be integrated into the general school system, a development that would lower the demand for special-needs school teachers. Fifth, vocational schools are being expanded into what is known as centers of vocational competence which will assume a range of new tasks, both in initial vocational training and in continuing and advanced vocational training.

The introduction of the Bologna Process in teacher training has come in for criticism from universities. Even so, the present overview of the structural school reforms set to be implemented clearly indicates that the only system capable of coming effectively to terms with the problems emerging in teacher employment is the bachelor's/master's system.

The Picture of Teachers in Germany

In the course of the nineteenth century, the picture of teachers evolved from the pastor's "auxiliary" for popular education to the "professor" educated in the neohumanist tradition for higher education and then to the picture of the academically trained, professional "teaching civil servant" who, while providing neutral and correct instruction, is no longer responsible for the education or the fate of the children entrusted to him or her and for whom instruction is a task or job like any other. This picture could well change again in the near future because teachers will soon find themselves faced with new tasks that will require them to alter their self-conception.

Students are different today, and they need to be treated differently. We have discovered informal learning, the Hidden Curriculum. We have come to understand that performance in school rests in large measure on nonschool attitudes and behaviors. Moreover, schools now assume responsibility for the further course of life of their students and, in particular, for their vocational careers. While the behavior of students, both in classrooms and in peer groups, has become markedly individualized, it has at the same time become markedly collectivized; informalization is becoming increasingly important. Today teachers need not only academic qualifications but also, and once again, socio-educational qualifications. In the future, the picture of teachers could well come to resemble more that of "coaches" than that of teaching civil servants.

School Autonomy

In Germany, schools were invariably dependent state institutions, organized and administered by school administrations; even school principals were dependent civil servants who had little leeway for the decisions they made—and were in no way comparable to British headmasters. It was only through teachers' conferences that teachers were involved at all in the development of school lessons. When it came to school administration, teachers had nothing to say, and, if at all, their views were heard only in informal conferences. This situation is changing fundamentally.

Schools are becoming increasingly autonomous, not only in educational terms but also as far as financial and personnel matters are concerned; that is, schools are gaining substantial and growing scopes to make decisions on their own. This goes not only, for example, for the definition of educational priorities or the selection of students but also for the recruitment of new teachers or school-related expenditures. Even though the ongoing school reforms are highly likely to strengthen the hand of school principals, another outcome will be that teachers will be involved far more than ever in managing schools as organizations. No longer restricted to responsibility for the instruction they themselves give, teachers will be increasingly responsible for schools as a whole. For teachers, these are both new rights and new tasks.

Continuing Teacher Training

In the past the duty of teachers to continue their training was formulated in very general terms; there was no right to continuing or advanced training. This, too, is changing. The new demands placed on the teaching profession necessarily imply a need for continuing training. This training will no longer take place while school is in session, as teachers will have to attend training courses on weekends and during school vacations. Such training will play a role in the promotion of teachers and become an element of the new salary structure for teachers. Teachers will, for this reason, have a right to continuing training that will include the continuing professional training in which they have always engaged but will expand to cover methodological training, information technology training, and management training.

A New Teacher Right

As mentioned above, in the future teachers in Germany will very likely no longer be civil servants but instead have the status of public-sector employees. In view of the fact that civil service status for teachers is outdated in any case, the difference will not play a major role in practice.

One thing that will be important is the new salary structure for teachers. If performance-linked salaries are adopted for teachers, the questions will be what performance is expected of a teacher and who is to measure this performance. Should teacher performance be measured in terms of output or in terms of student performance, for instance, meaning the results that students achieve on performance tests? Should teachers be evaluated by their superiors, their peers, or their students' parents? At present, Germany does not have new salary laws but an agreement in principle. If performance-linked salaries are adopted, then teachers will have a right to collective bargaining, including the right to strike.

Conclusion

The rights enjoyed by teachers in Germany are situated somewhere between those enjoyed by administrative officials and those enjoyed by members of the free professions. Teachers have the career security of the tax inspector, though without being wedged into a hierarchy like the latter. Teachers have the freedom enjoyed by free professionals like doctors, with the professional self-image that goes along with it, though without having to assume liability, like doctors, for professional malpractice.

German teachers regard themselves as experts in given subject matter such as for Pythagoras but not as experts for people, for a child, or for a youth. German teachers see themselves as responsible for good lessons, but not for the learning successes of their students. German teachers are convinced that parents are responsible for rearing their children and that parents are obliged to support the work of school by, for instance, assuming responsibility that their children do their homework. German teachers do not see themselves as responsible for education in family and peer groups.

The reason why the German school system is difficult to manage today is that hierarchical command-and-control management simply no longer works. The German school system is unaccustomed to management keyed to participation or pecuniary incentives. However, the ongoing reforms of the German school system will not succeed unless they are carried out as a coproduction involving administration and the teaching profession. For this reason, too, the time has come to reform teacher rights.

Bibliography

Avenarius, Hermann and Hans Heckel Schulrechtskunde, 7th ed., 2000, Luchterhand, Neuwied.

Birch, Jan K. and Ingo Richter (eds.), Comparative School Law, 1990 (Richter on West Germany, Switzerland and Austria, and the European Communities), Pergamon Press, Oxford.

DeGroof, Jan (ed.), The Legal Status of Teachers in Europe, 1995 (Kreitz and Teichler on Teacher Mobility and Füssel and Püttner on Germany), Acco, Leuven.

Richter, Ingo, Recht im Bildungssystem, 2006, Kohlhammer, Stuttgart.

Roeder, Peter M., et al. (eds.), Pluralism and Education, 1995 (Avenarius on Germany), Institute of Governmental Studies Press, University of California, Berkeley.

9

Malaysia

Tie Fatt Hee

Introduction

The Federal Constitution[1] in Malaysia is the primary piece of legislation governing the legal rights of teachers. The educational service, which includes public schools, is considered to be a part of the civil service.[2] Teachers who serve in public schools are regarded as employees of the public service. In this respect, federal law acts to establish, govern, and regulate the qualifications for the appointment and conditions of employment of teachers in the educational service as well as their conduct.[3]

At the same time, the law governing the legal rights of teachers in public schools is based on the twin principles that all teachers in the public schools are civil servants who hold their offices at the pleasure of His Majesty the King[4] and that he determines the qualifications for appointments and conditions of service. The pleasure of His Majesty the King applies to tenure of the offices of teachers and extends to a wide range of other matters such as appointments, promotions, transfers, salaries, leaves, and other benefits. Public school teachers, as civil servants and as servants of the Ruler, owe their undivided loyalty to His Majesty the King, the Federal Constitution, and the government of the day.

The Federal Constitution also provides for the establishment of an Education Service Commission (ESC).[5] The ESC has the authority to appoint, confirm, place on the permanent or pensionable establishment, promote, transfer, and exercise disciplinary control over members of the education service. The powers and functions of the ESC are normally exercised by a board appointed by the King. However, the board does not have the power of first appointment of teachers to the permanent or pensionable establishment. Teachers who are aggrieved by the exercise of powers or functions by the board may seek review by an Appeal Board appointed by the King.[6]

The Federal Constitution confers substantial rights on teachers. The constitutional rights of teachers encompass equal protection before the law,[7] a right to due process, and privacy rights. All teachers are entitled to the same privileges as those provided to other professionals in the civil service. Teachers have constitutional protection from any form of discrimination based on religion, race, descent, place of birth, or gender in any law.[8] The Federal Constitution sets out the mandatory procedural rules and regulations when officials exercise the power to dismiss or reduce the rank of teachers.

In addition to the Federal Constitution, another set of civil service rules and regulations sets forth the procedures, legal rights, and conduct of members of the teaching profession. This is known as the Public Officers (Conduct and Discipline) (Chapter "D") General Orders 1980, sometimes referred to as the "General Orders" ("GO"). The GO is a code of conduct for all civil servants that acts as a guide for public school teachers.

The GO also lays down the types of punishment that can be imposed on teachers who commit misconduct and the procedures for disciplinary action. Public school teachers are required to abide by the provisions contained in the GO. Similarly, the Disciplinary Authority is required to abide strictly to the procedures set out in the GO when conducting disciplinary proceedings against teachers. The procedures in the GO are set out in a clear, systematic, and comprehensive manner. Most of the provisions in the GO are designed to protect the legal rights of teachers. An example of how the GO functions can be found in the GO's provision that teachers are entitled to the right to natural justice under the principle of *audi alterem*.

Employment Rights of Teachers

In Malaysia, the employment rights and obligations of public school teachers are grounded in contracts and statutory provisions. The federal government and the Ministry of Education set the qualifications for teaching positions and teacher employment. In order to be eligible for employment as teachers, individuals can enroll in one of the following teacher education programs: a Diploma in Education program at the teachers' institute, a Bachelor of Education program at a university, or a Postgraduate Diploma in Education program.

Teacher trainees in the Diploma in Education program are usually offered scholarships by the Ministry of Education. Theses trainees are contractually bound to serve the government for a period of five years after their studies. Newly qualified teachers are normally offered contracts of employment by the Ministry of Education after medical tests and taking oaths that they have not committed criminal offenses.

Malaysian teachers do not have a right to be assigned to particular schools and can be posted to any school by the Ministry of Education. Teachers are placed on probation for a period of one to three years and subsequently offered permanent positions on confirmation.

Teachers serve the government as a form of right of employment for a continuing period until the mandatory retirement age of 56. Most teachers retire successfully and receive monthly pensions for life at the end of their service unless their employment is terminated due to breaches of contracts.

In *Government of Malaysia v. Thelma Fernandez & Anor,*[9] a teacher trainee entered into an agreement with the government to pursue a training course at a teachers' training college and thereafter to serve as a teacher in a government school for a period of five years. The agreement provided that should the trainee refuse to serve, refuse to continue to serve, resign, or leave the service of the government without its consent, then the trainee and sureties would be jointly and severally liable to refund on demand all monies paid by the government in respect of the defendant's course of training.

After completing the course and having served the government as a teacher for a period of two and a half years, the defendant left the service, alleging that his post as a primary school teacher was not commensurate with his education. The teacher argued that the clause in the agreement that provides a refund of all monies to the government was a non-enforceable penalty. The Court decided in favor of the government, holding that the penalty was not an unconscionable sum compared to the loss incurred by the State in its long-term plan to train teachers and ensure the success of its education policy in overcoming the shortage of qualified teachers.

Generally, teachers in Malaysia are promoted based on seniority and experience in the educational service. The normal career path is promotion from an ordinary teacher to senior subject teacher, senior assistant, and then principal. School principals have the authority to assess and evaluate the annual job performance of teachers. The promotion of teachers is also subject to successfully passing examinations. There are restrictions on performance-based promotion assessment, as teachers have very limited legal redress in the event of any abuse of the system.

The number of teacher unions in Malaysia is small, and union activity is mainly passive. Such an approach is attributable to the culture of general compliance with governmental policy and the public service employment factor. Membership in teachers' unions—especially the main union, the National

Union of Teaching Profession—consists mainly of non-graduate teachers. The effectiveness of teacher unions in their capacity as a form of checks and balances in safeguarding the interests of teachers is very limited due to some of the provisions in the GO that do not encourage active union participation.

In *National Union of Teachers in Independent Schools, West Malaysia v. Han Chiang High School, Penang* (*National Union*),[10] the school and the appellant teacher union were involved in a dispute over a collective agreement on wages and conditions of employment. A second dispute concerned the school's wrongful dismissal of some teachers. The Industrial Court decided that the union had no *locus standi* to act in the dispute on behalf the school teachers based on the allegation that none of the teachers belonged to the union.

The first issue that arose in *National Union* was whether the Industrial Court erred in law and in fact in concluding that since the services of the teachers were lawfully terminated, they were not union members. The second issue was whether the Industrial Court exceeded its jurisdiction. In allowing the appeal, the High Court expressed its opinion that the Industrial Court's judgment, that the union lacked *locus standi* because the teachers were not members, was actually an adjudication of the dispute of the wrongful dismissal of teachers who were union members.

According to the High Court, it was important to note that the Industrial Court did not have the jurisdiction to resolve the dispute since the matter was referred to the Minister. Instead, the High Court pointed out that the disagreement was wrongly referred to another division of the Industrial Court. The High Court thus held that there was an absence of evidence supporting the Industrial Court's finding that the union had no members. The High Court added that the Industrial Court erred in assuming that the union had no members to represent based on its perception that no union members were present before it when it ruled.

The Federal Constitution provides procedural safeguards that must be followed before teachers are dismissed or reduced in rank.[11] However, no safeguards are available when teachers are transferred from their schools following written directives from the Ministry of Education. This is based on the general principle laid down in the contract of employment for civil servants. Under this provision, teachers who join the government service are liable to be transferred and cannot claim to have a legal right of non-transferability.

In other words, since the government has the right to decide where and when transfers are to be made, appeals against transfer orders are unlikely to succeed. In one case, a teacher unsuccessfully challenged his being transferred from one school to another that was located more than 400 kilometers away. After the Minister of Education rejected the challenge, the teacher applied for a declaration that the transfer was void and inoperative. At the first instance, the Court decided in favor of the teacher, finding that the power of transfer must be exercised in a bona fide, honest, and reasonable manner.[12]

The Ministry of Education subsequently appealed to the Federal Court.[13] The Federal Court determined that the government has discretionary powers to decide on the transfers of civil servants and could transfer an officer such as the teacher because of the public interest. As a result, teachers can be transferred to from one school to another when the government is faced with a shortage of teachers, especially in some of the critical subjects. Moreover, this dispute reiterates the propositions that the courts do not interfere with the actions of the Ministry of Education in transferring teachers unless individuals can demonstrate that they were moved in bad faith and that no constitutional provisions allow teachers to bring their grievances before the courts. Thus, aggrieved teachers have no cause of action when the Ministry of Education transfers them from their schools.

Academic Freedom

Academic freedom in Malaysia is not a contentious legal issue at the moment, as there is minimal intrusion by authorities into teachers' classroom teaching. Teachers enjoy considerable freedom to teach in a manner that they deem fit and proper. On the other hand, the right of teachers to academic freedom appears to be restricted in terms of providing input and feedback on the curriculum.

The Ministry of Education has prescribed a standard national curriculum for all public schools in the national education system. The national curriculum includes core subjects that shall be taught, specifying the knowledge, skills, and values that students are required to acquire at the end of schooling.[14] Teachers tend to follow strictly as well as rigidly the prescribed curriculum since all students in public schools sit for a common national examination.

Overall, the academic freedom of teachers is limited to discussion on issues that are general in nature. Teachers are allowed to exercise their right to speak freely about their subject matter while using appropriate materials and teaching methods without being subject to any form of strict supervision and control.

Freedom of Speech and Expression

The Federal Constitution in Malaysia guarantees that teachers have the right to freedom of speech and expression.[15] In a multi-ethnic, multi-cultural, and multi-religious country, one has to consider the sensitivities of other races when exercising the right to freedom of speech and expression.

Remarks that are racist, distorted, and derogatory in nature create tension, hatred, and frustration. Abuse of the right to freedom of speech and expression can be highly divisive since it can foster feelings of animosity, mistrust, and hatred and eventually lead to a disintegration of a country, as evidenced from the past experiences of some other nations.

In education, teachers are supposedly role models for the younger generation. In this aspect, education and the law in Malaysia have been fortunate at this point of time as teachers are able to exercise their freedom of speech and expression with wisdom and maturity. It is done with restrain, respect, and sensitivity to the need to maintain national unity and racial harmony. Litigation in this area does not exist, as the prevalent culture of toleration and respect among teachers has played an important role in preserving peace and harmony among teachers and students from different diverse racial backgrounds.

Overall, teachers do not encounter difficulties associated with the right to freedom of speech and expression. Teachers in Malaysia, like their colleagues in the United States, do not lose their constitutional right to freedom of speech and expression when they accept the offer of employment in the public service. In addition, teachers have the right to assemble peaceably and without arms[16] as well as the right to form associations and teacher unions.[17]

It is pertinent to note that Parliament is vested with the authority to impose laws to restrict the freedom of speech and expression when it is deemed necessary or expedient in the interest of the security of the country or to provide against contempt of court, defamation, or incitement to any offense.[18] Similarly, the right of teachers to assemble peaceably can be curbed when it is deemed necessary in the interest of the security of the nation and public order. Further, the right of teachers to form associations can be restricted when it is necessary or expedient in the interest of the security of the country, public order, or morality.[19]

The rules and regulations governing freedom of speech and expression among public servants apply to public school teachers. The GO provides the primary set of regulations governing teachers' freedom of speech and expression. Teachers who comment on matters of public concern are expected to abide by the GO's provisions.[20]

As public civil servants, teachers cannot by oral, written, or other means make public statements regarding any government policy, program, or decision on any issues; provide any factual information about one's department; or offer an explanation concerning any incident or report related to one's own department. Moreover, teachers cannot distribute statements, information, or explanation that they make or that anyone else makes, except with the written approval of the Minister of Education.

In a related vein, teachers cannot make public statements that are detrimental to governmental policies, programs, or decisions. At the same time, teachers cannot embarrass the government or make comments about the strengths or weaknesses of governmental policies, programs, or decisions. In this context, public statements refer to statements or comments made to the public, to the press, or during public lectures or speeches or through visual or spoken means.

Freedom of Religion

Malaysian teachers have a constitutional right to profess and practice and propagate their religions.[21] However, this is not an absolute right, as there is a provision in the Federal Constitution that prohibits the practice and propagation of those forms of religion that threaten public order, public health, or morality. The government has banned all types of deviationist teachings. State law and federal law also control and restrict the propagation of religious doctrines or beliefs among persons who are of the Muslim faith.

The right to freedom of religion may include individuals' right to express their religion through the way they dress. On the other hand, it is highly unlikely that individuals' freedom to exercise their religious practices and beliefs extends to acts that are carried out while only function as teachers. In other words, teachers probably cannot perform religious rituals and absuances at work. To this end, it may be argued that practices may be religious in nature but are disallowed by authorities if they do not constitute essential and integral parts of religions.

Teachers who wear religious attire to school based on the argument that it is encouraged by their religion and is a constitutional right may not be allowed to do so. It is likely that the Court would prohibit teachers from wearing "serbans"[22] or "purdahs"[23] to school. In this context, it is worth reviewing the landmark case concerning the right of students to wear religious attire to school based on their religious beliefs.

A principal expelled three students who refused to obey school regulations related to school uniforms after they continued to wear "serbans" to school despite numerous warnings not to do so. In fact, the school had established its own regulations on school uniforms. While the Ministry of Education has its own set of regulations on school uniforms, it was silent with regard to wearing "serbans" to school. The students contended that the principal acted *ultra vires* when the school established its own set of regulations. In addition, the students alleged that the expulsion order constituted an infringement of their constitutional right to freedom of religion and expression.

The Federal Court asserted that the principal acted *intra vires* but that the school regulations against wearing the "serban" did not infringe on the students' constitutional rights to freedom of religion. The Court pointed out that school authorities have vast experience in managing school discipline with its own rules and regulations. In sum, courts are reluctant to interfere with the management of schools, particularly disputes over discipline, unless it can be shown that officials acted in bad faith.

In an earlier case,[24] a female governmental employee challenged her being prohibited from wearing a "purdah" to the office. The Supreme Court held that there was no infringement of her constitutional right to practice her religion. The Court explained that both the wearing of "serbans" and "purdahs" are closely associated with religious practices and observances.

These two cases reveal that the courts introduced the test of integrality when considering the constitutional right to wear religious attire. In both instances, the courts were of the opinion that the practices were not an integral part of the religion of Islam. Based on these judgments, it may be argued that teachers do not appear to have a right to wear "serbans" or "purdahs" to school.

Participation in Politics

In the education system, Malaysian teachers are grouped into professional categories based on academic qualifications: graduate and non-graduate teachers. Graduate teachers, who are considered to be in the management and professional group, are strictly prohibited from taking part in politics or wearing symbols that are associated with political parties.[25]

Specifically, the government prohibits these teachers from making oral or written public statements regarding opinions on anything that has become controversial among various political parties; publishing or distributing books, magazines, or pamphlets that provide opinions related to political parties; campaigning to gather votes and support candidates during general elections, during by-elections, or in any elections to contest for positions in political parties; acting as agents for candidates in elections; contesting for posts in political parties; and holding positions in political parties. On the other hand, non-graduate teachers have some flexibility since they are allowed to become ordinary members of political parties,[26] provided that they inform their Heads of Department.[27]

In *K Ramasen v. Minister of Education, Malaysia & Anor*,[28] a teacher stood for election in three general elections despite the fact that the ministry warned him not to, even though it did not take any disciplinary actions against him for disobeying its directive. Nevertheless, the teacher was dismissed when he contested in a by-election.

The teacher argued that he was dismissed in bad faith since he was victimized for his political beliefs and convictions. In rejecting his application, the Court noted that the teacher failed to prove that he was dismissed in bad faith. Instead, the Court reasoned that the teacher's dismissal was lawful since a conflict of interest was likely to occur when a person who has been elected to a political office is permitted to continue to work as a teacher.

In its analysis, the Court added that despite being warned by his superior, the teacher continued to be active politically although he knew that it was morally wrong. The Court concluded that the teacher admitted that he knew of the restriction imposed on civil servants related to participation in elections.

Teacher Sanctions, Due Process, and Dismissals

Teachers in Malaysia enjoy security of employment once they are confirmed in their posts and are placed in the permanent scheme of service. Cases of teacher sanctions and dismissals from employment are rare. The Disciplinary Authority is required to abide by a set of rules and procedures set out in the GO before it decides to sanction or dismiss teachers.

The Federal Constitution has established two important legal principles before sanctions or dismissals can be effected. First, teachers, as members of the education service, shall not be dismissed or reduced in rank by authorities who are subordinate or equal in rank to the teachers who are being tried.[29] Second, teachers shall not be dismissed or reduced in rank without being given reasonable opportunities of being heard.[30]

Orders to dismiss teachers are not valid when they are not afforded reasonable opportunities to be heard.[31] Breaches of this fundamental principle of natural justice would mean that the teachers were denied natural justice. It is mandatory for the Disciplinary Authority to abide strictly by the procedural and substantive due process requirements before it can enforce sanctions or dismissals of teachers.

In most circumstances, the reasons for teacher dismissal involve being absent from work, sexual harassment, corruption, dishonest behavior, insubordination, and drug abuse. The Disciplinary Authority has the discretion to impose a range of punishments such as warnings, fines, losses of emoluments, postponements of salary increases, reductions in salaries, reductions in rank, or dismissals according to the severity of the offenses.

Teachers, as role models to younger generations, are expected to demonstrate certain standards of behavior among colleagues and students, both professionally and ethically. As public servants, teachers are prohibited from allowing their personal interests to override their public duties.[32] At the same time, teachers should not behave in such a way as to give rise to conflicts between personal interests and their public duties[33] or to behave in such a way that brings disrepute to the public service.[34] The GO regulations disallow dishonest behavior and untrustworthiness,[35] irresponsible behavior,[36] and dereliction of duty.[37]

Disciplinary actions can be taken against teachers when they are absent from work without leave or without prior permission or without reasonable justification.[38] Misconduct can be grounds for the termination of employment before the expiration of teachers' probationary periods as well as of those who are on permanent contracts.[39]

Commencement of Legal Proceedings against Teachers

When faced with court actions in the exercise of their public duties, teachers must obtain the prior permission of the Director General of the Public Service before being allowed to commence any proceedings in matters related to their employment.[40] If teachers receive notice about the commencement or proposed commencement of legal proceedings related to their employment, they must report it to their Heads of Department in order to obtain instructions on how and whether the notice of court process should be received, answered, or defended.[41]

Teachers can apply to the Director General of the Public Service to obtain legal assistance in legal proceedings that arise from their employment.[42] The Director General of the Public Service may approve or reject teachers' applications for legal assistance subject to advice from the Attorney General based on the amount of legal aid that is approved, the advocate and solicitor who would be employed by the teacher, and other conditions that the Attorney General deems fit.[43]

Dismissal or Reduction in Rank

Teachers can be dismissed or reduced in rank in disciplinary proceedings on the condition that they have been informed in writing of the reasons for the decisions to be taken against them. There must be due inquiries made into the accusations against the teachers, specific charges, evidence substantiating the charges, and adequate notice of the decisions to sanction or dismiss. In addition, teachers must be given reasonable opportunities to be heard.[44]

Teachers lose the right to be heard when charges for criminal offenses have been proved against teachers; the Disciplinary Authority is satisfied that due to reasons which cannot be recorded, it is not reasonable and practical to follow the provisions; the King is satisfied that the action was taken for national security; orders for detention, supervision, restricted residence, or deportation have been issued against the teachers; or forms of bond have been issued related to national security, crime prevention, prevention detention, restricted residence, deportation, or immigration.[45]

In cases of misconduct, the Chairman of the Disciplinary Authority must consider whether violations complained of are of a type that should be punished with dismissals or reductions in rank or with lesser punishments.[46] In cases where the punishments do not amount to dismissals or reductions in rank, the Disciplinary Authority must inform teachers in writing about the facts of the violations of discipline that they committed and provide them with opportunities to make written representation no fewer than 21 days from the date when the facts were received.[47]

When teachers are found guilty of offenses that do not merit dismissals or reductions in rank, the Disciplinary Authority can impose one of the following punishments: warnings, fines, losses of emoluments, postponements of annual salary increases, or reductions in salary.[48]

The procedures related to teacher dismissals or reductions in rank are more complicated as a result of the severity of the punishments where there is a consequent loss of earning and employment. The Disciplinary Authority must establish a *prima facie* case under such circumstances.[49] Teachers who receive statements regarding the facts of the violations of discipline and reasons why dismissals or reduction in rank would be imposed can make written representations to exculpate themselves within 21 days.

If teachers do not make any representation within the stated time period, or where the representation fails to exculpate the teachers from the violation, the Disciplinary Authority can decide whether to dismiss or reduce the rank of teachers.[50] An investigation committee that consists of more than two government officers may be appointed to obtain further details and clarification for individual cases. The officers must be in more senior positions than the teachers under investigation.

Witnesses may be called for examination to substantiate the allegations made against teachers. Teachers must be given opportunities to be present physically and question the witnesses.[51] After considering the representations from the Investigation Committee, the Disciplinary Authority must impose appropriate punishments if teachers are found guilty.

Teachers must inform their Heads of Department when criminal proceedings have been commenced against them. If criminal proceedings result in convictions, teachers are suspended from duty from the dates of their convictions while waiting for decisions from the Disciplinary Authority.[52]

Principles of Natural Justice

Decisions made to dismiss teachers without regard to the principles of natural justice are void. All members of the education service have the constitutional right to be given an opportunity to be heard before being dismissed or reduced in rank. In exceptional circumstances, when criminal charges have been proved against teachers, the right to be given reasonable opportunities of being heard is compromised.[53] According to Article 135 (2) of the Federal Constitution:

> No member of such a service as aforesaid shall be dismissed or reduced in rank without being given a reasonable opportunity of being heard: Provided that this Clause shall not apply to the following cases:
>
> (a) where a member of such a service is dismissed or reduced in rank on the ground of conduct in respect of which a criminal charge has been proved against him;

In *Tan Tek Seng v. Suruhanjaya Perkhidmatan Pendidikan & Anor* (*Tan Tek Seng*),[54] the plaintiff, a senior assistant of a primary school, was charged with two counts of criminal breach of trust by a public servant under s 409 of the Penal Code. The Sessions Court convicted the plaintiff and sentenced him to six months' imprisonment.

On appeal, the High Court bound over the plaintiff conditionally on his entering into a bond to be of good behavior for a period of three years under s 173A (ii) (b) of the Criminal Procedure Code[55] ("the CPC") in the sum of RM5,000 without sureties. However, the ESC took a more serious approach and dismissed the plaintiff on the basis that his conduct brought irreparable damage to the reputation of the civil service, an offense under paragraph 4 (2) (d) of the GO. The ESC effected the dismissal under orders 33 and 35 (1) of the GO.

The plaintiff, in a later appeal, alleged that the dismissal was not valid, claiming that the issue was whether the High Court's binding over order under s 173A (ii) (b) of the CPC could have been construed as a "conviction" under orders 3, 33, and 35 of the GO. The Court rejected the plaintiff's claim, ruling that the word *conviction*, as defined in order 3 of the GO, includes "a finding of guilt by a criminal court in Malaysia." Although no conviction was recorded when a binding over order under s 173A (ii) (b) of the CPC was effected, the Court pointed out that it first had to determine whether the charge had been proven. A declaration that the charge was proved, the Court asserted, would have meant that there was a concurrent finding of guilt, which is within the ambit of the definition of *conviction* in order 3 of the GO. The term *convicted* that appeared in General Order 3 reads as follows:

> In these General Orders unless the context otherwise requires—
>
> "convicted" or "conviction" includes a finding or an order involving a finding of guilt by a criminal court in Malaysia or elsewhere, or by a competent body conferred with the power to conduct summary investigation under any written law that the person charged or accused has committed an offence.

The Court upheld the decision of the ESC to dismiss the plaintiff under the GO, observing that under the circumstances, a criminal charge had been proved. Based on the facts, the Court was of the view that Article 135 (2) of the Federal Constitution, which provides for a reasonable opportunity to be heard, was not applicable. Subsequently, the senior assistant appealed to the Court of Appeal.[56]

There were two distinct arguments on appeal, namely, the constitutional right of the plaintiff to be heard and the severity of his punishment. First, the Court of Appeal agreed with the decision of the High Court that the plaintiff was not entitled to a hearing before being dismissed. The Court posited that the constitutional protection provided by Article 135 (2) of the Federal Constitution was withdrawn when the teacher was found guilty of the offense.

On closer examination, the Court of Appeal pointed out that it was accurate that paragraph (a) of Article 135 (2) Federal Constitution contains the word *proved* and not *convicted* and that the lower court decided that a binding order had to be made under s 173A (ii) (b) of the CPC. As such, the Court thought that there had to be a plea or finding of guilt that resulted in the offense's being proved within the terms of paragraph (a) of the proviso to Article 135 (2) of the Federal Constitution.

The teacher's second argument was that as a member of the public service who was bound over under s 173A (ii) (b) of the CPC, he could only be subject to disciplinary punishment of either dismissal or reduction in rank under orders 33 and 35 of the GO. Moreover, the Court of Appeals acknowledged that the Disciplinary Authority had to consider mitigating factors before dismissing the teacher, including the record of the criminal proceedings and the circumstances of the case, especially the recommendations of the State Education Department. If the Disciplinary Authority found that the teacher committed misconduct, it was obligated to proceed as to the types of punishments set forth in the GO. The Court explained that these punishments included warnings, reprimands, fines, salary forfeitures, stoppages or deferments of increments, reductions of salary or rank, or dismissals.[57]

In its analysis, the Court of Appeal recognized that the Disciplinary Authority had to act in a reasonable and fair manner when determining the types of punishments imposed on public servants. If anything, the Court continued, when the Disciplinary Authority acts arbitrarily or unfairly or imposes a punishment that is disproportionate to the misconduct, its order can be quashed. As such, the Court of Appeal highlighted the need to consider the recommendations made by the State Education Department and the judgment of the earlier court. The Court of Appeal thus disagreed with the High Court's decision and held that since the order of dismissal was too severe in nature, the only penalty that the teacher could have been subjected to was a reduction in rank.

In sum, *Tan Tek Seng* stands for the proposition that the principles of natural justice must be complied with in cases involving the dismissals or reductions in rank of teachers and that the punishments must be commensurate with the severity of the offenses. Under the principle of natural justice, dismissal can be used only as a last resort in cases of severe misconduct.

Emerging Issues

As noted, teachers can sue the government if they have obtained the approval of their Heads of Department. However, this process can be cumbersome and time-consuming, leading to the barring of actions on the grounds that they were filed outside limitations periods which require litigation to commence within three years of complained-of actions.[58] Unfortunately, this obstacle can discourage teachers from taking actions against the government.

In one case, for example, a teacher sought a letter of consent from the Ministry of Education to sue two police officers who were alleged to have acted in bad faith and maliciously against him.[59] When the teacher finally filed the suit nine years after the incident occurred, the Court of Appeal dismissed his claim as statute barred. Clearly, this is an issue that must be addressed if teachers are going to be able to protect their rights.

Another emerging trend involves two related aspects of teacher transfers. First, teachers have limited legal redress to challenge transfers that they allege are made in bad faith. Second, teachers who seek to improve their academic qualifications may receive scholarships or financial grants to further their studies at universities. When teachers complete their studies, they may be transferred to schools that are located at great distances from their homes.

If teachers are unable to appeal in either of these situations, the result can lead to feelings of frustration and unhappiness that will undoubtedly impact teacher performance. Thus, attempting to resolve staff shortages in some schools while maintaining the rights of teachers to challenge their being transferred is a delicate, and sometimes onerous, task, and it is an area that must be addressed in the interest of promoting quality education in Malaysia.

Conclusion

The Federal Constitution in Malaysia provides a strong legal framework for the protection of the rights of teachers. Teachers possess a number of legal rights. The law has granted public school teachers rights to employment, freedom of speech and expression, freedom of religion, and freedom of association. Insofar as these rights are not absolute, they can be constrained by the need to protect the nation, the rights of fellow citizens, public order, and public health and morality.

Notes

1. The Federal Constitution, a written constitution grounded in the basic principles of the British government and constitutional conventions, is described as based on the "Westminster" model. More specifically, it is modeled along the Indian Constitution.
2. Article 132 Federal Constitution.
3. Article 132 (2) Federal Constitution.
4. Article 132 (1) Federal Constitution.
5. Article 141A Federal Constitution.
6. Article 114 (5b) (ii) Federal Constitution.
7. Article 8 Federal Constitution.
8. Article 8 (2) Federal Constitution.
9. [1966] 1 LNS 55.
10. [1989] 2 MLJ 224.
11. Article 135 Federal Constitution.
12. *Loot Ting Yee v. Tan Sri Sheikh Hussien bin Sheikh Mohamed & Ors.* [1982] 1 MLJ 321.
13. *Pengarah Pelajaran, Wilayah Persekutuan & Ors v. Loot Ting Yee* [1982] 1 MLJ 68.
14. See Section 18 Education Act 1996, which states that the national curriculum shall be used by all schools in the National Education System.
15. Article 10 (1) (a) Federal Constitution.
16. Article 10 (1) (b) Federal Constitution.
17. Article 10 (1) (c) Federal Constitution.
18. Article 10 (1) (a) Federal Constitution.
19. Article 10 (1) (c) Federal Constitution.
20. General Order 19 (1).
21. Article 11 (1) FC, with the exception of Clause 4.
22. A "serban" is a piece of cloth that is worn around the head and is related to religious practice. It is sometimes referred to as a turban.
23. A "purdah" is a piece of cloth that is worn to cover the whole face except the eyes. It is usually black in color and normally worn by female muslims conceal their faces.
24. See, generally, *Hajjah Halimatussadiah bte Hj Kamaruddin v. Public Services Commission Malaysia & Anor* [1994] 3 MLJ.
25. General Order 21 Public Officers (Conduct and Discipline) (Chapter "D") General Orders 1980.
26. General Order 21 (5).
27. General Order 21 (6).
28. [1986] 1 LNS 70.

29. Article 135 (1) Federal Constitution.
30. Article 135 (2) Federal Constitution.
31. Article 135 Federal Constitution.
32. General Order 4 (2) (a).
33. General Order 4 (2) (b).
34. General Order 4 (2) (d).
35. General Order 4 (2) (f).
36. General Order 4 (2) (g).
37. General Order 4 (2) (j).
38. General Order 22 (1).
39. See, generally, *Sulnayah Mohd Isa v. Sekolah Kanak-Kanak Pekak Selangor & Anor* [1999] 6 CLJ 234.
40. General Order 22 (1).
41. General Order 22 (2).
42. General Order 22 (3).
43. General Order 22 (4) (a) through (c).
44. General Order 25 (1).
45. General Order 25 (2) (a) through (d).
46. General Order 26.
47. General Order 27 (1).
48. General Order 38 (a) through (g).
49. General Order 28.
50. General Order 28 (3).
51. *Id.*
52. General Order 32 (5).
53. Article 135 (2) (a) Federal Constitution.
54. [1995] 2 MLJ 476.
55. S173A (ii) (b) Criminal Procedure Code reads as follows:

(ii) when any person is charged before the Court with an offence punishable by such Court, and the Court finds that the charge is proved, but is of opinion that, having regard to the character, antecedents, age, health or mental condition of the person charged, or to the trivial nature of the offence, or to the extenuating circumstances under which the offence was committed, it is inexpedient to inflict any punishment or any other than a nominal punishment or that is expedient to release the offender on probation, the Court may, without proceeding to record a conviction, made an order either—(a) dismissing the charge or complaint after such admonition or caution to the offender as to the Court seems fit; or, (b) discharging the offender conditionally on his entering into a bond with or without sureties, to be of good behavior and to appear for the conviction to be recorded and for sentence when called upon at any time during such period, not exceeding three years, as may be specified in the order.

56. *Tan Tek Seng v. Suruhanjaya Perkhidmatan Pendidikan & Anor* [1996] 1 MLJ 261.
57. See General Order 36.
58. See section 2 of the Public Authorities Protection Act 1948.
59. *Alias bin Ismail v. Hairuddin bin Mohamad & Anor* [1997] 3 MLJ 724.

10

The Netherlands

Ben P. Vermeulen

Introduction

This chapter provides a brief description of the legal position of teachers in the Dutch educational system. It primarily discusses the rights of teachers in primary and secondary education.

The legal status of the Dutch teacher is, to a large extent, determined by the constitutional norms and principles regulating the school system. The basic structure of this system, as laid down in Article 23 of the Constitution,[1] is binary. This binary structure is linked to the dichotomy that Dutch law makes between public law, regulating the vertical–hierarchical relation between the State and citizens, and the civil law that concerns the horizontal relation between individuals (including civil law corporations). It consists of two types of schools, public-authority schools and private, non-state schools, which like, Yin and Yang, complement and supplement each other.[2]

Public-authority (or public) schools are generally governed by local authorities, often by the municipal executive. While these schools do not enjoy autonomy in terms of a freedom to ground their educational principles in specific religions or beliefs, they are free to choose their pedagogical approaches such as Montessori or Dalton.

The education provided in public schools is regulated by law; it must be non-denominational based on the principle of neutrality. In light of this principle, public schools are not allowed to select teachers based on denominational criteria. Insofar as the status of teachers is controlled by public law, they are public servants. This means that administrative courts are competent to resolve cases between teachers and public schools.

Public schools, which are freely accessible to all, have a certain primacy since the government has to guarantee that within a small distance from home there should be a public school available for every pupil. Aside from that, both subsystems—public-authority schools and private schools—have equal status. Public and non-state (private) schools receive funding according to identical or equivalent criteria since the strict church–state separationism that characterizes the United States school system is absent in the Netherlands.

Non-state schools, also called independent or private schools, are run by corporate bodies under civil law as foundations or associations, although these schools are, in general, fully government funded and enjoy a level of autonomy safeguarded by the Constitution: the freedom of education.

This freedom consists of three rights: the right to shape a school according to a religious or philosophical worldview while offering education of a distinctive religious or philosophical character (*vrijheid van richting*); the pedagogical and organizational autonomy (*vrijheid van inrichting*), which overlaps the prior right; and the right to establish a school in order to provide the type of education covered by the two previously named rights (*vrijheid van stichting*).

The right to allow non-state, government-funded schools a distinctive religious or philosophical character, the *vrijheid van richting*, may be regarded as the core of the freedom of education. It is this aspect of the *vrijheid van inrichting* (the pedagogical and organizational autonomy) that is guaranteed most when it concerns schools founded on distinct religious grounds. The freedom to organize schools and provide education based on specific religious or philosophical views is explicitly safeguarded in Article 23 of the Constitution, which declares that when the government issues quality standards (funding conditions for private schools), this freedom must be respected, especially in relation to the choice of teaching materials and the right to appoint teachers (sections 5 and 6 of this provision). The right to establish non-state schools, *vrijheid van stichting*, is also strongly linked to the *vrijheid van richting*, the freedom to give such a school a distinctive religious or philosophical character.

The *vrijheid van inrichting*, the pedagogical–organizational autonomy, is less protected when school policies are based on non-denominational considerations. For instance, the discretion school boards have in hiring teachers is wider when they act based on religious adherence than when grounded in "secular" standards such as purely pedagogical criteria.

The majority of non-state primary and secondary schools, which accounts for two- thirds of all schools, have, at least formally, a Christian character.

However, it must be stressed that most of the Catholic and Protestant schools no longer have strongly distinctive religious characters, presenting themselves as "open" and pluralistic.

As now has become clear, non-state or independent schools have the right to select teachers on the basis of criteria derived from their denominational or pedagogical ethos. Even so, this right may not be exercised arbitrarily; it is limited by specific provisions.

The legal relationship between a school board and an individual teacher must be characterized as a civil law contract, although its material content, or the substantive norms regulating it, are, to a large extent, derived from the aforementioned public law provisions and principles. Labour cases in this field are dealt with by civil courts.

Although there are fundamental differences in the legal positions of teachers in public and private schools, their material conditions are fairly equal. The level of such items as salaries and vacation rights is primarily regulated by more or less similar labor agreements between trade unions and employers' organizations; their social security rights are set by law.

The Right to Provide Education

In Dutch education law, school organizations, which are represented by boards and management, have a strong legal position, while teachers, to a large extent, are subordinate employees. School boards and management are ultimately responsible for the choice of educational materials, pedagogical methods, didactic arrangements, and the organization of education in general. This may seem curious because the freedom of education in its original intent was not primarily a right of institutions or school boards to organize and provide education.

Originally, the freedom of education was regarded as the right of individual educators, the autonomy of competent teachers to found schools and to teach there, thus earning their daily bread. The framers of the 1848 Constitution interpreted the phrase "Providing education is free," currently laid down in Article 23(2), in a literal sense. It guaranteed the *droit d'enseigner*, the individual freedom to teach and educate. As the explanatory memorandum stated, this provision protects "the right for everyone who, within the limits of the law, can manifest his competence and morality, thereby freely communicating his knowledge and skill."[3]

On the other hand, the fairly weak position of teachers in the current school system is not that remarkable. In fact, even in 1848, the opinion that freedom of education was an exclusive right of ambitious teachers was rejected.

Apart from this right of the teacher, the claim of parents to have their children educated in conformity with their religious, philosophical, and pedagogical convictions—the *droit d'apprendre*—was regarded as a second, independent legal foundation of the freedom of education. This freedom also encompassed "the right of parents to have their children educated according to their fundamental views, entrust them to the care of those individuals who, because of their competence and moral standing, have obtained their teaching authority."[4]

In the course of the long political dispute that would come to be referred to as the *Schoolstrijd*, or the *school struggle*,[5] which resulted in complete equal funding of public and non-state schools in the 1917 Constitution, the rights of both individual teachers and parents were absorbed in the right of collective providers, the school boards administering private schools.

The parental right was always regarded as one to select between various schools, not as an individual claim to a specific curriculum within a chosen school. Moreover, gradually school boards started hiring teachers, thereby replacing the individual teacher–entrepreneurs. To this end, the Schoolwet-Mackay (School Act) of 1889 stipulated as that as a condition of receiving government funding, private schools had to be managed by foundations or associations. Subsequently, the constitutional amendment of 1917 made it clear that the freedom of education belongs to the boards and their institutions, not to individual teachers whom they employ.

Of course, a legally protected autonomous position of teachers with regard to public education also seems problematic due to the dominance of (local) government in public schools under Article 23(4) of the Constitution and due to the requirement that the law regulates the content and structure of public education pursuant to Article 23(3) of the Constitution. It must be further stressed that there is a strong demand in society and politics, reacting to failures of top-down educational innovations in the 1990s, to give teachers some guarantee of their autonomy as professionals, especially in pedagogical and didactic matters. This is discussed further under the heading on the autonomy of the teaching profession.[6]

Equality

Provisions in the Dutch Constitution and statutes, as well as in international and European law, express the principle of equality, demanding equal treatment of individuals and of minority groups. According to the first sentence of Article 1 of the Dutch Constitution, persons have to be treated equally in equal cases. The second sentence of this provision prohibits discrimination.

What equal cases are, and what discrimination is, depends on value judgments as to what cases "count" as equal and what reasons "count" as sufficient justification of differential treatment. Article 3 of the Constitution declares that Dutch nationals have equal rights to be appointed to public service, which includes public schools. Pursuant to Article 23(3) of the Constitution, education provided by public authorities must pay due respect to everyone's religions or beliefs. These three provisions imply that public-authority schools must be neutral and accessible for all. These provisions further suggest that school officials may not select teachers on the basis of criteria such as religion, race, or culture.

Human rights treaties that address the principle of equality are also relevant to the status of teachers. For example, among the most important self-executing treaty norms is Article 26 of the International Covenant on Civil and Political Rights; this Article contains the general principle of equality. This principle is also protected in the European Convention by Article 14 in conjunction with another Convention right as well as by the Twelfth Protocol to the Convention. Article 5 of the International Convention for the Elimination of Racial Discrimination (ICERD)[7] demands that State parties eliminate racial discrimination while guaranteeing the right of equality to all in the enjoyment of fundamental freedoms and social rights. Additionally, this provision prohibits direct and indirect discrimination.

Article 1(1) of the ICERD defines "racial discrimination" as

> any distinction, exclusion, restriction or preference based on race, colour, descent, or national or ethnic origin which has the purpose or effect of nullifying or impairing the recognition, enjoyment or exercise, on an equal footing, of human rights and fundamental freedoms in the political, economic, social and cultural or any other field of public life.

At the same time, community law is relevant. Council Directive 2000/43/EC of June 29, 2000, implementing the principle of equal treatment between persons irrespective of racial or ethnic origin,[8] must be mentioned in this regard. Article 2, in conjunction with Article 3 of this directive, forbids direct and indirect discrimination on the basis of race and ethnicity in the fields of labor, social security, education, and housing.

Articles 2 and 3 of Council Directive 2000/78/EC of November 27, 2000, also demand equal treatment in labor relations irrespective of religion or conviction as well as disability, age, or sexual orientation.[9] However, under Article 4, section 2 of this directive, churches and other denominational organisations, including private schools, may differentiate on the basis of religion or belief when individuals' religions or beliefs constitute genuine occupational requirements with regard to the ethos of a particular organisation. This implies that religious organisations may, under certain conditions, still require their staff members to adhere to the distinctive ethos that is present in a school.[10]

Finally, there is the 1994 General Equal Treatment Act, *Algemene Wet Gelijke Behandeling* (AWGB). The AWGB, which, to a large extent implements the constitutional norms, European Union directives, and treaty provisions on anti-discrimination, intends to provide "more substance" and more effectiveness to the principle of equality.

The AWGB not only applies to vertical relations between government and citizens in public schools, but also, to a certain extent, applies to horizontal relations between individuals and private organisations such as private denominational schools. Even so, churches and their organizations are fully exempted from the AWGB's Article 3.

The structure of the AWGB is founded on the assumption that differentiations based on suspect grounds such as political persuasion, race, sex, or religion are prohibited in specified areas such as work, commercial transactions, and education.[11] Article 5(1) of the AWGB, for instance, prohibits differential treatment on these grounds in such cases as the conclusion and termination of labour contracts, appointment of civil servants and the termination of their engagements, and terms of employment. Thus, teachers in public and private schools are protected against discrimination.

The AWGB distinguishes between so-called direct and indirect differential treatment. Direct differential treatment explicitly refers to suspect criteria such as religion or race and is always prohibited unless the AWGB contains an explicit exception. Indirect differential treatment is treatment in which a criterion is applied that seems to be neutral but in practice, in its effect, is primarily disadvantageous to persons sharing common characteristics such as religion or race. Indirect differential treatment may not only be justified when a specific exception in the AWGB applies but can also be justified by so-called "objective reasons" or legitimate interests that are not spelled out in its terms, overriding the disadvantages suffered by groups particularly affected by that treatment (Article 2(1) of the AWGB).

By way of illustration, if a school specifically prohibits female teachers from wearing Islamic veils, their policies must be qualified as direct differential treatment, only justified when the law provides for an explicit exception. For public schools, the AWGB does not contain such a provision; there may be an exception for private schools under Article 5(2) of the AWGB, discussed below. However, if schools adopt ostensibly neutral dress codes such as forbidding any head coverings, there is no question of direct differential treatment. Still, because it disproportionally affects religious persons, it is a form of indirect differential treatment, which is prohibited unless a school board is able to refer to a legal provision that enables it to act or is able to provide strong objective arguments such as safety, order, or educational purposes justifying such a policy.

The first paragraph of Article 5(2) of the AWGB does not eliminate the freedom of faith-based schools and other denominational organizations to lay down requirements concerning the fulfilment of positions that they may regard as necessary in order to realize their religious or philosophical principles. Such requirements may not lead to differential treatment based solely on political persuasion, race, sex, nationality, sexual preference, or civil status. Differential treatment due to religious grounds is permitted. The aim of this exemption is, of course, to respect the freedoms of religion and education, allowing denominational organizations to select teachers on the basis of criteria flowing from their specific ethos.

In line with the famous *Maimonides* judgment,[12] the AWGB grants denominational schools based on a religious ethos the freedom to apply criteria derived from their religious "missions" in selecting their teachers (and pupils) as long as they do so consistently.[13] This implies that if denominational organizations select their employees on denominational grounds on a case-by-case basis rather than in a consistent manner, they cannot appeal to the exception of the AWGB and thus will be in breach of Article 5. In practice, this implies that the majority of non-orthodox organizations, even though based on religions or beliefs, are fully bound by the non-discrimination principle.

The interpretations of the AWGB given by the Equal Treatment Commission, or *Commissie Gelijke Behandeling*, play a dominant role. This Commission is a public authority that, at the request of private persons or organizations or on its own accord, examines the AWGB-conformity of acts of the government or private organizations such as boards of faith-based schools in equal treatment cases.

The Commission is not a judge: it provides opinions that are not legally binding. However, these opinions are considered important because they are often regarded as authoritative interpretations of the AWGB, in general, to be followed by the courts. Since its inception, the Commission has offered important views concerning religious issues in education and other areas.

Commission cases involving religious issues in schools often address dress codes,[14] particularly the Islamic headscarf. While it is clear that pupils in Dutch public schools are allowed to wear headscarves, it is not entirely evident that teachers may, too, because that might be regarded as a violation of the principle of the neutrality of public education contained in Article 23(3) of the Constitution.

At least according to the Commission, the neutrality principle does not entail the prohibition of headscarves as long as teachers do not express their religious views during their lessons.[15] Conversely, if teachers in public schools express their religious opinions too fervently or try to convert pupils, they violate this principle, which demands reticence in matters of religion, and may be fired.[16]

A case that has attracted a considerable amount of publicity involved a female Muslim teacher at a public school who, after returning from her vacation in Morocco, refused to shake hands with males for religious reasons. The school board dismissed the teacher, arguing that her conduct breached its code of conduct. The Commission decided that the dismissal amounted to indirect differential treatment because it primarily affected Muslim women. Further, the Commission thought that the application of the code was not justified by objective reasons under Article 2(1) of the AWGB.

Instead, the Commission decreed that the dismissal was disproportionate since the teacher was prepared to greet men otherwise, such as with a friendly nod.[17] The school board did not accept this outcome and brought the case before the district court, which ruled that the relationship between it and the teacher had become so strained that the dismissal was justified. Still, the Court granted the teacher financial compensation.[18] This was a pragmatic judgment. The Court was unwilling to give a clear answer whether the teacher's refusal to refuse to shake hands with males is always a ground for dismissal.

Apart from conflicts involving Muslim teachers, the AWGB has not generated much controversy in education law cases. This may be surprising because during the many years of the legislative process that resulted in the AWGB, there was a fierce debate concerning whether orthodox Christian schools should be allowed the right to refuse to hire homosexual teachers. On the basis of the text of the law and its legislative history, this prohibits officials from applying criteria, even those arising from a school's ethos. That led to differential treatment on the ground of sexual orientation as well as on the basis of the legislative history.[19] Accordingly, it must be assumed that the refusal to hire teachers who live with partners of the same sex violates the AWGB in principle.[20]

Due to the small number of cases before the Equal Treatment Commission, it may be assumed that homosexuality is not a big issue. Nevertheless, the European Commission recently stated that the AWGB probably is not in conformity with community law in that the act still leaves school boards too wide a discretionary margin in this issue[21] and has demanded clarifications of the Dutch government.[22] If the European Commission starts an infraction procedure against the Netherlands, a repetition of the ideological debate of the 1990s may be expected.

Fundamental Freedoms in Schools

To what extent can teachers appeal to the freedom of religion and the freedom of speech in their relations with school boards and management? Article 6, section 1 of the Dutch Constitution provides that "(e)veryone shall have the right to manifest freely his religion or belief, either individually or in community with others, without prejudice to his responsibility under the law."

Freedom of religion comprises not only the freedom to establish and have a religion, including the right to change one's religion or not to have a religion, but also the freedom to behave in accordance with a specific religion or to profess or propagate a religion in ritual, cult, and clothing.[23] Article 9 of the European Convention on Human Rights likewise protects religious freedom.

Article 7, section 1 of the Dutch Constitution provides that "(n)o one shall require prior permission to publish thoughts or opinions through the press, without prejudice to the responsibility of every person under the law." Moreover, Article 7, section 3 of the Constitution provides: "No one shall be required to submit thoughts or opinions for prior approval in order to disseminate them by means other than those mentioned in the preceding paragraphs, without prejudice to the responsibility of every person under the law." Article 10 of the European Convention also guarantees the freedom of expression.

In discussing the relevance of these fundamental rights adequately, some distinctions must be made. It is necessary to differentiate between international human rights that are guaranteed, in particular, by the European Convention and constitutional rights. Further, it is essential to differentiate between private and public education.

As to European Convention rights, such as those flowing from its Articles 9 and 10, it is necessary to stress that they are drafted to regulate vertical relations between individuals and states, not horizontal relations between private parties or between individuals and private organizations.[24] The Convention rights therefore are not applicable as such in disputes between private school boards and teachers. Still, this does not preclude that these rights may have an indirect *Drittwirkung*, in that they may be used as means of interpretation and specification of civil law principles. However, in general, appeals to Convention rights as such or as means of interpretation are likely to fail in court because it is generally assumed that teachers, through their labour contracts, have waived these rights.

In such a case, a court in Amsterdam noted that the headmaster of a Catholic school who became a member of a religious sect that required him to express his new beliefs by wearing orange clothing could be dismissed. The Court was of the opinion that the Convention does not protect persons from the loss of religious freedom contractually in agreements with their employers.[25] Additionally, when teachers appeal to religious freedom in disputes with their denominational schools by consistently relying on their own religious bases, they generally fail since the school boards' freedom of education prevails.[26]

In public education, on the other hand, the Convention is directly applicable. Public schools are governmental agencies that must respect Convention rights. Even so, these rights can be restricted under the restriction clauses such as Articles 9(2) and 10(2) of the Convention. It must be assumed that public schools have a wide margin of discretion in limiting the freedom of religion and expression of their teachers because of their functioning as professionals within educational contexts. This margin is even wider when the pluriform and neutral character of public education is at stake.[27]

Like Convention rights, constitutional guarantees of the freedom of religion and of expression are only directly applicable in legal relations between individuals and private groups on the one hand and public authorities on the other; they do not apply to legal relationships between private parties. Further, it is often assumed that these rights have been given up by contract[28] or have to give way to the fundamental rights of the schools as freedom of education or freedom of association.[29] For example, it was decided that membership of the Communist Party was incompatible with the obligations that a religion teacher at a Christian school accepted when he signed his employment contract.[30]

An interesting case concerned a member of Parliament of a radical right-wing party whose contract as a teacher was judicially dissolved, without an award of damages, because the relationship had become strained. Of particular relevance was that the judge stressed that it must be expected of the teacher that he refrain from making political statements in his lessons.[31] This judgment therefore should not be interpreted as positing the rights of teachers to express their political convictions at school and *a fortiori* in their lessons.

As mentioned, when discussing the relevance of the European Convention, it must be assumed that since public schools "belong" to the State, they must respect the constitutional rights of their teachers. A basic principle of the current 1983 Constitution is that fundamental rights apply unimpaired to public servants, including teachers in public schools.[32] To this end, a district court found that the dismissal of a teacher because of his radical political opinions, which he expressed only outside school, violated his right to freedom of expression. The Court explained that it was not in any way established that the teacher indoctrinated his pupils or otherwise expressed his views in class.[33]

A qualifying comment is necessary at this point. The neutrality of public education in Article 23(3) of the Constitution places serious limits on the expression of religion and opinion in public schools. It may even be doubted that constitutional rights apply within public schools.[34] Articles 125a and 125b of *Ambtenarenwet*, the Public Servants Act, suggest that these rights are solely written to protect expressions outside government organizations.

Put another way, such freedoms as expression, association, and religion demand that public servants may not be restricted in their expressions outside their function unless constitutional provisions contain adequate restrictions clauses which are implemented in Acts of Parliament. However, since these restrictions are inapplicable within the civil service, they are irrelevant in public schools. To this extent, the scope of constitutional freedoms probably is not as wide as the ambit of the corresponding Convention rights.

In sum, the direct relevance of treaty and constitutional rights in education law cases is limited. Apart from the legal–technical arguments just discussed, an important reason is that the free space for religious and other expressions within educational institutions is subject to limitations that are inherent in the fact that teachers are part of a collective pedagogical process in which restrictions apply as to place because the time and mode of expression are unavoidable. For instance, an appeal to religious freedom in order to claim a right to perform a ritual during class would probably be dismissed as frivolous. The same outcome is likely to occur in cases where individual teachers believe that their freedom of expression allows them to deviate from curricula or methods that school teams agreed on. If such cases result in legal conflicts, then school boards and management teams are most certain to prevail.

Dutch perspectives notwithstanding, the European Convention recently has become involved in the discussions on a so-called *burqa ban*. A bill was introduced by the Freedom Party (PVV) of Geert Wilders that intends specifically to prohibit women from wearing a burqa, an Islamic veil that fully covers the face in every public place, including schools.[35] The Council of State concluded that since this proposal is discriminatory and violates the freedom of religion, it is incompatible with the European Convention. Second, Henk Kamp, MP for the Liberal Party (VVD), introduced a bill that intends to prohibit all clothing that covers the face.[36] Although this provision is *prima facie* neutral, the question may be raised whether it is (in)compatibile with the freedom of religion and non-discrimination norms as enshrined in the Convention.[37]

Professional Competence and Pedagogical Autonomy of the Individual Teacher

It seems that the legal relationship between school (boards) and teachers is one-sided. Of course, the appointment of teachers is regulated by fundamental rights provisions, in particular by equality norms. These norms are also relevant when terminating labour relationships. However, within school organizations teachers seem to be but subordinate employees who must follow the orders of boards and management.

The assumption that the legal relationships are purely hierarchical is a one-sided view. It seems that the position of teachers is better described as a duplex ordo. Indeed, on the one hand teachers are employees, bound by legal professional standards, the missions of their schools, and the instructions of their employers. At the same time, teachers are professionals who *qualitate qua* have a certain amount of pedagogical autonomy.[38] This autonomy is only partially guaranteed in the education acts. Further, there is often an implicit attribution of competence by teachers. To this end, teachers determine the day-by-day routine in their classes and choose when to send troublesome pupils away and which pupils pass tests.

The assumption that teachers are professionals with rightful claims to some autonomy flows in part from the competence requirements that they must fulfil. Article 23, paragraph 2 of the Dutch Constitution allows the law to formulate requirements for teacher competence. Article 32a of the Primary Education Act, "Wet op het primair onderwijs"; Article 36 of the Secondary Education Act, "Wet op het voortgezet onderwijs"; and Article 4.2.3 of the Adult and Vocational Education Act, "Wet educatie en beroepsonderwijs" all provide abstract definitions of competence requirements—pedagogical–didactic knowledge, insight, and competences as well as professional competence. These requirements are further defined and specified in governmental decrees, the *Besluit bekwaamheidseisen onderwijspersoneel*.[39] In general, teachers in primary and secondary schools, as well as those in institutions for vocational training, must have diplomas testifying that they fulfil these requirements.

Given the professional autonomy of teachers, it is evident that they must be allowed a large margin of appreciation in assessments and evaluations. In general, judicial scrutiny of teacher assessments and evaluations, in the course of cases brought by parents and pupils, is marginal; it is not up to judges to act like super-examiners who repeat assessment procedures. For instance, whether students have passed or have the capacity to follow advanced courses of study is primarily up to teaching professionals, not judicial bodies. Only if teachers fail to follow procedural norms or act in an arbitrary manner are there possible grounds to declare their behavior unlawful.[40] More or less the same standard applies when there is a conflict between teachers and school boards/management concerning assessments within the sphere of teachers' competence. As long as there are no clear indications that teachers acted against formal and procedural regulations and their decisions are not evidently arbitrary, it must be assumed that they acted correctly.[41]

At the same time, the autonomy of individual teachers cannot be invoked to obstruct pedagogical policies accepted by the majority of teaching staffs. If a school's management, in conformity with the views of most of its teachers, chooses to make a fundamental change in teaching methods, for instance, adopting a system of pupil-oriented supervision instead of class teaching, then individual teachers lack the authority to continue their traditional style of so-called "frontal" class teaching.[42]

The Autonomy of the Teaching Profession[43]

One fundamental issue has yet to be discussed. The status of professional autonomy has solely been examined from the perspective of individual teachers. However, the issue is not only the position of individual teachers but also the legal position of the teaching profession as such, the collectivity of professionals.

In most Western countries there is widespread pessimism concerning the quality of education. It seems self-evident that the quality of education depends on the quality of the educators. Still, there are some trends that are detrimental to maintaining and raising the quality of the educators, the teachers themselves. On the one hand there is, in general, a shortage of persons willing to become teachers. This inevitably leads to a lowering of professional requirements.

There is also a strong trend to accept unqualified teachers who must earn their qualifications within a few years after being hired. Additionally, pedagogical innovations in the 1990s have been detrimental to the profession. These innovations were to some extent imposed by changes in legislation but to a larger extent were propagated by government advisors and the education inspectorate, which was motivated by the pedagogical ideal of child-centered learning as well as by school boards/managements which used this ideology to cut the number of teachers.

The result of these innovations and policies was a stress on general competences and skills, to the detriment of traditional subjects such as languages and mathematics as well as teaching methods. These innovations required teachers to relinquish their positions as individual professionals devoted to teaching the essence of their subject(s) in their classes, the so-called "frontal" teaching, and to become supervisors, merely assisting pupils in their own development.[44]

These developments led to wide-scale dissatisfaction: parents believed that their children did not learn the basics any longer, pupils demanded a return to traditional teaching in class, and teachers were demoralized. In February 2008 a parliamentary committee, chaired by Dijsselbloem MP, concluded that the innovations not only failed but also were, to some extent, counterproductive. The committee proposed a renewed stress on basic subjects and more central standardized tests, combined with pedagogical autonomy for schools and teachers.[45]

One of the topics raised by the Dijsselbloem report is how to strengthen pedagogical autonomy. That question is not easily answered. At least three parties are involved: school boards and management, responsible for the entire curriculum; teams of teachers, responsible for parts of the curriculum; and individual teachers, responsible for their specific classes and subjects. It is clear that schools cannot operate without central coordination. To deny boards and management the final say with regard to the basics of the curriculum seems to be unworkable. On the other hand, the current situation in which (teams of) teachers have no legal status as to such matters as the choice of didactics, methods, and educational material is unsatisfactory. It is plausible to assume that in the near future legislation will be enacted that ensures teaching teams, not individuals, co-partnerships in the decision-making process.

The university model may be a source of inspiration. The Dutch university may be described as a federation, consisting of three different levels of authority. There is a central administration, or *College van bestuur*, that primarily deals with financial matters, coordination, and fundamental strategic choices. Then the different disciplines are administered by the faculty management, which deals with the basic structure of the curriculum. Finally, teams of academics/professionals are responsible for their individual courses. The Higher Education Act attributes competences to all these three levels. Within their own spheres, faculty members and teams have a fair amount of autonomy. Moreover, the Higher Education Act requires that one member at a central and faculty level, typically the vice chancellor or the dean, is a professor, thereby ensuring that the financial expertise is somewhat counterbalanced by academic professionalism.

It seems obvious that a "federal" model cannot fully replace the unitary system currently in force in primary, secondary, and vocational education. Nevertheless, it seems just as unavoidable that at least a certain degree of decentralization will have to be realized.

Conclusion

The Dutch system is a binary one, consisting of public schools run by public authorities and non-state, private schools. These schools are funded on an equal basis and have to meet similar quality standards. Public schools must be neutral and, to that extent, be open for all teachers. Private schools may select staff on the basis of denominational criteria and, in general, enjoy freedom of education. The discretion of public and private school boards in selecting their staffs is restricted by equality norms. These norms leave private school boards a larger margin of discretion but only if they base their decisions on the consistent application of criteria derived from their denominations. Otherwise, the terms of employment in public and private schools are similar.

The relevance of constitutional and human rights such as freedom of expression and freedom in schools is limited. In general, boards prevail in legal conflicts concerning teachers' religious and other expressions in schools. However, these rights may be relevant in discussion of the so-called *burqa ban* since bills seeking to ban this style of dress by teachers in schools have been introduced in Parliament. It seems that such a general prohibition, which is also applicable in schools, is incompatible with the freedom of religion.

A serious political issue is the professional autonomy of teachers, which has been restricted due to recent top-down educational policies. There is general consensus that this autonomy should get stronger protection. However, since it is not certain how the the law is to be implemented, the future is far from clear.

Notes

1. The relevant sections of Article 23 of the Constitution read as follows:

(1) . . .
(2) All persons shall be free to provide education, without prejudice to the authorities' right of supervision and, with regard to forms of education designated by law, its right to examine the competence and moral integrity of teachers, to be regulated by Act of Parliament.
(3) Education provided by public authorities shall be regulated by Act of Parliament, paying due respect to everyone's religion or belief.
(4) The authorities shall ensure that primary education is provided in a sufficient number of public-authority schools in every municipality. Deviations from this provision may be permitted under rules to be established by Act of Parliament on condition that there is opportunity to receive the said education, whether or not in a public-authority school.
(5) The standards required of schools financed either in part or in full from public funds shall be regulated by Act of Parliament, with due regard, in the case of private schools, to the freedom to provide education according to religious or other belief.
(6) The requirements for primary education shall be such that the standards both of private schools fully financed from public funds and of public-authority schools are fully guaranteed. The relevant provisions shall respect in particular the freedom of private schools to choose their teaching aids and to appoint teachers as they see fit.
(7) Private primary schools that satisfy the conditions laid down by Act of Parliament shall be financed from public funds according to the same standards as public-authority schools. . . . .

2. Cf. also J. Henk, J.M. Hoefnagel, & Ben P. Vermeulen, "Recent developments in Dutch legislation on education," *European Journal for Education Law and Policy* 1997, no. 1, pp. 155 ff.

3. *Handelingen II* 1847/1848, p. 355. Cf. B.P. Vermeulen, *Constitutioneel onderwijsrecht*, Den Haag 1999, p. 17.

4. *Id.*, Cf. D. Mentink, "Vergeten" onderwijsrecht. Over overheidszorg en de relatie tussen school en opvoeding, in P. Boekholt (ed.), *Tweehonderd jaar onderwijs en de zorg van de staat*, Assen 2002, pp. 79–80.

5. For a short sketch, see D. Mentink and B.P. Vermeulen, *Artikel 23 Grondwet*, Den Haag 2007. Religious–political school struggles were also fought in Belgium and France, with divergent results: the Belgian system resembles the Dutch, whereas in the French system secular republicanism, favouring the public school, has prevailed.

6. The relevant provisions of the Constitution read as follows:

> Article 1: "All persons in the Netherlands shall be treated equally in equal circumstances. Discrimination on the grounds of religion, belief, political opinion, race or sex or any other grounds whatsoever shall not be permitted."
>
> Article 3: "All Dutch nationals shall be equally eligible for appointment to public service."
>
> Article 23(3) is cited in paragraph 1.

7. ". . . States Parties undertake to prohibit and to eliminate racial discrimination in all its forms and to guarantee the right of everyone, without distinction as to race, colour, or national or ethnic origin, to equality before the law, notably in the enjoyment of the following rights: . . . (e) economic, social and cultural rights . . . ."

8. OJ L 180, 19.7.2000, pp. 22–26.

9. OJ L 303, 2.12.2000, pp. 16–22.

10. This provision reads as follows:

> 2. Member States may maintain national legislation in force at the date of adoption of this Directive or provide for future legislation incorporating national practices existing at the date of adoption of this Directive pursuant to which, in the case of occupational activities within churches and other public or private organisations the ethos of which is based on religion or belief, a difference of treatment based on a person's religion or belief shall not constitute discrimination where, by reason of the nature of these activities or of the context in which they are carried out, a person's religion or belief constitute a genuine, legitimate and justified occupational requirement, having regard to the organisation's ethos. This difference of treatment shall be implemented taking account of Member States' constitutional provisions and principles, as well as the general principles of Community law, and should not justify discrimination on another ground.
>
> Provided that its provisions are otherwise complied with, this Directive shall thus not prejudice the right of churches and other public or private organisations, the ethos of which is based on religion or belief, acting in conformity with

national constitutions and laws, to require individuals working for them to act in good faith and with loyalty to the organisation's ethos.

11. The AWGB does not forbid differentiations on the grounds of race, etc. when the purpose of such differentiation is to put ethnic or cultural minority groups in a favourable position in order to diminish or abolish inequalities (positive discrimination/action), and this measure is proportionate to this goal (Article 2(3) AWGB).

12. Hoge Raad 22 January 1988, *Administratiefrechtelijke Beslissingen* 1988, 96.

13. Commissie Gelijke Behandeling, 4 December 2001, *Rechtspraak Onderwijsrecht* 2000–2002, 48.

14. A comparative survey of European state practice—with an extensive discussion of the French position—can be found in Dominic McGoldrick, *Human Rights and Religion: The Islamic Headscarf Debate in Europe*, Oxford 2006.

15. Commissie Gelijke Behandeling, 22 December 1999, decision 1999-103, *Administratiefrechtelijke Beslissingen* 2000, 71.

16. Commissie Gelijke Behandeling, 16 August 2007, decision 2007-153.

17. Commissie Gelijke Behandeling, 7 November 2006, decisions 2006-220 and 2006-221. The Minister for Immigration Affairs and Integration suggested in response to these decisions that the Commission should be abolished.

18. Rechtbank Utrecht, 31 August 2007, *Administratiefrechtelijke Beslissingen* 2007, 307.

19. *Kamerstukken I* 1992/1993, 22014, nr. 212c, p. 11.

20. Commissie Gelijke Behandeling, 29 April 1999, *Administratiefrechtelijke Beslissingen* 2000, 71; Commissie Gelijke Behandeling, 15 June 2007, 2007-100.

21. Directive 2000/78/EG, OJ 2000 L303/16. The AWGB is the main instrument implementing this directive.

22. *Kamerstukken II* 2007/2008, 27017, nr. 34.

23. *Kamerstukken II* 1990/1991, 22014, nr. 6, pp. 39–40.

24. That this treaty is written specifically to regulate the vertical relation between individual and state is clear from the text of the freedoms it protects, and from Article 34 of the Convention, that grants the right to complain solely to individual persons, groups of individuals, and non-governmental organizations, and only concerns complaints about Convention violations by states.

25. Kantongerecht Amsterdam, 11 February 1983, *Administratiefrechtelijke Beslissingen* 1983, 277.

26. Hoge Raad (Supreme Court), 9 April 1976, *Nederlandse Jurisprudentie* 1976, 409.

27. Cf. ECHR, 7 December 1976 (Kjeldsen, Busk Madsen, Pedersen); ECHR, 15 February 2001 (Dahlab); ECHR, 29 June 2007 (Folgero).

28. Commissie van Beroep Katholiek kleuter-, basis- en buitengewoon onderwijs in Zuid-Nederland, 12 March 1979, *Administratiefrechtelijke Beslissingen* 1979, 347.

29. Vgl. Hoge Raad, 22 January 1988, *Administratiefrechtelijke Beslissingen* 1988, 96 (Maimonides).

30. Commissie van beroep voortgezet onderwijs Besturenraad protests-christelijk onderwijs, 30 January 1975, *Administratiefrechtelijke Beslissingen* 1975, 115. Zie ook

Kantongerecht Zwolle, 7 March 1991, *NJCM-Bulletin* 1991, 302. Other decisions in the same vein are mentioned in B.P. Vermeulen, "Commentaar op artikel 6 Grondwet," in Akkermans/Koekkoek (eds.), *De Grondwet*, Zwolle 1992, pp. 136–37.

31. Kantongerecht Den Haag, 22 October 1984, *Nederlandse Jurisprudentie* 1985, 286.

32. *Kamerstukken II*, 1975/1976, 13872, no. 3, p. 11.

33. Centrale Raad van Beroep, 26 May 1987, *Administratiefrechtelijke Beslissingen* 1987, 520.

34. Cf. B.P. Vermeulen e.a., *Overwegingen bij een boerkaverbod*, Den Haag 2006, pp. 37–40.

35. *Kamerstukken II* 2007/2008, 31108.

36. *Kamerstukken II* 2007/2008, 31331.

37. The opinion of the Council of State on this bill has not yet been published.

38. Onderwijsraad, *Leraarschap is eigenaarschap*, Den Haag 2007.

39. *Staatsblad*, 2005, 460.

40. Pres. Rechtbank Amsterdam, 29 September 1994, *Kort Geding* 1994, 366; Pres. Rechtbank Arnhem, 3 September 1998, *Kort Geding* 1998, 281; Vz. Rechtbank Amsterdam, 29 July 1999, *Administratiefrechtelijke Beslissingen* 2000, 104; Afdeling Bestuursrechtspraak Raad van State, 13 March 2002, *Administratiefrechtelijke Beslissingen* 2002, 348; Vz. Rechtbank Leeuwarden, 23 December 2005, LJN: AU9582; Rechtbank Amsterdam, 23 April 2007, LJN: BA4253. Cf. B.P. Vermeulen, P.J.J. Zoontjens, "Het 'algemene' bestuursrecht en het 'bijzondere' onderwijsrecht," in: *De Awb en de bijzondere wetgeving*, Den Haag 2000, pp. 167–68.

41. Commissie van Beroep BVE SGO, 22 February 2005, zaak no. 102685.

42. Centrale Raad van Beroep, 5 November 1987, *Tijdschrift voor Ambtenarenrecht* 1988, 10; Commissie van Beroep Islamitische Scholen, 10 December 2005, no. 102989.

43. P.W.A. Huisman & B.P. Vermeulen, "De juridische positie van de leraar in balans," in J.M.M. van der Ven and B.P. Vermeulen (eds.), *De docent: onderdaan of autoriteit?*, Den Haag 2007, pp. 11–73.

44. It must be stressed that this account is one-sided. Many teachers in the beginning promoted these changes as well, and the current criticisms overlook the valuable elements of this pedagogical theory.

45. "Parlementair Onderzoek Onderwijsvernieuwingen," *Kamerstukken II* 2007–2008, 31007, no. 6.

11

New Zealand

Paul Rishworth and Sean Kinsler

The Legal and Constitutional Sources of Education Law

New Zealand is a Westminster-style parliamentary democracy with a single House of Representatives, a mixed proportional representation system, and an independent judiciary. Broadly speaking, New Zealand's Constitution mirrors that of the United Kingdom, the old colonial parent. The Queen of Great Britain and Northern Ireland is also the Queen of New Zealand, where she is represented by a Governor-General. Like the United Kingdom's, the New Zealand Constitution is unwritten, contains no formal constitutional rights, and permits almost unquestioned Parliamentary supremacy. New Zealand courts have no power to review the validity of Parliament's laws or declare them invalid for unreasonably abridging human rights.

New Zealand does have a Bill of Rights which affirms a range of rights and freedoms derived from the International Covenant on Civil and Political Rights. Although the New Zealand Bill of Rights Act, passed in 1990 as ordinary legislation, confirms the supremacy of Parliament, the practice of regular elections, a wide franchise, and public scrutiny of political debate ensure a degree of rights protection that is comparable to other liberal democracies in the world today.

The provisions of the Bill of Rights Act are crafted to provide a political-democratic protection against unreasonable limitations of the rights and freedoms of citizens. The guaranteed rights limit the power of the executive branch and all public actors. As to the legislative branch, the Bill of Rights Act requires the Attorney-General to draw to members' attention to any potentially rights-infringing provisions contained in legislation introduced to the House of Representatives.

Coupled with a statutory expression of the principle that legislative abridgment of fundamental human rights must be clear and express and that courts must read ambiguities in a rights-favouring way, the Bill of Rights Act ensures that Parliament will only be taken to have unreasonably limited rights and freedoms where that result is clearly intended and is supported by sufficiently clear statutory language. Further, moves to abridge rights are politically contentious, and New Zealand's small size means they rarely escape considerable attention. As a result, New Zealand can boast few deliberate abridgments of fundamental rights since the Act was introduced 17 years ago.

The Treaty of Waitangi, signed in 1840 by Maori chiefs and a representative of Queen Victoria, is New Zealand's founding constitutional document, even though it is not itself a source of law. Under the Treaty, the Maori tribes of New Zealand ceded their sovereignty, or at least a power to govern, to the English Crown, and in return Maori indigenous rights were affirmed. In light of its brevity, but also because of textual discrepancies between the respective Maori and English translations of the Treaty (the Maori text arguably reserving considerable power to Maori that the course of history has not respected), it is usual now to speak of the "principles" of the Treaty.

These principles are generally taken to denote an ethos of partnership between the executive government and Maori in matters concerning governance and economic development. In practice, this entails a duty to consult and give effect, as far as politically possible, to Maori aspirations. In the educational sphere, particular emphasis is placed on the preservation of the Maori language and culture. State schools are required to facilitate this, and there is also provision for schools in which Maori language is the language of instruction.

Educational policy in New Zealand is determined by the Cabinet on the advice of the Minister of Education. This is where broad decisions as to the form of the education system and the content of the curriculum are made. However, the operational management of primary and secondary schools lies with each state school's locally elected board of trustees, exercising powers through school principals who serve in effect as boards' chief executives and are accountable to the boards.

The sources of law relating to teachers' rights are to be found in the general law of contract, employment, and tort as well as in those statutes governing the public education regime such as the Education Act 1989 and the State Sector Act 1988. Section 3 of the Education Act provides that all children have a right to receive a free education in a state school between the ages of 5 and 19, even though parents may elect to educate their children in private schools.

The State has a corresponding duty to facilitate access to education as well as the substantive duty to educate.

School boards of trustees comprise between three and seven parent representatives elected from the parent community of schools as well as a school's principal, a representative of its teachers, and sometimes a student representative. The Board of Trustees exercises "a pervasive governance role."[1] Boards employ the principals and all staff and are empowered to run schools on behalf of the State.

Boards are also deemed to be "Crown entities." Public law standards of behaviour are therefore required of boards and principals in the execution of powers relating to their core function: performing the State's duty to provide access to education and to educate. They must act in a fair and reasonable manner and in conformity with the purposes for which their powers were conveyed. As with other State actors, when engaging in market behaviour such as entering contracts, boards are simply subject to the general law of the land.

When school boards employ principals and teaching staff, the rights and obligations of both parties are therefore determined by the general law together with an additional "overlay" comprising the nationally negotiated collective employment agreements (there being different agreements for principals, teaching staff, and administrative staff), along with the extra statutory obligations that are placed on public sector employers by the State Sector Act 1988.

The Employment Rights of Primary and Secondary School Teachers

The starting point in teacher employment is that teachers at all levels of the compulsory education system must be registered. Registration was introduced in 1990 and made compulsory in State kindergartens, primary schools, and secondary schools in 1996; in early childhood centers in 2005; and for Kura Kaupapa Maori (State schools where teaching is in the Maori language) in 2006. The Education Standards Act 2001 created the New Zealand Teachers' Council, which performs registration functions under the Education Act. The Council replaced an earlier, equivalent body, the Teacher Registration Board.

While any persons may apply to the Teachers' Council to be registered as teachers, the provisions of the Education Act 1989 require employers only to appoint those who are currently registered and hold practising certificates to teaching positions. Teachers must maintain their practising certificates while employed. Employers are expressly prohibited from employing persons whose registration has been cancelled and not renewed unless those individuals are under the general supervision of one who holds a practising certificate. The Council hosts an online register of all teachers who hold registration and practising certificates in New Zealand; it also identifies teachers who have had their registration cancelled.

There are currently three levels of registration: Full, Provisional, and Subject To Confirmation. The Teachers' Council, in deciding whether to grant full registration (under s 122), must be satisfied that an applicant is of good character, fit to be a teacher, satisfactorily trained to teach, and has satisfactory recent teaching experience.

Provisional registration is intended for recent graduates of approved training courses applying for registration for the first time (s 123). Experienced teachers, should they be ineligible for registration under s 122, can apply for registration subject to confirmation under s 124. A registration granted under s 124 expires in three years if confirmation is not granted (s 127(1)(a)). The test for registration is similar to that under s 123: along with the requirements noted, applicants must either have previously been registered under s 122 of the Education Act or have had adequate and suitable teaching experience.

The Teachers' Council may take into account "any relevant matters" when deciding whether a person is satisfactorily trained to teach. The Council must take into account both the applicants' qualifications and whether they have satisfactorily completed training recognised by the Teachers' Council as suitable for people who want to teach. The Ministry of Education lists 14 approved education providers in New Zealand for primary school teachers and 10 approved education providers for secondary school teachers.

When evaluating whether persons are of good character and fit to be teachers, the Teachers' Council must obtain police "vets" of applicants (s 124B (1)). (A "vet" is an inquiry into whether a person has any criminal convictions or has come to the attention of police in connection with offences against children.) This does not limit any other matters that the Teachers' Council may take into account in evaluating character and fitness to be a teacher. It is worth noting also that the vet shows up both convictions and those summary offences for which persons received a "discharge without conviction," this being a possible outcome of a minor crime when a judge is persuaded that the consequences of conviction outweigh the gravity of the offence.

In *McDowell v Police*,[2] for example, a woman found guilty of assault sought a discharge without conviction on the basis that it would have prejudiced her ability to undertake teacher training and an eventual teaching career. The judge granted the discharge under the Sentencing Act but took notice of a Crown submission that any subsequent police vet would reveal to the Teachers' Council the charge of assault, regardless of whether a conviction was imposed, and that the guidelines of the relevant teacher training institute, Christchurch College of Education, had essentially the same result.[3] In this sense, then, those seeking to become teachers are subject to a more intense level of "character scrutiny" than individuals entering most other employment, even in the public sector. However, this is not dissimilar to the requirements of other professions.

In considering whether periods of employment were satisfactorily completed by persons under s 125, the Teachers' Council may take into account any relevant matters, including the views of the professional leaders of schools, early childhood service, or the fact of service to other educational institutions. Dissatisfied applicants have a right of appeal to the District Court.

Section 77A of the State Sector Act 1988, which relates to all public sector employment, imposes a duty on school boards of trustees to be "good employers." Additionally, when making employment decisions, boards must have regard for the "aims and aspirations of Maori people," the aims and aspirations and the cultural differences of ethnic minorities, the employment requirements of women, and the employment requirements of people with disabilities.

In appointing applicants to positions, boards must give preference to those best suited to the jobs and, to facilitate this, must advertise vacancies in such a way as to enable suitably qualified persons to apply. Advertising must also comply with the Human Rights Act 1993; that is, it must not evince any intention to discriminate.

The State Sector Act confers on the State Services Commissioner the powers of an employer for the purposes of the Employment Relations Act 2000. This includes the power to lock out or suspend striking workers in the context of employment negotiations as well as the power to direct that staff not be paid for the duration of strike periods. This settles tensions that arose under the old regime, where it had been possible for school boards to continue to pay striking teachers, something that a number of boards were prepared to do in consequence of the fact that while boards are their employers, teachers' salaries are negotiated between the teacher unions and government. It was possible, therefore, for boards (largely parent representatives without budget responsibility for the salary component of their schools' finances) to support teachers in strike actions.

Strikes in the education sector remain unlawful unless relevant unions notify the Commissioner at least three days before their commencement. Private schools are not bound by the provisions of the State Sector Act, but they must comply with the provisions of the Employment Relations Act.

Sanctions and Processes of Dismissal for Misconduct

Misconduct has consequences within employment relationships between teachers and school boards as well as between teachers and the New Zealand Teachers' Council. The rules canvassed above therefore add an extra layer to ordinary employment law for teachers. The Teachers' Council's role of controlling registration and practising certificates exists alongside causes of action and remedies available in all employment situations.

Teacher registration is maintained over a period of time by requirements to renew practising certificates every three years. When renewing practising certificates, teachers must prove that they have had satisfactory teaching experience for two of the previous five years.

Under s 127(2), when teacher registrations expire, teachers' names must be removed from the register kept under section 128. However, expiry of registration in any of the above ways does not prevent the Teachers' Council from also cancelling teacher registrations and putting teachers' names on the cancelled teachers list.

The law relating to cancellation of teacher registration is found in s 129 of the Education Act 1989. This section was amended in 2004. Previously, the Teachers' Council's power to consider cancelling teacher registrations usually depended on requests from the professional leaders, such as the principal, of the teachers' learning centres. Under the new section, the Teachers' Council can initiate cancellation proceedings without such requests.

The Council must cancel teachers' registrations if it is satisfied that persons are no longer of good character, not fit to teach, not satisfactorily trained to teach, or have not had satisfactory recent teaching experience. It may also cancel registrations if it is convinced that initial registrations were wrongly granted through error or fraud; if, following inquiries into teachers' competence, the Council is convinced that teachers are not competent to teach and should be deregistered; or if, following complaints and investigations into teacher misconduct or criminal convictions, the relevant Disciplinary Council requires the Teachers' Council to deregister teachers.

Any persons dissatisfied with Council decisions cancelling their teaching registration under s 129 can appeal to the District Court under s 126.

An example of such an appeal occurred in *Mrs. C v The Teacher Registration Board.*[4] Mrs. C had been convicted of fraud committed at her previous place of employment, the Auckland College of Education, where she was employed in a non-teaching position. Mrs. C had lost her subsequent job as a teacher after her previous employers, following their statutory duty, informed the Teacher Registration Board (the Teachers' Council's predecessor) of her illegal behaviour. The Board, then considering Mrs. C's application for renewal of her practising certificate, notified her that this gave grounds for deregistration and informed her of her right to be heard. Her explanations were not to the Board's satisfaction, and she was deregistered.

Mrs. C then appealed to the District Court on the basis that the Board made a wrongful predetermination because it assumed that the convictions, without more evidence of misconduct, meant that she was not of good character or fit to be a teacher. In addition, Mrs. C argued that when the Board was considering whether a person was of good character or fit to be a teacher, there was a mandatory requirement under s 130C of the Education Act 1989 to take into account and give weight to the views of the principal and the school board of trustees. Both of these sources filed affidavits supporting Mrs. C's continued registration.

The Court ruled that while there had been no predetermination, the Board had taken an overly narrow approach, focussing on the convictions without taking notice of other relevant considerations. Still, while finding fault with the Board's decision-making process, the Court declined to use its ability under s 126(3) of the Act to substitute its own judgment for that of the Board. Instead, the Court took a further option available under s 126(3), namely referring the decision back to the Board for reconsideration.

The Education Act 1989 places the burden of mandatory reporting on employers. Under this law, which came into effect on September 1, 2004, all employers must immediately advise the Teachers' Council when they dismiss teachers (s 139AK(1)); when teachers resign; if within the previous 12 months they advised teachers that they were dissatisfied with, or intended to investigate, any aspect of the conduct of teachers or the teachers' competence (s 139AK(2)); when they receive complaints about teachers' conduct or competence within 12 months after they have left their employment (s 139AL); when they have reason to believe that teachers have engaged in serious misconduct (s 139AM); or when they are satisfied that despite undertaking competency procedures with teachers, individuals have not reached the required level of competence (s 139AN).

Under s 139AO, it is an offence punishable by summary conviction (a fine not exceeding NZ$5,000) if employers or former employers fail without reasonable justification to satisfy the reporting requirements. The exception to the employers' burden is in s 139AP, which maintains that teachers themselves have the burden of reporting convictions punishable by imprisonment for 3 months or more to the Teachers' Council within 7 days of their convictions.

The natural justice provisions relating to the Teachers' Council's ability to cancel registration are set out in s 129(2) of the Act. The Council cannot cancel registrations without taking all reasonable steps to ensure that teachers or authorised persons are given notice of the reasons for the proposed cancellations (s 129(2)(a)); it must also give the teachers or authorised persons a reasonable opportunity to make submissions and be heard, either in person or by counsel or other representative, on proposed cancellations (s 129(2)(b)).

The powers of the Teachers' Council in relation to deregistration and cancellation were tested in *Kerr v Teachers' Council 9 (Kerr)*.[5] A school board became aware of an alleged sexual relationship between a teacher and a pupil and asked the Council to consider whether to cancel his registration. The Council resolved to do so and notified the teacher of its intentions. Before consideration could take place, the teacher voluntarily deregistered himself.

The key issue was whether the Council had jurisdiction to cancel the registration and publicly list as such a teacher who requested his own deregistration. J. Wild found that it did. Nevertheless, given the shifting content of the Education Act 1989, it is unsurprising that *Kerr* was legislated into irrelevancy by the insertion of s 127A into the Act through a 2006 amending statute. The section now affirms that teachers may voluntarily deregister themselves only if the Teachers' Council is satisfied that they are not the subject of an investigation by the Council under Part 10A of the Act.

The Teachers' Council is empowered to make rules (regulations) relating to misconduct and incompetence under s 139AJ of the Act. The current delegated legislation relating to complaints of this nature is the New Zealand Teachers' Council (Making Reports and Complaints) Rules 2004 (SR 2004/144).

Section 9 of the rules sets forth the criteria for reporting serious misconduct by teachers. For serious misconduct, employers must suspect on reasonable grounds that teachers engaged in the physical, sexual, or psychological abuse of children or young persons; the latter may include, but is not limited to, physical abuse of other persons, or damage to property, inflicted in front of children or young persons; threats of physical or sexual abuse; and harassment.

Serious misconduct also includes being involved in inappropriate relationships with any persons under the age of 16 years; being involved in inappropriate relationships with students with whom teachers are, or were when the relationships commenced, in contact as a result of their positions as teachers; the neglect or ill treatment of any children or young persons in the teachers' care; the neglect or ill treatment of any animals in the teachers' care; theft or fraud; involvement in the use of controlled drugs; permitting, or acquiescing in, the use of controlled drugs by any children or young person; viewing, accessing, or possessing pornographic material while on school premises or engaged on school business; viewing, accessing, or possessing pornographic material that depicts children or young persons in sexual acts with humans; breaching a school's standards or rules concerning the use of alcohol at the school or while on school business; or any other act or omission that could be the subject of a prosecution for an offence punishable by imprisonment for a term of 3 months or more.

Section 10 of the Rules sets forth the criteria for reporting teacher incompetence. For the purposes of s 139AL(3)(b) of the Act, the criterion for reporting competence issues about teachers is that employers would not, if asked, sign teachers' practising certificate renewal applications due to doubts about whether the teachers meet the satisfactory teacher dimensions.

In terms of the performance and assessment of teachers, these indicators are covered by either individual or collective employment agreements. Primary and secondary teachers covered by their current collective agreements are not subject to performance-related pay. Remuneration in these agreements is governed by pay scales and various non-performance-related allowances. Even so, all schools, whether State or private, are subject to the jurisdiction of the Education Review Office (ERO).

Schools must maintain professional development programmes. Boards as employers may, subject to the general law of employment set out in the Employment Relations Act 2000 and to the terms of the relevant teachers' collective agreement, institute disciplinary or competence proceedings against their staff members. For teachers other than the principal, this would generally be instigated and managed by the principal. For principals, it would be managed by the Board itself.

Ideological Issues Facing Teachers

Though employment disputes abound, few cases implicating the "core" constitutional rights of teachers have been litigated. Still, as with the rights of students, guidance can be drawn from comparable jurisdictions, patterns can be discerned, and predictions made.

The right to freedom of association in s 17 of the Bill of Rights Act is limited by restrictions on sexual relationships with students and justifiably so. However, do good character or "fitness" requirements intrude into the personal belief systems of teachers? Do they restrict the rights to the freedom of association or to expression?

In *Balfour v Attorney-General (Balfour)*,[6] a primary school teacher found out in the 1980s that his personal file held by authorities in Wellington had a note attached to it from a District Senior Inspector of Secondary Schools describing him as a "long practising and blatant homosexual." The teacher claimed that this damaged his career development. The teacher's damages claim of negligence and for breach of statutory duty was unsuccessful in the early 1990s. The sense is that the teacher's supposed "considerable degree of effeminacy" offended the sensibilities of the relatively small New Zealand communities in which he worked throughout the 1970s and early 1980s. In the early 1990s, when the case was heard, the Court of Appeal utilized the notion of a "moral suitability" to teach in conducting the balance between a teacher's rights and the wider responsibilities of the education system.[7]

The international human rights instruments and their relevance to global civil society have been recognized in New Zealand's legal culture since the beginning of the 1990s. To the extent that human rights norms play a much larger role in national culture today than 17 years ago, the law is an expression of this. One result is that *Balfour* would be handled very differently today.

At the same time, the concept of "moral suitability" is surely synonymous with current "good character"; neither has the sort of predictive certainly associated with formal qualification requirements, and one can expect prevailing social norms to enter the legal fabric through these sorts of junctures. The "local governance" of schools through community-representative boards and the associated school politics are the primary mechanism for resolving disputes impacting students' rights to education. As seen, though, the Teachers' Council does have a range of centralized enforcement functions. It also promulgates a Code of Ethics, and one can probably expect to see current values exerted through these mediums in a broadly similar way as they have been historically.

The Code of Ethics, for instance, stipulates teachers' "obligations to society." In fulfilling these obligations, teachers are to strive to provide active support for policies and programmes which promote equality of opportunity for all, to work collegially to develop schools and centres which model democratic ideals, and to teach and model those positive values which are widely accepted in society and encourage learners to apply them and critically appreciate their significance.

The abstract nature of these requirements is certainly ripe for conflict. What is the best way to encourage learners to critically appreciate the significance of positive values which are widely accepted in society? More importantly, how may those teachers who might have fringe political commitments or subscribe to minority religious beliefs best promote mainstream values?

The distinction between action and belief is probably necessary to prevent an excess of intrusion by the State into the rights that teachers enjoy as citizens in a liberal democracy. The distinction between private and professional life is also relatively easy to maintain. A police officer who, in his spare time, played aggressive and satanic music in a band called *Dawn of Azazel* was seemingly able to maintain an effective work-life balance. The issue sparked interest in the media, but no litigation emerged. The personal life of the man had no bearing on his professional duties as a court escort. The situation should be no different if the man were a teacher or if a teacher's political beliefs or religious practices were at the fringe of community standards. However, this is all subject to the important proviso that the relevant belief system cannot impinge on a teacher's capacity to perform his or her professional duties.

For this reason, "good character" has tended to be defined along criminal or quasi-criminal lines. The distinction between thought and conduct is reflected in the disciplinary convention that failures of moral standards (even where these are assessed as against a local community's sense of right or wrong rather than a standard based on what the community is prepared to tolerate)[8] are linked to possible or actual harm to current or future students.

Public perceptions are clearly relevant to the integrity of the educational system. In *Richardson v The Teacher Registration Board*,[9] a district court confirmed the Board's decision to deregister a plaintiff–teacher on the ground that she was unfit to teach because she fabricated to a parent a story about having taken urgent action to prevent a child's attempted suicide. No such attempt took place, and the student was placed at risk as a result of the teacher's fabrication. Like Mrs. C above, these actions implicate fitness concerns because they represent a failure to adhere to society's conventional norms of social behaviour, regardless of whether they are expressed through the criminal law.

In order to withstand judicial review, the Teachers' Council cannot fetter its discretion by incorporating a policy that uses the existence of a conviction as a bright line or predetermining factor when considering registrations. This fact suggests that conventional moral standards of wrongdoing incorporate notions of fair play, culpability, and personal development. Minor convictions, especially when historical and where persons acknowledge responsibility, are often not factors that give great insight into individuals' character, and they do not serve much predictive function in evaluating whether persons are likely to be harmful to the interests of students.

Conduct is required for misconduct, and the overriding principle in evaluating the scope of misconduct that warrants deregistration is the protection of students and potential students. Teachers' freedom of personal beliefs, therefore, including political, moral, or religious beliefs, would have to be manifested as conduct harmful to the interests of children to be justifiably limited by the State, and there is no justification out of context for an association between unpopular belief and unfitness to teach.

What about academic freedoms and the associated freedom of expression? The school curriculum is designed by the Minister of Education, who has the power under the Education Act to promulgate national education guidelines, foundational curriculum policy statements, and statements outlining the scope and content of the curriculum. These decisions do not lie with individual teachers, and there is no academic freedom to depart from or augment the curriculum.

Teachers can exercise their right to express themselves freely and consistently with their responsibilities, but content must be relevant to learning outcomes and teachers cannot further political or religious agendas in their classes. By way of illustration, the possibility of teaching intelligent design theory alongside evolutionary theory in high school biology is a debate that would take place at a political level.

The Human Rights Commission recently sponsored the production of a "Statement on Religious Diversity," and New Zealand delegates to an Asia Pacific Interfaith Dialogue in May 2007 called for a school curriculum including a provision for education about diverse religions and cultures. From the perspective of students' rights, this might offend the right to be free from religious education at all while implicating issues of parental choice in relation to private schooling.

From the perspective of teachers, the duty may plausibly lead to a conflict between personal religious commitments on the one hand and a professional duty to teach impartially on the other. However, this is not of great concern. Such tensions between moral belief and professional duty are common in other professions, and where such conflict exists, professional duty tends to prevail. The lead taken in the United States, where the speech rights of teachers are subordinated to the educational aims of the State and the interests of students, can probably be thought to apply here, as speech protection in New Zealand is assuredly generally weaker than that provided by the First Amendment to the United States Constitution in other contexts.

Teachers, along with all New Zealanders, have rights conferred under the Human Rights Act 1993 (against discrimination) and the New Zealand Bill of Rights (more general civil and political rights). It can be expected that the ordinary operation of employment law and administrative law gives effect to these rights. That is to say that one would not expect disciplinary action for conduct which is, in fact, protected under the Bill of Rights. Certainly, there have been no cases with that result.

Emerging Issues

New Zealand is currently in the middle of a male teacher shortage. As of April 2006, the Ministry of Education reported that there were 12,175 male and 27,361 female teachers in New Zealand. Cash incentives have been offered to men to undertake primary and secondary level teacher training qualifications.

Coupled with a belief that (particularly) boys require male role models from outside their families, the shortage has resulted in one school's piloting a male-only teacher training programme with an aim to eventually employ its graduates.[10] The programme could fall foul of the anti-discrimination provisions in New Zealand's rights legislation, the Bill of Rights, and Human Rights Acts, though commenting to the media, the Human Rights Commission expressed the belief that it was possible the college could justify its apparent discrimination if it proved boys had been disadvantaged in the past.[11]

Responding to the publicity, the government put its hat into the ring, commissioning several reports addressing the issue.[12] These tended to conclude that the lack of male role models was one factor among several tending to contribute to the relative underperformance of boys in the primary and secondary education system. Even so, these observations fell short of the construction of the "feminization" of schools as a specific threat to the future of masculinity.[13]

The issue of pay parity between primary and secondary school teachers also arises periodically. Currently, both primary and secondary school teachers are on a unified pay scale, the Education Payroll Centre setting salaries according to individual teachers' qualifications and teaching experience. The respective unions, the New Zealand Educational Institute and the Post Primary Teachers' Association, argue over the appropriateness of parity between themselves and between preschool-level care providers. The issue is currently being reviewed as part of a wider government inquest into inequalities in public sector employment.

A major issue in the education sector as a whole is the expectation placed on locally elected school boards to manage their teaching staffs along with the inevitable performance and competency issues that arise. Boards are generally well-intentioned amateurs who must rely substantially on their appointed principals in dealing with employment issues, even though principals often need outside advice, too, and certainly if the employment dispute is with a principal.

In recognition of these and other difficulties for boards, publicly funded support agencies have been established which employ consultants whose advice may be freely sought on employment disputes as well as on other matters of school governance. School boards are also usually insured for the cost of employment-related litigation, as insurers' lawyers conduct the defence once disputes proceed to litigation.

Conclusion

In the New Zealand context, teachers' rights are associated mostly with employment and registration issues, generally revolving around the requirement for due process by employers and the Teacher's Council. Process aside, when courts review appeals, they pay close scrutiny to the substantive reasoning of school boards or the Council when they exercise judgment in respect of teachers.

Courts must act without bias or predetermination, properly applying the legislated or contractually agreed-upon standards. In this sense, then, teachers' rights are ensured by the same general administrative law and employment law duties that are owed to all persons by those who wield power. Those general duties are, of course, overlaid with the specific requirements of the education sector, notably the collective employment agreements and the professional standards enforced by the New Zealand Teachers Council.

Most disputes in the employment law field for teachers turn out to be about performance and competency issues, while most in the registration field concern misconduct of a criminal or moral nature. The relatively low level of litigation over "teachers' rights" outside the employment law field is, it can be suspected, due to the New Zealand custom of low-level resolution of claims.

Schools in New Zealand are not yet the site of ideological conflicts over, say, the teaching of evolution or the place of religion. This is not to say that such issues do not arise from time to time, but they are generally not taken to courts in the context of disputes about teachers' conduct. New Zealand is a relatively small society in which national publicity and attention can be given to seemingly minor disputes or controversies. Such an approach tends to bring these controversies into the daylight and prompts informal resolution.

Index of Cases

Abbotsford School District 34 Board of Trustees v Shewan (1998) 70 BCLR 40 (BC Court of Appeal).

Balfour v Attorney-General [1991] 1 NZLR 519.

Hobday v Timaru Girls' High School Board of Trustees (Employment Court, Christchurch, CED 16/94 Judge Palmer).

Kerr v Teachers' Council (HC, Wellington, CIV-2002-485-000860, 6 April 2004, Wild J.).

McDowell v Police (HC, Christchurch, A 133-02, 13 February 2003, John Hansen J.).

Mrs C v The Teacher Registration Board [2000] DCR 803.

Richardson v The Teacher Registration Board [2000] DCR 595.

Notes

1. *Hobday v Timaru Girls' High School Board of Trustees* (Employment Court, Christchurch, CED 16/94 Judge Palmer).
2. (HC, Christchurch, A 133-02, 13 February 2003, John Hansen J.).
3. *Id.*, pp. 2–3.
4. [2000] DCR 803.
5. (HC, Wellington, CIV-2002-485-000860, 6 April 2004, Wild J.).

6. [1991] 1 NZLR 519.
7. *Id.*, at 529.
8. Compare *Abbotsford School District 34 Board of Trustees v Shewan* (1998) 70 BCLR 40 (BC Court of Appeal).
9. [2000] DCR 595.
10. Nelson College.
11. "Men Only Teacher Training Planned," *New Zealand Herald*, 19 January 2007. The Human Rights Act 1993 and the New Zealand Bill of Rights Act 1990 each allow so-called "affirmative action." In the case of a State school, s 19(2) of the Bill of Rights would apply, thereby removing from the concept of unlawful discrimination in s 19(1) "measures taken in good faith for the purpose of assisting or advancing persons . . . disadvantaged because of discrimination."
12. The Achievement of Boys (Education Review Office, 1999); Promoting Boys' Achievement (Education Review Office, 2000); Ministry of Education, Explaining and Addressing Gender Differences in the New Zealand Compulsory School Sector (Alton-Lee & Praat, 2001).
13. See Robert Hyndman, *Connecting School Culture to Boys' Learning*, LLM Thesis, University of Waikato, 2007.

12

Singapore

Mui Kim Teh and Kenneth Stott

Introduction: Singapore—An Island

Singapore is a small island in a strategic location, but it has no natural resources. In order to survive, Singapore needs foreign capital, technology and markets, and "brainpower" to work within the economic system, and it needs the capacity to access the most lucrative global markets. Education is a crucial concern for Singapore's leaders in the running of the country because, alongside innovation, education is seen as a significant economy driver. Policies are initiated to nurture students so that the nation has future leaders to meet the challenges of an increasingly service- and knowledge-based economy. What are the laws, then, that govern the smooth running of education in Singapore?

Under the Singapore constitution, all persons are equal before the law and entitled to the equal protection of the law (Article 12(1) of the Constitution of Singapore). As regards to education, Article 16 ensures that there is no discrimination against any citizen of Singapore on the grounds of religion, race, descent, or place of birth in the administration of any educational institution maintained by a public authority. Article 16 also prohibits discrimination in the providing of funds through public authority financial aid for the maintenance or education of students in any educational institution, regardless of whether it is maintained by a public authority and whether it is within or outside Singapore.

Insofar as Singapore is a multicultural society, each religious group can request permission to establish and maintain institutions for the education of children and provide instruction in its own religion. For this reason, there are Christian schools, such as Anglican, Methodist, Roman Catholic, and Presbyterian; Islamic religious schools; and a Buddhist primary school. These schools can apply for financial aid from the government under the Education (Grant-in-Aid) Regulations. Schools in receipt of "grant-in-aid" from the government are known as aided schools and are subject to the various conditions stipulated in the regulations. One of the conditions is that schools may not refuse any person admission to study in the school on the grounds of religion or race.

With such an array of religions and denominations, coupled with considerable ethnic diversity, there is always the potential for social schism, but one of the government's strategies in education, designed to limit the possibility of social division, has been the choice of language. English is the common language of the country, as it is seen as an international language that will link Singapore to the rest of the world's economies. In addition, English has served as a unifying force for the different ethnic groups and cultures.

Legislation and Education

The Education Act was first enacted in 1957. At that time, the ruling party, the People's Action Party, had just come to power in a united front with the Communists to fight British colonialism. Thus, a review of the Education Act shows very strict licensing regulations, presumably with the intention of controlling the use of classrooms for Communist propaganda. The Education Act governs the registers of schools, managers, and teachers while setting out conditions for teacher registration.

Regulations, in the form of subsidiary legislation, which are made under the Education Act, regulate issues such as school management, school staff, qualification of teachers, school premises and equipment, playgrounds, lavatories, school health, workshops, laboratories, discipline, money, and school accounts and syllabi. School regulations also prohibit political propaganda in schools and the control of textbooks by any group beyond the Ministry of Education. These regulations were enacted in 1958 for political reasons; therefore, many lawyers are of the view that they no longer represent the present political and education climate and should be significantly amended.

The most relevant piece of legislation is the Education (Grant-In-Aid) Regulations, which is subsidiary legislation of the Education Act. As mentioned above, this piece of legislation enables the government to render financial aid to non-government-registered schools that apply for aid where the conditions stated in the regulations are satisfied. The conditions regulate, *inter alia*, admission policies, curriculum, examinations, school buildings and facilities, and school terms and holidays.

In order to ensure consistency and a good standard of teaching across the nation, the Ministry of Education feels the need to exercise control over teachers. Hence, before these aided schools employ prospective teachers, they are required to obtain the Ministry of Education's approval. This obviously gives considerable control of education to the government, and there is little latitude, even for schools with strong historical ties to particular religious affiliations.

The other significant pieces of subsidiary legislation that impact teachers in Singapore are the Public Service (Disciplinary Proceedings) Regulations and the Public Service Commission (Delegation of Disciplinary Functions) Directions, under Articles 110 and 116 of the Constitution, and the Education Service Incentive Payment (Connect Plan) Regulations, under the Education Service Incentive Payment Act. These are discussed later in the chapter.

Primary education in Singapore was made compulsory in 2003. In acceding to the Convention on the Rights of the Child (CRC), Singapore expressly reserved the right not to make primary education compulsory, the reason being that "such a measure is unnecessary in our social context where in practice virtually all children attend primary school" (United Nations, 2001). However, with the government's rhetoric indicating that every Singaporean counts, and with Singapore purported to be a progressive country, it would have been an anomaly had education not been made compulsory.

Under the Compulsory Education Act (CEA), it is a criminal offence if parents fail to enroll their children in school and ensure their regular attendance. Children who are home-schooled or who attend full-time religious institutions can be exempted from the CEA, but parents must apply for exemption from the Ministry of Education and satisfy the relevant criteria in the CEA.

A speaker in Parliament observed that six years of primary-level education will not adequately prepare a person to meet even the most basic challenges of a knowledge-based and globalised economy (Chiang, 2000). Although the CRC requires State parties to "make primary education compulsory and available free to all" (Article 28), some might argue that the Singapore government should nevertheless consider the spirit of the CRC when setting the criteria for compulsory education in Singapore and ensure a minimum of at least 9 to 10 years of compulsory education, so as to more adequately prepare young people for the future.

Apart from having a basic knowledge of legislation referred to above, principals and teachers arguably have had little legal literacy or understanding of areas of law that impact their jobs, such as the law of negligence, special needs, and educational malpractice, since they have largely been protected from the fear of litigation by the Ministry of Education. However, things are changing, and schools and the people in them have become increasingly vulnerable to the demands, sometimes excessive, of a knowledgeable and articulate parent body. Indeed, amongst parents, the language of "rights" has become relatively prevalent in recent years. Perhaps for this reason, since 2005, the Attorney General Chambers and the legal department in the Ministry of Education have been jointly running annual one-day legal awareness seminars for school leaders.

With the growing number of young teachers joining the teaching profession, the notion of "rights," which in the past was of little significance to teachers, is now becoming important. Regardless of whether teachers are aware of them, teachers have employment rights, privileges, and entitlements; the next section discusses some of the issues involved.

Employment Rights of Teachers in Government Schools

Hiring Process and Contract

Applicants who are interested in the teaching profession apply to the Ministry of Education to become teachers. Applicants are divided into two categories: those with teaching qualifications and those without teaching qualifications. Newly appointed teachers receive letters of appointment informing them of their appointments along with the terms and conditions of service. All teachers in government schools (and some teachers in aided schools) are civil servants. As such, on appointment, teachers are subject to the usual terms and conditions of civil servants and any public disciplinary regulations governing their employment. These terms and conditions are incorporated into the contracts that teachers sign with the government and are set out clearly in the Instruction Manual, which is accessible to all civil servants.

Once appointed, individuals without teaching qualifications must undergo training at the National Institute of Education (NIE), which is based in one of the country's universities, although it is closely affiliated with the Ministry of Education. The entry requirement for NIE is to pass the Entrance Proficiency Test (EPT) or gain an exemption from it if applicants meet specified academic criteria.

All trainee teachers must sign the Teachers' Training Deed (TTD). If trainee teachers break the bond, they must pay liquidated damages based on the number of months or years outstanding in the bond. The amount is prorated based on the expenses incurred by the government for the tuition, fees, and salaries during the NIE training. There is an additional 10% compound interest. Under the TTD, trainee teachers are required to complete and pass the training course in NIE. Trainee teachers who are unable to meet the requirements of the course, in particular, the teaching practicum, and where NIE refuses re-admission of trainees, must reimburse the government for the training costs.

An attractive feature of the teaching profession in Singapore is the Education Service Incentive Payment Act. Under this legislation, both aided school teachers and government school teachers qualify for "awards," which are annual monetary contributions to teachers below the "superscale" grade in the Education Service. The amount of contribution is determined by the length and continuity of service and other qualifying conditions stipulated in the regulations, such as not having a criminal record or not being guilty of professional misconduct.

Career Path

Beginning teachers undergo a Structured Mentoring Programme where they receive a structured induction process and are then matched with trained mentors who can share experiences and practices while familiarising them with a school's culture. In order to help teachers continuously upgrade themselves, the Ministry of Education has implemented a system called the Professional Development Continuum Model (PDCM), in which teachers are able to take courses that accumulate toward advanced certification. Under this model, teachers can even take a PDCM–master's course at the NIE while they are still in-service.

Career advancement for teachers depends on their performance and potential. In order to cater to the different aspirations of teachers, the Ministry of Education has introduced the "Education Service Professional Development and Career Plan" (Edu-Pac), which is designed for teachers to develop their potential to the fullest. Edu-Pac comprises three career tracks. If teachers like interacting with students and wish to remain indefinitely in classrooms, the Teaching Track allows teachers to advance through several steps to the top level of Master Teacher.

In terms of remuneration, some Master Teachers receive equivalent remuneration to the school principal. In 2005, even after the career scheme had been operating for a few years, the number of master teachers was in single figures, out of a population of 28,000 teachers, providing an indication of the demanding standard that must be attained.

The second track is the Leadership Track, which gives teachers the opportunity to take on leadership positions in schools or at the Ministry of Education's headquarters. However, teachers must satisfy the demands of this track before being selected for it or in order to progress successfully.

The final track, the Senior Specialist Track, is geared toward specialised areas, where deep knowledge and skills are essential for breaking new ground in educational developments. Those on this track are usually deployed in the Ministry to work on such tasks as curriculum development and assessment.

Assessment and Evaluation of Teacher Performance

The Ministry of Education uses a competency-based system called the "Enhanced Performance Management System" to appraise teachers. This appraisal is conducted formally on a yearly basis and teachers are evaluated for their performance and potential. In order to ensure a fair and accurate assessment, principals and heads of department are encouraged to meet with their teachers regularly to review the teachers' work, priorities, and targets.

Performance assessment is graded using letters A to E. Teachers who have been previously assessed to be of a high grade, for example, Grade A teachers, are measured against the performance standard expected of that grade. In assessing teachers' potential, the concept of "Currently Estimated Potential" is used. The objective of this concept is to plan teachers' training and development activities, career advancement opportunities, and promotion or succession possibilities.

In using the Enhanced Performance Management System and the Currently Estimated Potential framework, the potential and performance of teachers in Singapore are "ranked" into performance bands. In order to prevent the subjectivity of a principal's rendering an assessment as "unfair," a ranking panel, comprising a principal, vice-principal(s), and heads of departments, with a cluster superintendent (such as a superintendent overseeing a group of schools) as moderator, is convened before the ranking procedure is finalised.

Although the system of assessment is well intended, it has also led to teachers' appealing against "D" or "E" grades, feeling that they have been victimised and finally requesting to be posted to other schools, for teachers have a right to appeal against assessments and evaluations of their performances. Teachers can write to the Ministry of Education to appeal against a school's decisions. However, very often, teachers choose to refer such appeals to the Singapore Teachers' Union, which makes appeals on behalf of the aggrieved teacher.

Unions

There are four teachers' unions in Singapore: the Singapore Chinese Teachers' Union, the Singapore Tamil Teachers' Union, the Singapore Malay Teachers' Union, and the Singapore Teachers' Union (STU). The STU is the largest teachers' organisation in Singapore and started as early as 1946. The STU's main objective is to protect the interests of all education officers, and it prides itself on its efforts over the years to provide teachers with improvements in salaries and conditions of work.

The STU currently has more than 13,000 members from a teaching workforce of approximately 28,000. The STU assists members with work-related problems while advising them about their terms and conditions of service. The STU is part of a strong tripartite relationship between the government, trade union, and the employer. Further, rather than take an adversarial approach, the STU tries to provide solutions for teacher members through collaboration, cooperation, and dialogue with the agencies concerned.

Most teachers are ordinary branch members of the STU and are eligible for all grievance-handling services in addition to the social, recreational, and professional benefits that membership provides. Education officers, like principals, are general branch members who are only eligible for social, recreational, and professional benefits provided by the STU. In other words, the STU is not permitted to represent principals in matters related to terms and conditions of service.

Academic Freedom, Free Speech, and Religious Rights of Teachers

One must agree, even from the brief synopsis of the development of education in Singapore, that since becoming an independent state in 1965, Singapore's progress has been nothing short of remarkable. Still, amidst the bouquets, there has been the occasional brickbat, usually associated with the style of government. The style has been described variously as paternalistic, authoritarian, inflexible, and even rigid (Teh, 2004). Despite the government's rhetoric in recent years to change the rules of engagement and "out of bounds" markers, the effects of such a *modus operandi* cannot be overcome so easily. Even a simple request for non-confidential information can result in officers' seeking clearance from the Ministry. Such is the conditioning over the years that even relatively senior personnel may practise self-censorship in situations where there is no logical reason to do so.

When a retired teacher learned that we were writing a chapter on teachers' rights and free speech in Singapore, she expressed considerable surprise, saying, "What rights? What free speech?" However, we are convinced that prevailing perceptions of Singapore are not entirely accurate. In the area of free speech, the country is genuinely attempting to make progress.

The "Remaking of Singapore" report in June 2003 acknowledges that, out of economic necessity, there is an urgent need for a change in the mindsets of Singaporeans, and Dr. Balakrishnan, the then-Minister of State for National

Development and Chairman of the Remaking Singapore Committee, explained that "the centre of gravity, of power, will alter, the rules of engagement will change and OB (*out of bounds*) markers, the avenues for expressions, regulations, all these will change" (Lee, 2003, italics added).

Indeed, one of the fundamental freedoms in a modern society is the freedom to speak openly and without fear of retribution. Article 14 of the Singapore Constitution explicitly guarantees every citizen of Singapore the right to freedom of speech. However, the government may impose by law such restrictions "necessary or expedient in the interest of the security of Singapore . . . public order or morality and restrictions designed . . . to provide against contempt of court, defamation or incitement to any offence."

The government is the employer of most teachers in Singapore. As public officers, teachers are expected to conduct themselves in a manner which upholds the integrity of the public service. Teachers are therefore expected to act within the policies governing public officers. Although the Singapore Constitution guarantees freedom of speech, there are policies that regulate this freedom. For example, when teachers are invited to make or provide materials for any form of broadcasts and telecasts, and if the issues or materials relate either directly or indirectly to their official work, they must first obtain permission from the Ministry of Education before they can accept an invitation. Again, when teachers are invited to be editors or contributors to publications concerning politics, government policies, and practices, they must obtain approval from the Ministry before becoming involved. Breaches of this policy may subject teachers to disciplinary proceedings and sanctions.

Apart from the above restrictions, the whole climate of free speech for teachers is changing for the better. Teachers are not only given the opportunity to be involved in school processes, but they are also afforded many platforms to express their views. One such platform is the online forum for teachers where a wide range of views is discussed, such as teacher grading, school ranking, and life in school. These views are monitored by a corporate communications department in the Ministry of Education, and a link called "Ask Senior Management" is given to teachers to pose questions and suggestions to top officials in the Ministry. Further, the Ministry of Education invites teachers and administrators to attend Focus Group Discussions before and after policy implementations.

As regards religious freedom, Article 15 of the Singapore Constitution guarantees citizens of Singapore the right to profess and practise and propagate their religions. Like Article 14, the government only intervenes when acts contrary to general laws relating to public order, public health, or morality are carried out. Insofar as Singapore is a multi-racial country, made up mainly of

Chinese, Malays, and Indians, there is no official state religion. As such, Singapore considers itself a secular state.

Since religion is a sensitive issue, the Ministry of Education strictly prohibits teachers in both government and mission schools from engaging in any form of proselytisation. This is to prevent teachers from using their positions and special relationships with their students to influence them to adopt or convert them to a particular faith. Teachers' religious freedom to profess and practice their religion is thus subject to the national interest of maintaining the multicultural and multi-religious sensitivity and harmony in the country.

Although there is no anti-discrimination legislation *per se* in Singapore, the Ministry of Education has implemented policies to prevent discrimination on the grounds of religion. For example, aided schools are not permitted to compel students to engage in any religious activity against their wishes. In addition, schools cannot set attendance at religious activities as a condition for students to be admitted. This is in stark contrast to the practice in some other countries, where it is accepted that if children enroll in a particular religious denomination's school, they are accepting the conditions attached to such an enrollment. In Singapore, since most "mission" or religious-based schools are funded largely by the government, the conditions the school can impose are commensurately limited.

Teacher Sanctions, Due Process, and Dismissal

Under Article 110 of the Singapore Constitution, the Public Service Commission (PSC) has the duty "to appoint, confirm . . . and exercise disciplinary control over public officers." Under Article 116 of the Constitution (in particular, the Public Service Commission (Delegation of Disciplinary Functions) Directions), the PSC may delegate its disciplinary functions to another public officer, and this function is ordinarily delegated to the Permanent Secretary of the Ministry of Education. Teachers who are public servants appointed by the PSC cannot be dismissed or disciplined without adherence to the Public Service (Disciplinary Proceedings) Regulations.

For non-public servants, the terms of their contracts with their schools apply. A major difference is that of sanctions for offences committed by aided school employees. Insofar as aided school employees are not government officers (except for civil servants who have been seconded to teach in the aided school), they cannot be subjected to disciplinary action under the Public Service Commission. However, under the Education (Grant-in-Aid) Regulations, the Permanent Secretary of Education has the power to direct the School

Management Committee of aided schools to take disciplinary actions against their employees.

The Public Service (Disciplinary Proceedings) Regulations provide directions for disciplinary actions for teacher misconduct. When deciding whether there is misconduct, the PSC evaluates whether there is a nexus between the alleged misconduct and the suitability of a teacher as an employee of the government. Personality clashes and professional incompetence do not amount to misconduct.

One of the safeguards for teachers is that those who are subject to disciplinary proceedings must be given every reasonable opportunity to make their defence. An inquiry committee is formed to hear the evidence and defence concerning a teacher's alleged misconduct. Examples of misconduct include meting out corporal punishment without appropriate approval, committing a criminal offence, and neglect of duty.

Ultimately, what constitutes "misconduct" is decided by an inquiry committee. Evidence and witnesses on behalf of the government and teachers may be called, and teachers are also entitled, if they wish, to be represented. If teachers are union members, they invariably ask the union to defend their case. On conclusion of a hearing, an Inquiry Committee prepares a report for the Public Service Commission. Based on an Inquiry Committee's finding, the Public Service Commission determines whether officers are guilty of offences and, if so, recommend suitable sanctions.

The disciplinary sanctions meted out for teacher misconduct or offences include verbal or written warnings, the withholding of increments, fines, the withdrawal of allowances, reductions in salary, reductions in rank, retirement in the public interest either with or without reduction in retirement benefits, and, finally, dismissal.

Emerging Issues

Recruitment

Teachers will always be a critical part of the education system in Singapore because of their role in nurturing and building up the nation's only major resource, its people. In 2005, the Ministry of Education reduced the primary-one class size from 40 to 30. The effect of this change was the need to recruit and deploy more teachers to schools. In fact, in the Financial Year 2007 Supply Debate, a Ministry of Education political figure spoke of targeting a pupil-to-teacher ratio of below 20-to-1 for primary schools by 2010 (Lui, 2007a).

As the benefit of having a smaller teacher–pupil ratio becomes more apparent, it will not be surprising if a smaller class size regime is implemented across all schools, namely, primary and secondary, in the coming years. Further, while for most countries that would be an impossible aspiration, Singapore has demonstrated a commitment to education that is unmatched internationally. Such a massive financial commitment is evidenced by the remarkably high standard of school buildings; the central infrastructure to guide curriculum, examinations, and range of related educational matters; and the enormous investment in professional development. For example, those selected for training as principals are given six months in the NIE, full time, to prepare for their principalships and are even sent overseas for a short period of time. This represents a significant investment in education and its ability to provide major economic benefits to the nation.

As a natural consequence of reducing the teacher–pupil ratio, an ongoing priority for the Ministry of Education will be the recruitment and retention of teachers. In the interim, the Ministry of Education introduced a scheme called "Adjunct Teaching" in 2004, whereby trained teachers who have left the service are appointed to support schools when teachers go on long-term leave, professional development, or part-time teaching. Under this scheme, schools are given the additional teachers but have the flexibility to decide how they should be deployed.

Training and Evaluation

Teaching is increasingly recognised as an important profession in Singapore. Gone are the days where teaching was seen as something that one could do if no other jobs were available. In a public perception survey conducted in 2004, the public ranked the teaching profession first in importance, ahead of doctors and lawyers (Lui, 2007b). From the education reforms taking place in Singapore in recent years, the Ministry of Education is also moving "from a bureaucracy-dominated education system to one characterized by greater autonomy at school level" (Gopinathan & Sharpe, 2001, p. 24).

The rising importance of the teaching profession and the devolving of central power to schools, together with the changing attitudes of parents, may well mean a growing community demand for greater accountability in the teaching profession. Such accountability could be over such issues as the schools' duty of care regarding the physical safety of children, the schools' duty to prevent bullying from occurring on school grounds, and, for students with special education needs, identification and meeting of those needs.

As Stewart and Knott (2002, p. 3) note, "school principals and teachers are highly visible in the community and are personally as well as structurally accountable." The Ministry of Education is taking the right step forward in recruiting school counsellors for every school and special needs officers to help teachers with special learning needs. Still, much needs to be done. One area of improvement could be the pre-service and in-service training of teachers. Initial teacher training and professional development should not just emphasise skills in teaching and learning but should also teach skills and knowledge on such issues as the legal duty of care, diagnosing learning disabilities, and other legal issues that may have an impact on the teaching profession.

As advised by Russo and Stewart (2001, pp. 18–19), "educators need a sound understanding of the law associated with the many legal questions that they confront on a daily basis," and a good starting point is for teachers, during pre-service or in-service training, to acquire at least basic legal literacy to meet the increasingly complex challenges of the teaching profession.

The assessment and evaluation of teachers will be an important issue for the teaching profession in relation to the retention of teachers, especially if good teachers become disaffected and leave. The Ministry of Education has indicated that officials are continually taking feedback and suggestions from teachers and school leaders on how to improve the "Enhanced Performance Management System."

With Singapore being one of the few countries that link teachers' rewards to reviewed performance and evidence of ongoing professional development, other countries will be looking closely at how teachers in Singapore and, consequently, its students, actually benefit from such an evaluation system. In other words, is there compelling evidence that the enormous costs associated with such projects yield commensurate benefits?

Conclusion

There is no doubt that Singapore has made considerable progress in relation to teachers' rights in recent years, although it is understandable that it has moved cautiously. That is because any latitude given to teachers as a group needs to be considered in light of societal dynamics and changes.

Such changes have been taking place, slowly but surely, over the past decade and a half, under the leadership of Prime Minister Goh Chok Tong, who took over the reins of government in 1990, and then Lee Hsien Loong, who has continued Goh Chok Tong's moves to provide increasing scope for the people's voice. Such voice is gradually increasing in volume and extent, but it is still monitored and controlled, and with good reason, since, it is argued, unbridled freedom of expression could easily destroy the fabric of a society that has been built up, with consummate success, it has to be said, over the past forty years. It is in this context that the rights of teachers, and the capacity to articulate and exercise those rights, have to be seen.

We need to be clear, though, about whether we are really talking about "rights" or about "entitlements." Many of the conversations we have had have related to the ways in which the government has given teachers the opportunity to say and do things. However, rights are not *granted* by governments. Rather, rights are *protected* by governments.

Thus, there are limits as to what a government can do in terms of taking away a right, a situation that is unlikely to be the case in Singapore. In contrast, an entitlement is something that is granted. On the surface, it would seem that much of what we have had to say about teachers and new opportunities has essentially been about entitlements, and, of course, entitlements can be removed. This is not a criticism, because any analysis of those entitlements would show that the government has been immensely generous to teachers and provided unparalleled opportunity for career and professional development.

The distinction, though, between rights and entitlements is not problematic, because they are probably interrelated. In fact, entitlements may be seen as a part of rights since they provide the specificity about the content of rights by giving quantifiable detail. Thus, teachers in Singapore may have rights in relation to vacation leave, but the entitlements specify precisely how much and when and the conditions attached to the leave.

As we have shown, there are emerging issues in education in Singapore because society is changing. At the risk of over-generalisation, people are more educated, more articulate, more conversant with their rights, and more willing to express themselves than they were even just a decade or so ago. People have been brought up with relatively high living standards and with high expectations. Consequently, people are demanding and are unwilling to settle for less than the best.

It is no surprise that, in such conditions, the word *rights* has become prominent. Principals report that a previously acquiescent parent body has become more conscious of their rights and their children's rights, and parents have not been slow to make their dissatisfaction known to principals and teachers. In this context, since educators unaware of their legal duties and responsibilities are inevitably vulnerable, this is why we argue that today's generation of teachers needs—and, indeed, it may be their "right"—guidance in and an understanding of legal literacy.

The influence of globalisation is immense, and the internationalisation of education in Singapore through exposure to many other systems of education has not only convinced educators that Singapore has a successful system but also made them aware of the conditions of their counterparts in other systems. On the whole, the lot of Singapore teachers is a happy one, with excellent conditions and top-quality resources. Even so, there is always the potential for teachers in Singapore to focus on the rights of their overseas counterparts and to compare and contrast their relative freedoms. At the moment, that does not pose any problems, but it could provide challenges in the future.

Singaporean teachers' rights and entitlements are considerable. The entitlement to various forms of leave, allowances, professional development, and career enhancement and progression is probably unique. Whether teachers' rights in more fundamentally serious areas will emerge is a matter for conjecture. With the emphasis on creativity and innovation, which are essential characteristics in a competitive global economy, there needs to be a spirit of openness, and the government, to its credit, recognises this.

It is doubtful that teachers, particularly those brought up in a culture of compliance and conformity, can break away from the mould and exercise newly granted freedoms. Of course, younger teachers are entering the profession, and their experience in Singaporean society has probably been qualitatively different to their elders, and perhaps change will occur. But change takes time—a luxury Singapore does not have. Despite that, the outlook is good. The key issues, such as elevating the status of the profession and retaining teachers, are being addressed, and if teachers can build the confidence to respond positively to the government's initiatives, the future for Singapore education looks encouragingly rosy.

Bibliography

Compulsory Education Act (Chapter 51), 2003.

Constitution of the Republic of Singapore, 1965.

Chiang, C. (2000). Parliamentary Debates, Singapore. Parliament No. 9. Session No. 2. Volume No. 72. Sitting 9. Sitting Date 09-10-2000. Column 892.

Education Act (Chapter 87), 1957.

Education (Grant-in-Aid) Regulations, 1983.

Education Service Incentive Payment Act, (Chapter 87B), 2002.

Education Service Incentive Payment (Connect Plan) Regulations, 2002.

Gopinathan, S. & Sharpe, L. (2001). The teacher is the key: professionalism and the strategic state. In E. Thomas (Ed.), *Teacher Education: Dilemmas and Prospects*. London, Kogan, 23–32.

Lee, R. (2003). "Remake S'pore? Start with yourself first." *The Straits Times*, 12 June.

Lui, T.Y. (2007a). *Teachers Workload and Assessment of Teachers*. Financial Year 2007 Committee of Supply Debate.

Lui, T.Y. (2007b). *Speech By Radm (Ns) Lui Tuck Yew, Minister of State, Min-*

istry of Education. Nie Teachers' Investiture Ceremony, Nanyang Technological University, 17 January.

Ministry of Education, Singapore (2000). *Principal's Handbook.*

Ministry of Education, Singapore (2002). *Teachers' Handbook.*

Ministry of Education, Singapore (2005), "No proselytisation allowed in schools". Web: http://www.moe.gov.sg/forum/2005/20051025a_print.htm

Ministry of Education, Singapore (2006). "Singapore Staff Appraisal (Education Service)."

Ministry of Education, Singapore (2007). Frequently Asked Questions. Web: http://www.moe.gov.sg/teach/FAQ.htm.

Public Service (Disciplinary Proceedings) Regulations, 1990.

Public Service Commission (Delegation of Disciplinary Functions) Directions, 1997.

Russo, C.J. & Stewart, D.J. (2001). The place of educational law in the international community. *Educational Law Journal, 2(1)*: 18–25.

Singapore Teachers' Union. Web: http://www.stu.org.sg/

Stewart, D.J. & Knott, A.E. (2002). *Schools, Courts and the Law*, Prentice Hall.

Teh, M.K. (2004). Globalisation, Rights and Issues in Education Law in Singapore. *International Journal for Education Law and Policy, 1(1–2)*, (Special Conference Edition): 154–66.

United Nations. (1989). Convention on the Rights of the Child.

United Nations. (2001). United Nations Treaty Collection: Declarations and Reservations. Web: http://www.hri.ca/fortherecord2001/documentation/reservations/crc/htm.

13

South Africa

Marius Smit, J. P. Rossouw, and Rassie Malherbe

Introduction

South Africa is sometimes described as the world in one country. This statement refers not only to the country's breathtaking natural beauty but also to its inspiring and challenging cultural diversity. For historical reasons, South Africa is a geographic region in which African, European, and Eastern (Indian and Malay) cultures have converged in one country. The diversity of school communities in South Africa covers the demographics of race, including colour and ethnicity, culture, religion, language, gender, socioeconomic status, and location, whether urban or rural.

The historic elections of April 1994 marked a shift from authoritarian to constitutional democratic rule in South Africa. The Constitution adopted during the 1990s is the supreme law, and any law or conduct inconsistent with it is justiciable in a court of law.[1] Together with the Constitution and the common law, a host of statutes on education forms the legal framework for the rights of educators.[2]

South African common law is based on the Roman-Dutch Law of the seventeenth century but includes a blend of English law principles such as the *stare decisis* doctrine (or precedent system) for High Court decisions.[3] Accordingly, case law serves as another source of law for the rights of educators in South Africa.

Legislative and Administrative Transformation of the Education System

After 1994 the government embarked on an ambitious program to transform South African society with the aim of redressing past injustices and inequalities. Authorities on democratisation across the world agree that the South African transition process is among most complicated in the world.[4] Accordingly, the rights of educators should be understood within this context of a society engaged in a process of profound change.

A recent World Competitive Report ranked South Africa low in respect to human resource management and development.[5] Following a lengthy planning and negotiation process which included participation by educational institutions as well as business and labour organisations, the Department of Education formulated the policy with the objectives of unifying the previously fragmented educational system while integrating education and training. As a result, the legislative framework for the educational system was established by the promulgation of such laws as the National Education Policy Act (1996; NEPA), the South African Schools Act (1996), the Employment of Educators Act (1998; EEA), and the Further Education and Training Act (1998).

In 1994, one third of South African educators were considered to be underqualified or even unqualified.[6] In order to address this problem in the workforce, the government enacted the South African Qualifications Authority Act (1995), the Skills Development Act (1998) and the Employment Equity Act (1998). These statutes encompass an integrated national framework with the objectives of improving the skills and qualifications of the workforce while redressing unfair discrimination in education, training, and employment opportunities.

The government agencies responsible for the administration of these statutes are the South African Qualifications Authority (SAQA), whose duties include the formulation of quality standards and the investigation of compliance with the required quality outcomes, and the National Skills Authority, whose main function is to allocate funding for Sector Education and Training Authorities (SETAs).

In 1997 the National Educator Audit highlighted an oversupply of educators nationally even though there were local shortages for certain educators qualified to teach mathematics, science, and technical subjects.[7] The government embarked on a rationalisation and restructuring programme which resulted in the closure of 150 of the educator training colleges by 2001.[8] Today these institutions have been merged with the remaining 24 higher education institutions (universities and technikons) involved in educator education. These institutions currently produce about 5,000 educators annually.[9]

There is a downside, though. Demographic trends indicate that the South African educator population is ageing and that the cumulative attrition rate, that is, the rate of educators leaving the workforce due to retirement, death, and resignations, for example, has risen over the past five years.[10] As a result of the low rate of supply of new educators and the high attrition rate, it is estimated that by 2010 South Africa will experience a shortage of 60,000 educators.[11]

Recognised Teaching Qualifications and Professional Registration

In terms of the National Policy Framework for Teacher Education,[12] a four-year Bachelor of Education degree, which includes the equivalent of one full-time year of supervised practical teaching experience in schools, is the standard qualification for those wishing to teach in any learning area, subject, or phase. For those with appropriate first degrees in other fields of study, either an Advanced Diploma in Education, a Post Graduate Certificate in Education, or a Higher Diploma in Education would be the required qualification to teach in any learning areas, subjects, or phases.

The minimum qualification required to teach is a three-year teaching Diploma. Universities have been allowed to offer this qualification, although students are required to complete a fourth year before qualifying as teachers. Insofar as this Diploma may be offered in both contact and distance modes, it can attract student teachers who might not meet degree entrance requirements as well as assist those who need to start earning earlier.

In terms of the South African Council of Educators Act (SACE), it is compulsory for all qualified educators to register with the Council of Educators, and no persons may be employed as educators by any employers unless they are registered with the Council.[13] In South Africa, education is regarded as a profession.[14] The term *educator*, the South African term for teacher, denotes more than an obligation to teach: it signifies the duty and calling to provide a broad and encompassing education over and above the teaching of learning area outcomes. In this regard, educators are reminded to be role models, mentors, and life coaches as well as teachers.

In keeping with their professional status, the discipline, work ethic, and conduct of educators are regulated by SACE. The Council, as the professional body responsible for educator professionalism, has the statutory right in terms of SACE to discipline educators who act unprofessionally, are guilty of misconduct, or bring the profession into disrepute.[15] Penalties for offences might include the removal of persons' names from the register of educators, suspensions, fines, or criminal prosecutions, depending on the circumstances.

The SACE Code of Conduct prescribes the desired conduct that educators should demonstrate toward learners (or students), parents, members of the community, colleagues, and employers. In essence, the Code of Conduct requires educators to behave in a manner that enhances the dignity and status of the profession, to avoid bringing the profession into disrepute, and to carry out their duties in a professional manner.

Employment Rights of Educators

The main statutory instrument regulating the education profession is the Employment of Educators Act.[16] This Act stipulates the conditions of service such as salaries, duties, and terms of service; the appointment procedures, including promotions and transfers; the termination of service provision, which includes retirement, discharge, or resignation; and the procedures to be followed in disciplinary cases.

Contracts and Employment Conditions

The national Minister of Education determines the salaries and other conditions of service of educators according to their ranks and grades. However, such calculations take place consistent with the collective negotiation procedures prescribed by the Labour Relations Act.[17] This Act codified the labour rights of all workers, including educators, and includes collective rights such as the right to organise as unions, negotiate employment conditions by collective bargaining, resolve disputes, and, ultimately, take recourse to strike actions.

All teachers' unions are required to be members of the Education Labour Relations Council (ELRC). Collective bargaining on behalf of educators who are employed by the State takes place annually when the ELRC confers with the Minister of Education as well as other Cabinet ministers such as the Minister of Public Service and Minister of Finance by virtue of their responsibilities.

Other educators employed by school governing bodies or independent schools must negotiate the terms of their employment on an individual basis. For these educators, the Basic Conditions of Employment Act of 1997 regulates and standardises the minimum conditions for fair employment of any workers, including educators, and includes stipulations with regard to working hours, leave, particulars of remuneration, and ancillary matters.

Educators whose employment conditions are not subject to collective agreements negotiated by the ELRC are thus entitled to negotiate at least the minimum fair conditions in accordance with the Basic Conditions of Employment Act. Even so, these educators usually manage to contract more advantageous market-related terms by virtue of the demand and general shortage of competent and qualified educators.

Discrimination Based on Gender and Marital Status

In the matter of *Association of Professional Teachers v Minister of Education*, the second applicant, Rademan, a married woman who was employed as the principal of a primary school, applied for a subsidy on a housing loan from the provincial Department of Education.[18] The Department rejected the application on the basis that, in terms of the Public Service Code, a married woman qualified for a housing subsidy only if her husband was permanently medically unfit to obtain paid employment.

The Court found that Rademan was receiving a lesser financial reward for her work than a single female teacher or a married male teacher and that the sole cause of her failure to receive equal treatment was the disqualification contained in her employer's policy. The Court maintained that the policy directly discriminated against a class of women on the basis of their gender, coupled with their marital status and deemed dependency on a male spouse. Such discrimination was based on circumstances which were wholly irrelevant to the employment relationship between the parties. The Court held that the policy constituted an unfair labour practice but postponed its order to enable the parties to negotiate a suitable package to remedy the unfair labour practice.

Hiring Process of Educators

Educators Must Consent to Appointments, Promotions, or Transfers

The first requirement for valid transfers or appointments is that affected educators must give their prior consent to the intended appointments, transfers, or promotions.[19] In *Simela v MEC for Education, Eastern Cape*, the provincial Department of Education failed to obtain such consent when the entire professional staff of a school was "seconded" to other schools as a punitive measure.[20] The educators were given copies of the report of a task team, which concluded that they were all guilty of various acts of misconduct. The educators sought a court order restraining the Department of Education from taking any steps to effect their transfers and applied for reinstatement to the posts from which they had been transferred.

The Court ruled that the provisions relating to the transfers (or appointments) of educators in the Employment of Educators Act require the consent of the affected educators but that no such consent had been obtained. The Court added that fundamental to the notion of fair administrative action is that people have the right to be heard before their liberty, property, existing rights, or legitimate expectations are prejudicially affected. The Court thus viewed the summary transfer and "shotgun" approach of removing the entire staff from their posts on the basis of untested allegations as unconstitutional, inherently unfair, disproportionate, and contrary to the interests of education. As to relief, the Court declared the transfers void and reinstated the educators in their posts.

Recommendation by School Governing Bodies

The second requirement is that no appointments or transfers to public schools may be made unless the recommendations of the school governing bodies have been obtained.[21] In the matter of *Grove Primary School v Minister of Education, Western Cape*, the Court decided that a collective agreement between the Department of Education and the Education Labour Relations Council to transfer all teachers unilaterally who were in excess to existing vacancies, without regard to the rights of approval of the particular school governing bodies, was illegal.[22]

The matter of *FEDSAS, Limpopo v Departement van Onderwys, Limpopo*, illustrates the requirement to obtain a school governing body's recommendation to transfer or appoint educators to schools.[23] In this matter, the principal of a primary school received letters from the Department of Education of the Limpopo Province informing the governing body that a number of educators who were in excess at other schools were to be transferred to the school.

The school governing body conducted interviews and recommended some of the educators for transfers. However, the governing body informed the Department of Education that a number of educators were unsuitable and that the transfers of these educators were not recommended. The Department ignored these recommendations and gave notice that the educators in excess at the other schools would be transferred temporarily in terms of section 8(5) of the Employment of Educators Act until further notice. FEDSAS, a federation of school governing bodies, applied for an order preventing the Department of Education from transferring the educators.

The Court noted that the Department of Education was not entitled to transfer the educators in terms of a collective agreement because the agreement did not involve the governing bodies as required by the Act. The Act contains the specific provision that any appointments, promotions, or transfers to any posts at public schools may only be made on the recommendations of the school governing bodies.[24] The Department of Education also contended that this provision of the Act was unconstitutional because it enabled governing bodies to discriminate unfairly against previously disadvantaged educators. The Court dismissed this argument on the basis that the Department failed to follow the correct procedure by bringing a separate application of unconstitutionality to be adjudicated before hearing the merits of the case.[25]

Correct Interviewing Procedures—Ensuring Equity and Substantive Equality

The procedures that must be followed when appointing educators are described in the regulations of the Employment of Educators Act under the heading "Personnel Administration Measures." The legality of the interviewing, selection, and recommendation process has been challenged in a number of court cases concerning the appointment of educators (*Carnavon High School v MEC for Education, Northern Cape; Douglas Hoërskool v The Premier of the Northern Cape Province; Kimberley Girls High School v Head of the Department of Education, Northern Cape Province; Settlers Agricultural High School v Head of Department of Education, Limpopo Province*).[26]

In the matter of *Douglas Hoërskool v Premier, Northern Cape*, the Court confirmed that the school governing body was correct to recommend only one candidate if the individual was the only qualified candidate to apply. *Settlers Agricultural High School v Head of Department of Education, Limpopo Province* involved the appointment of a principal to a vacant post. All the procedures, including the advertising of the post, the interviewing, and the recommendation requirements, had been complied with.

The governing body recommended that a white Afrikaans-speaking candidate be appointed as first choice of preference. However, the Department of Education appointed the second candidate on the short list because the departmental employment equity plan favoured a black female candidate as an affirmative action appointment. The Department contended that it could not be expected to simply "confirm and rubberstamp" a recommendation of a school governing body and that it was obliged to take all considerations and, in particular, the provisions of section 7(1) of the Employment of Educators Act into account.

In response, the governing body maintained first that section 6(3) of the Act did not entitle the Head of Department to substitute his choice of candidate for its candidate. Second, the governing body maintained that section 7(1)(a) required that the ability of the candidate be considered as a factor in conjunction with the need to redress past imbalances. The Court upheld both contentions of the governing body. The candidate recommended by the school governing body outscored the nearest competing applicant by a considerable margin during the evaluation process. The High Court held that since the best interests of the learners were of paramount importance, in accordance with section 28(2) of the Constitution, the most able candidate had to be appointed. Further, the Court interpreted the wording of section 6 of the Act as meaning that a singular recommendation of the governing body be appointed and not any candidate on a list of possible appointees.

In the matter of *Kimberley Girls High School v Head of the Department of Education, Northern Cape Province*, the High Court of the Northern Cape Division found that the Education Department's refusal to appoint the candidate recommended by a school governing body was valid because it did not give proper regard to the democratic values and principles referred to in section 7(1) of the Employment of Educators Act.

A vacancy for a teacher in English first language higher grade in respect of grades 10 to 12 was advertised. The Education Department sifted through the applications and furnished the school governing body with a list of twelve candidates. The governing body invited only three white female applicants to the interviews and omitted three black candidates who had excellent credentials on par with the other candidates. The governing body regarded it as reasonable to have set as an absolute prerequisite that candidates must be English first language speakers to be considered for the post.

The Court decided that the principles referred to in section 7(1) of the Employment of Educators Act impose positive obligations on the Head of Department to have regard to equality, equity, and democratic values.[27] The Court reasoned that the Head of Department is not a mere rubber stamp of the recommendation of governing bodies once the criteria of section 6(3)(b)(v) of the Act have been satisfied. The Court explained that the substantive equality and equity requirements of section 7(1) indicate that racial imbalances must be addressed in order to implement affirmative action programs. The Court ordered the governing body to re-interview all of the candidates, including the three disadvantaged candidates.

Kimberley Girls High School and *Settlers Agricultural High School* were resolved in different court jurisdictions. In terms of the South African precedent system, all the schools within the jurisdiction of the Transvaal Division of the High Court would be obliged to follow *Settlers*, while schools situated within the jurisdiction of the Northern Cape Provincial Division of the High Court would have to follow *Kimberley*.

In order to resolve the uncertainty as a result of the conflicting judgments of the respective High Courts, section 6(3) of the Employment of Educators Act was amended to provide that school governing bodies must recommend at least three candidates and the provincial Member of the Executive Council for Education (MEC) may appoint any of the recommended candidates.[28] The MEC may accordingly disregard a governing body's preferred candidate and may appoint any candidate on the list of three recommended candidates, even if he or she is a less suitably qualified or experienced candidate.

Best Interest of the Child

Section 28(2) of the Constitution provides that a child's best interest is of paramount importance in every matter concerning the child. *Governing Body of Point High School v Head of Western Cape Education Department* confirmed that despite the amendment to the Employment of Educators Act, which entitles the Department of Education to appoint any candidate from a list of three recommended candidates, the principle of the best interest of the child requires that the best candidate on merit should be appointed in order to adhere to this constitutional prerequisite.[29]

As important as racial and gender equity and redress might be, various South African rulings (*Western Cape Minister of Education v Governing Body of Mikro Primary School*;[30] *Laerskool Middelburg v Departementshoof, Mpumalanga Departement van Onderwys*)[31] confirmed that the best interests of the child principle overrides the interests of the education authorities, educators, or parents to promote redress and employment equity if such law or conduct is detrimental to the interests of the child(ren) involved.

Ideological and Constitutional Rights of Teachers

Academic Freedom

Academic freedom and the freedom of scientific research are guaranteed in section 16(1)(d) of the Constitution as part of the right to freedom of expression. This is of major significance. It means, first, that academic freedom is a constitutionally protected and judicially enforceable legal norm which must be given content.[32] It is not a luxury, a mere nicety to have. In recognition of the unique position of educational institutions, academics, and researchers in society, the Constitution makers regarded academic freedom as important enough to include it as one of the fundamental rights protected by the supreme Constitution.[33]

Second, it means that academic freedom forms part of the key freedom rights such as privacy; belief; opinion and conscience; expression; freedom and security of the person; and freedom of assembly, association, and movement, all of which protect individual freedom, the cornerstone and founding value of any civilized, democratic state. As sure as freedom of movement allows individuals physically to move about freely, academic or intellectual freedom, together with freedom of thought, conscience, opinion, and expression, ensures that individuals may follow wherever the explorations of their mind may take them.

The Constitution regards academic freedom as part of the right to freedom of expression under the influence of American law, where the right was first recognized in the 1950s as being a manifestation of the right to freedom of expression guaranteed in the First Amendment.[34] In contrast, the German Constitution expressly protects academic freedom,[35] as do the constitutions of Spain, Portugal,[36] Mexico, and Brazil.[37]

Briefly put, academic freedom refers to the freedom of those engaged in the practice of science to teach and engage in research as they deem fit and without interference;[38] neither from section 16(1)(d) nor from this definition can it be inferred that academic freedom applies only to those involved in higher education. Freedom of expression applies to everybody, and there is no reason why it should not also be a right of which teachers and even pupils can be bearers. This aspect is elaborated on below.

In their opposition to government pressure in the 1950s, South African scholars identified the key elements of academic freedom as the freedom from external interference of a university, specifically "to determine for itself on academic grounds who may teach, what may be taught, how it shall be taught, and who may be admitted to study."[39] The definition acquired legal status when Frankfurter incorporated it into American law in *Sweezy v New Hampshire*.[40] On the basis of this definition, the elements of academic freedom can be listed as follows:[41]

(a) Freedom to teach without outside interference. It includes the content, process, and methods of teaching as well as the evaluation or assessment of those taught.[42] Admissions requirements, standards, and criteria for awarding qualifications are logical corollaries to this right.
(b) Freedom to do research without outside interference. Research has been described as "a serious and systematic attempt in terms of content and form to find the truth"[43] and includes all research-related activities such as preparatory, managing, and supporting actions and the dissemination of results through publication.[44]
(c) Freedom to decide who shall teach and conduct research. This implies peer evaluation according to academic criteria and compliance with professional and ethical norms.[45]
(d) The right to tenure, which means that when academics comply with reasonable criteria, they are entitled to permanent positions.[46]

Formulated thus, it seems that academic freedom applies only to higher education, but it need not be the case. Normally, more serious limitations seem to be imposed on academic freedom within the school environment, but in principle teachers and students should also be able to enjoy some measure of academic freedom. Teachers are largely furnished fixed curricula and are not expected to do serious research, and students do not yet have the insight and skills to exercise academic freedom. However, this does not mean that those involved in school education cannot be the bearers of the right to academic freedom.

Teachers and students should at least be allowed to engage in debate, raise questions, voice their opinions, and write questioning and even critical papers. The best teachers are those who devise new methods to engage students and who succeed in challenging students to think beyond the prescribed and the obvious. Is not this a form of academic freedom that is being exercised for the benefit of the students?

From the above-mentioned elements of the right, it also follows that a distinction needs to be drawn between the individual and institutional components of academic freedom. Certain aspects of academic freedom have to be determined collectively or by institutions through their decision-making organs. It also follows that academic freedom includes the self-governing power of universities to decide for themselves on academic-related matters, in other words, matters related to the achievement of universities' missions as institutions aimed at teaching and research.[47]

In America, for example, institutional autonomy has developed from individual academic freedom,[48] while in Germany autonomy has been recognized alongside individual academic freedom on the basis of section 5(3) of the Constitution.[49] The right to academic freedom in section 16(1)(d) of the South African Constitution includes the right to institutional autonomy. It cannot be argued convincingly that section 16(1)(d) applies to natural persons only and therefore does not protect institutional autonomy. Section 8(4) provides that a juristic person is entitled to the rights in the Bill of Rights to the extent required by the nature of the rights and the nature of that juristic person. The nature of the right, which obviously has an institutional component, and the nature of the university clearly require that a university shall be recognized as a bearer of the right to academic freedom.[50]

Again, the question is to what extent schools may claim institutional autonomy. In terms of the South African Schools Act, schools function very much under the authority of the national and provincial education departments and probably cannot be compared to universities, which enjoy a greater measure of autonomy in terms of the Higher Education Act. However, this is once more a matter of degree and not of principle. Nothing in principle prevents the State from assigning more powers to schools over curricula, teacher appointments, admissions, and other academic matters as well as empowering schools to allow individual teachers as well as students a greater measure of freedom of choice in respect of such matters.

The State, in respect of individual academic freedom, as well as institutions, must respect, protect, promote, and fulfill the right to academic freedom.[51] This includes the duty of the State to provide the necessary financial and organisational assistance required to enjoy the right.[52] Any infringement of the right must be justified in terms of the general limitation clause, section 36. In this regard, the over-regulation of education and the uniform curricula prescribed by the South African education authorities leave much to be desired.[53]

There is a concern that education is seen by the government primarily as an instrument to pursue State-determined objectives instead of a service by which the State empowers citizens to achieve their highest potential. These two approaches may not necessarily be in conflict, but when they are, education as driven by the State can even become a hindrance to the optimal development of the people of South Africa.

Of course, academic freedom is not an absolute right, as the present is yet another age in which there is a worldwide tendency toward extended State control of education, *inter alia* due to such factors as financial considerations, increased accountability, changing needs and values of society, market forces, commercialisation, and globalisation, all of which tend to put academic freedom and institutional autonomy under pressure.[54]

Universities are indeed not ivory towers that can turn a blind eye to the rest of society, and the argument is not at all that they must be isolated from societal changes or that their academic freedom must remain untouched by such changes. Similarly, schools are supposed to contribute to the eradication of illiteracy and other legacies of the past while providing quality education to the nation. Nothing, though, takes away from the fact that academic freedom, in whichever way its content may change dynamically, is a judicially enforceable constitutional right worthy of protection like any other and that the State has a particular duty to respect, protect, and promote the right. Obviously, the academy at every level of education has the responsibility to meet the increased demand for accountability to society while, at the same time, it fends off excessive interference with the exercise of society's rights.

Freedom of Religion

The right to freedom of conscience, religion, thought, belief, and opinion in section 15(1) of the Constitution has important implications for education. The right protects not only one's beliefs but also one's right to promote, teach, and manifest those beliefs.[55] Included in this right is the right to join others in manifesting one's beliefs.[56] The question is how this right applies to teachers within the educational environment.[57]

First, it needs to be said that teachers also bear the right to religious freedom. They do not forfeit the right because they are teachers. Unlike the United States, there is not a strict "wall of separation" between the State and religion in South Africa, where teachers are not expected to leave their beliefs and convictions at the school gate. Of course, the State must still act impartially, and schools or teachers are not supposed to indoctrinate their students. However, this does not amount to a prohibition on schools to profess a particular ethos or on teachers to speak about their beliefs and engage with students in similar serious questions about life.

Section 15(2) of the Constitution makes this clear. The provision deals specifically with the manifestation or observance of one's religious convictions in State or State-aided institutions such as schools. It provides that religious observances may be conducted at State or State-aided institutions, provided that such observances follow rules made by the appropriate authorities, are conducted on an equitable basis, and allow free and voluntary attendance.

Section 15(2) confirms one element of religious freedom already contained in section 15(1), that of the right to manifest or observe one's beliefs, by emphasising that it is allowed in State or State-aided institutions, thus putting it beyond doubt that religious observances in public educational facilities are constitutionally protected. Obviously, teachers are also allowed to participate in such observances or conduct their own.

Section 15(2) distinguishes South Africa even further from the American position, where the so-called Establishment Clause has been abused to create a situation where all forms of religious observances have virtually been banned from public institutions such as schools.[58] The Constitutional Court is actually of the express opinion that the South African Constitution rejects the strict wall of separation doctrine found in the United States.[59]

Accordingly, section 15(2) corresponds with the traditional South African approach to religious freedom in terms of which the State has always been actively involved in the creation of favourable conditions for the exercise of religious freedom without favouring a particular religion, as may have been the case previously, because that would be inconsistent either with section 15(2) or section 9, the equality clause. In this respect, the traditional position in South Africa can be compared to the German Constitution, which imposes a positive duty on the State to further religious observances in schools.[60]

However, what exactly is protected by section 15(2)? Religious freedom entails the right to believe privately as one may choose and also to manifest those beliefs by expressing, confessing, and observing them publicly. It further entails that one may individually profess and manifest one's beliefs and that one may manifest them collectively by associating with others in worship, confession, and other acts of observance.[61] The right to conduct religious observances in schools protects pretty much all of this, for example, individual and collective scripture reading, prayers, moments of silence, worship, messages by clerics and others, campaigns by religious organisations, the display of religious symbols, and the observance of religious dress codes.

The exercise of freedom of religion in schools has particular implications. Generally in South Africa, there is much more tolerance for various ways in which religious beliefs may be manifested. Therefore, teachers should have the right not only to believe according to their own convictions but, within reason, also to manifest those beliefs among other things by the way in which they dress.

An orthodox Jewish teacher, for example, should be allowed to wear appropriate attire such as a yarmulke, while a Catholic teacher should be allowed to wear a cross. This can be inferred from two cases involving the religious attire of students. In *Antonie v Governing Body, Settlers High School*,[62] for instance, a learner who embraced the Rastafarian religion was suspended by the governing body for serious misconduct after she came to school wearing her dreadlocks under a cap. The suspension was set aside because adhering to religious dress codes did not, for the Court, amount to serious misconduct under the school's disciplinary code.

A similar approach was followed in *Pillay v KwaZulu-Natal MEC for Education*, in which a school's ban on the wearing of a nose stud as required by a learner's religion was held to constitute unfair discrimination on the grounds of religion and culture.[63] There is no reason why teachers should be treated differently, provided that their conduct does not amount or lead to the indoctrination of students.

At the same time, it should be emphasised that teachers may not be compelled to lead or participate in religious observances at school against their convictions. There should be no coercion. The same element of voluntariness which section 15(2) affords to students therefore additionally applies to teachers.

It should be further emphasised that section 15(2) accords constitutional protection to religious observances in educational institutions and that it does not endorse any form of religious neutrality as in the United States. So-called neutrality would be inconsistent with section 15(2), which prescribes the conditions that religious observances shall be equitable, free, and voluntary. For the same reason, the South African Constitution does not prohibit schools from subscribing to a particular religious ethos, as long as it is equitable, free, and voluntary so that learners and teachers with other convictions are not disadvantaged.

One aspect of the religious freedom of teachers that may be highlighted is the statutory prohibition on corporal punishment in schools. In *Christian Education SA v Minister of Education*, the applicants, an association of Christian private schools, called for an exemption to the ban on religious grounds.

The Constitutional Court, in recognizing the importance of the right to religious freedom and of corporal punishment as part of the religious beliefs of the applicants, applied section 36 in evaluating whether the limitation that the ban imposed on religious freedom was reasonable and justifiable.[64] The Court argued that the ban intends to promote respect for the dignity and physical and emotional integrity of all children. Any exemption, according to the Court, even on religious grounds, would have disturbed the whole symbolic, moral, and pedagogical purpose of the measure while undermining the State's duty to protect people from violence.

The Court thus decided that it was reasonable to expect the applicants to adapt their codes of discipline to the law, pointing out that parents remain free to punish their children based on their beliefs but are precluded from authorising teachers, acting on their behalf, to do so at school. The question is how this judgment affects teachers who also hold the belief that corporal punishment is biblically justified. Could teachers argue that the ban violates their religious freedom? Given the statutory ban, it seems as if the teachers would not succeed on this ground and would be expected to observe the ban.

Educator Sanctions, Due Process, and Dismissal

At the time of the implementation of the interim South African Constitution in 1994, labour legislation was regarded as one of the areas that needed the most urgent transformation. Unfair labour practices and different forms of discrimination in the workplace that prevailed necessitated rapid legislative initiatives from the new government. Consequently, the Labour Relations Act was adopted even before the final Constitution was promulgated in 1996.[65]

The Employment of Educators Act followed soon afterwards, providing for most aspects of labour relations of educators in public schools.[66] The purpose of this Act is to provide for the employment of educators by the State along with the regulation of the conditions of service, discipline, retirement, and discharge of educators. A significant part of the Act deals with teacher discipline.[67]

In the wake of decades of labour unrest and incessant disruptions of schools under the slogan "liberation before education" during the struggle against apartheid, large numbers of educators continued to make themselves guilty of disruptive behaviour. In numerous schools a culture of teaching and learning has not yet developed. This led to the amendment of the Employment of Educators Act in 2000 to include as Schedules 1 and 2 the detailed procedures that the Head of the Education Department as employer (or someone appointed by him) has to follow in the case of alleged misconduct, incapacity, or incompetence.[68] The continuation of educator misconduct had to be curbed while at the same time ensuring fairness of procedure, which is of the same importance as substantive fairness.

In order to ensure fairness toward employees in disciplinary procedures, the Labor Relations Act maintains that dismissal should be considered only when it is the only remaining option.[69] The disciplinary processes in labour and education legislation have moved away from a punitive approach to one that can be called "progressive discipline," a corrective approach according to which efforts are being made to correct the behaviour of employees through a system of graduated disciplinary measures such as counseling and warnings.

When considering dismissals, there must be a clear distinction between misconduct on the one hand and incapacity or poor work performance on the other. The possible actions taken against educators differ, as do the procedures, depending on which allegations are being investigated. In less serious types of misconduct, the prescribed disciplinary actions in the informal phase range from informal, verbal warnings to five written warnings by the principal before more serious steps may be taken. The formal phase starts with a final written warning and may eventually end in dismissal if all the prior sanctions have failed. Further training, counseling, rehabilitation programmes, or transferring educators to other positions are all steps that may be considered in cases of incapacity or poor work performance.

Judged by a number of cases, it is unfortunately clear that many departmental officials are not well informed about some crucially important legal principles that guide labour relations as, for instance, in *Simela & Others v MEC for Education, Province of the Eastern Cape.*[70] Moreover, from other cases and reports from the South African Council for Educators, it is equally evident that the actions of numerous educators continuously and seriously put the profession in disrepute.

In the Labour Court case of *MEC for Education and Culture v Mabika*, it was reported that two teachers absented themselves from work at their high school for a period of five months from June 12, 2002, until November 11, 2002.[71] Section 14(1) of the Employment of Educators Act indicates that unless employers direct otherwise, such educators shall be deemed to have been discharged from service on account of their misconduct. This provision implies that no hearings must take place because the educators have already terminated their contracts of employment. On the advice of the school governing body and a departmental official, a letter was written to the first and second respondents on August 6, calling on them to return to work by August 12, 2002, failing which they were to be charged with absconding.

The two educators referred a dispute to the Education Labour Relations Council, claiming that their dismissal was substantively and procedurally unfair. The arbitrator, who became the fourth respondent in this case, agreed that they were unfairly dismissed. The arbitrator thought that the teachers had not received the letter and that the dismissal was unfair because the applicants had not been granted a hearing.

The Labour Court noted that the arbitrator had not considered the effect of section 14(1)(a) of the Act and whether the letter complied with the requirements of that section. The letter informed the applicants that they were absent without leave and offered them the opportunity to make representations. The Labour Court further observed that the effect of section 14(1)(a) of the Act is that in such cases the deeming provision brings the contract to an end by operation of law after employees absent themselves from work without leave for 14 days.

A "deemed dismissal," the Labour Court asserted, did not therefore constitute a dismissal by the employer. The Labour Court pointed out that the letter was therefore irrelevant to the consequences that flowed from the provisions of section 14(1)(a) and did not convert a dismissal by operation of law into a dismissal by the employer. The Labour Court also declared that the respondent arbitrator by implication lacked jurisdiction to arbitrate the dispute.

The Labour Court set the arbitrator's award aside, ruling that the first and second respondents were not dismissed by their employer because their discharge occurred by operation of law. The Labour Court added that it followed that the employer could yet invoke the provisions of section 14(2), according to which it had the discretion to approve the reinstatement of the educator in the educator's former post or in any other post on such conditions relating to the period of the educator's absence from duty. Such instances of educator misconduct have a severely negative impact on the interests of South African learners, while the professional status of educators is thus lowered and their image seriously tarnished. This is a situation that can only be rectified though effective and consistent but fair implementation of the well-developed labour legislation.

HIV/AIDS and Employment Rights

The HIV/AIDS pandemic is of particular significance for all employees, including educators, because surveys confirm that South Africa has the highest rate of infection and incidence in the world. Not only does the impact of the disease affect the health benefits and working conditions of educators, but it also has a severely detrimental socioeconomic effect on the school population of South Africa.

According to the National Education Policy Act, educators may be compelled to disclose their HIV/AIDS status to school authorities. Educators with HIV/AIDS may voluntarily disclose their HIV/AIDS status to learners. Disclosure of educators' HIV/AIDS status to third parties may nevertheless be authorised by the informed consent of educators or if it is justified by statutory or other legal authorities. Unauthorised disclosure of HIV-related information could give rise to legal liability.

There is no reported case in this regard involving educators. In the landmark judgment in *Hoffmann v South African Airways* (SAA), the Constitutional

Court overturned a ruling by the High Court, reasoning that the company's refusal to employ an applicant who was HIV-positive had indeed infringed his constitutional right not to be subjected to unfair discrimination.[72]

The plaintiff applied to SAA for employment as a cabin attendant, went through a four-stage selection process, and was found, together with eleven other applicants, to be a suitable candidate for employment. This decision was subject to a pre-employment medical examination which included a blood test for HIV/AIDS. The plaintiff was found to be clinically fit, but his blood test revealed that he was HIV positive. The plaintiff was therefore regarded as unsuitable for employment as a cabin attendant and was not employed.

The plaintiff challenged the constitutionality of SAA's refusal to employ him in the High Court, alleging that this constituted unfair discrimination in violation of his constitutional right to equality, human dignity, and fair labour practices. SAA unsuccessfully opposed the application, alleging that its flight crews had to be fit for worldwide duty. SAA additionally argued that since crews had to be inoculated against yellow fever, and persons who were HIV positive could react negatively to this vaccine, they were prohibited from taking the shots. SAA feared that such individuals could contract yellow fever and pass it on to passengers since such persons were liable to contract opportunistic diseases. SAA argued that if they fell ill, such employees would not be able to perform emergency and safety procedures required of them as cabin attendants.

The decision of the Constitutional Court has far-reaching implications for the employment of persons who are HIV-positive. It also has significant ramifications with regard to employees' rights to equality of treatment generally and confirmed instatement or re-instatement as the appropriate redress for those who have been wrongfully denied employment or been dismissed on account of their health status in a country where it is estimated that 12.7% of educators are HIV positive.[73] *Hoffman* also protects HIV-positive educators against unfair discrimination or unfair labour practices.

Conclusion

South African society is undergoing fundamental transformation that includes the equitable provision of educational opportunities for all and fair employment conditions for educators. The challenges that educational authorities are facing and educators are experiencing reflect the complexities of the historical heritage and the socioeconomic encumbrances and multi-cultural diversities of South Africa.

Educators in South Africa are protected by law, and their fundamental rights guaranteed by the Constitution are substantial. Nevertheless, there is a long way to go in safeguarding the position of educators, not only in terms of their conditions of service but also with respect to their professional status. It is true that a happy teacher performs better. However, educators also have a grave responsibility to assist in improving the quality of school education. Educators would contribute in no small measure to the enhancement of their status and in commanding the respect of society they should enjoy as professionals if at all times they acted with the utmost responsibility and diligence in the interest of the youth of South Africa they serve. In the final analysis, what is at stake is the provision of the best possible education to South African youth.

Notes

1. Section 2 of the Constitution of the Republic of South Africa, 1996.
2. Rossouw, *Labour Relations in Education—A South African Perspective.* Pretoria: Van Schaik (2004) pp. 11–26.
3. Hosten, Edwards, Bosman, & Church, *Introduction to South African Law and Legal Theory* (2nd ed.). Durban: Butterworths (1995) pp. 355–56; 386–88.
4. Schlemmer, L. & Giliomee, H. (eds.). *The Bold Experiment—South Africa's New Democracy.* Halfway House: Southern Books Publishers (1994) p. 1.
5. Pons, A. & Deale, P. *Labour Relations Handbook.* Kenwyn: Juta (2001) p. 19.
6. Education Labor Relations Council. *Educator Supply and Demand in the South African Education System—Integrated Report.* Cape Town: HSRC Press. (2005) p. xvii.
7. Ramrathan, P. "Teacher employment: New evidence from tracer studies: Implications for large scale audits." 1999. *South African Journal of Higher Education* 13(3): pp. 164–69.
8. Parker, P. "Roles and responsibilities, institutional landscapes and curriculum mindscapes: A partial view of teacher education policy in South Africa: 1990 to 2000." In: Lewin, K., Samuel, M., & Sayed, Y. (eds.), *Changing Patterns of Teacher Education in South Africa.* Sandown, South Africa: Heinemann (2003) p. 10.
9. Parker (n 8), p. 17.
10. Crouch & Perry, "Educators." In: Kraak, A. & Perold, H. (eds.), *Human Resources Development Review 2003: Education, Employment and Skills in South Africa.* Cape Town: HSRC Press (2003) p. 43.
11. Crouch & Perry, (n 10) p. 44.
12. Department of Education. "National Policy Framework for Teacher Education and Development in South Africa," *Government Gazette No. 29832.* Pretoria: Government Printer (2006), pp. 13–15.
13. Section 21 of the South African Council for Educators Act 31 of 2000.
14. Oosthuizen, I.J. (ed.). *Aspects of Education Law.* (2nd ed.). Pretoria: Van Schaik Publishers (2003) pp. 105–06.
15. Sections 23 and 24 of Act 31 of 2000.

16. Employment of Educators Act 76 of 1998.

17. Labour Relations Act 66 of 1995.

18. 1995 9 BLLR 29 (IC).

19. Section 8(1)(a) of the Employment of Educators Act 76 of 1998.

20. *Simela v MEC for Education, Eastern Cape*, 2001, 9 BLLR 1085 (LC).

21. Section 20(1)(i) of the South African Schools Act 84 of 1996 and section 8(2) of the Employment of Educators Act 76 of 1998.

22. *Grove Primary School and others v Minister of Education, Western Cape*, 1997(4) (SA) 982 (C).

23. *FEDSAS, Limpopo v Department van Onderwys; Limpopo*, Unreported case no. 30801/2003 (TPD).

24. Section 6(3)(a) of the Employment of Educators Act 76 of 1998.

25. The final argument of the Department of Education was that it was entitled to transfer the educators temporarily in terms of section 8(5) of the Employment of Educators Act 76 of 1998. The Court dismissed this contention as well, declaring that section 8(5) was not intended to be used to transfer excess educators but merely provided for vacancies to be filled temporarily.

26. *Carnavon High School v MEC for Education of the Northern Cape*, 1999(4) SA (NC). *Douglas Hoërskool v The Premier of the Northern Cape Province*, 1999(4) SA 1131 (NC). *Head of Department, Department of Education, Limpopo Province v Settlers Agricultural High School*, 2003 (11) BCLR 1212 (CC). *Kimberley Girls' High School v Head, Department of Education, Northern Cape Province*, 2003 JOL 11106 (NC).

27. As prescribed for public administration by section 195(1) of the Constitution.

28. Education Laws Amendment Act 24 of 2005, date of commencement 26 January 2006 (Government Notice: 69, *Government Gazette* 28426 of 26 January 2006).

29. *Governing Body of Point High School v Head of Western Cape Education Department*, Unreported case no. 14188/2006 (WC).

30. *Western Cape Minister of Education v. Governing Body of Mikro Primary School*, 2005 (3) SA 436 (SCA).

31. *Laerskool Middelburg v Departementshoof, Mpumalanga Departement van Onderwys*, 2003 (4) SA 160 (T).

32. The right to academic freedom should therefore be the point of departure for every policy initiative regarding higher education—Zoontjes *Vrijheid van Wetenschap: Juridische Beschouwingen over Wetenschapsbeleid en Hoger Onderwijs* (1993) 20–22.

33. See, e.g., Du Plessis and Corder, *Understanding South Africa's Transitional Bill of Rights* (1994) 156–57, which explains why the right had already been included in the interim Constitution.

34. See, e.g., *Sweezy v New Hampshire*, 354 U.S. 234 (1957); *Keyishian v Board of Regents of the State of New York*, 385 U.S. 589 (1967).

35. Section 5(3): "Kunst und Wissenschaft, Forschung und Lehre sind frei. Die Freiheit der Lehre entbindet nicht an der Treue zur Verfassung."

36. On Portugal, see Magalhaes and Amaral, "Portuguese higher education and the imaginery friend: The stakeholders' role in institutional change." 2000. *European Journal of Education*, pp. 439–49.

37. For the protection of academic freedom in international law, see Article 15 of the International Covenant on Economic, Social and Cultural Rights (1967).

38. The right to academic freedom has been explored at some length in various contributions: Malherbe, "Die regsbeskerming van akademiese vryheid en universiteitsoutonomie in 'n nuwe Suid-Afrika," 1993, *Journal of South African Law*, pp. 359–83; Malherbe, "Die onderwysbepalings van die 1993 Grondwet," 1995, *Journal of South African Law*, 1: 8–10; Malherbe, "A constitutional perspective on higher education," 1999, *Stellenbosch Law Review*, 328: 344–49; Malherbe, "A fresh start II: Issues and challenges of education law in South Africa," 2000, *European Journal for Education Law and Policy*, pp. 57–68.

39. Quoted in Higgins, "Academic freedom in the new South Africa," 2000, *Boundary*, 2: 97 at p. 106; see also *The Open Universities in South Africa and Academic Freedom 1957–1974: A Review by the Academic Freedom Committees of the University of Cape Town and the University of the Witwatersrand*, Johannesburg (1974), pp. 11–12. Some regard this as an outdated liberal formulation—see Du Toit, "From autonomy to accountability: Academic freedom under threat in South Africa?" 2000, *Social Dynamics*, pp. 76–133; Southall and Cobbing, "From racial liberalism to corporate authoritarianism: The Shell affair and the assault on academic freedom in South Africa," 2001, *Social Dynamics*, 1–42.

40. 354 US 234, 263 (1957).

41. See Malherbe (n 39, 1999) 346. Cf. the 1915 Declaration of Principles of the American Association of University Professors, in which they defined academic freedom as the "freedom of inquiry and research; freedom of teaching in the university or college; and freedom of extra-mural utterance and action" (quoted by Chang [n 35] 919).

42. See the landmark German cases in BVerfGE 24, 25; BVerfGE 55, 37/68. See also Maunz-Dürig I, *Grundgesetz Kommentar* 5: 154; Von Munch I, *Grundgesetz-Kommentar* (1985) 320ff; Oppermann, "Praktische Konsequenzen der Entscheidung des Bundesverfassungsgerichts zur Wissenschaftsfreiheit," 1973, *Juristenzeitung*, pp. 433–41; Schmidt, "Wissenschaftsfreiheit als Berufsfreiheit," 1973, *Neue Juristische Wochenschrift*, pp. 585–90.

43. BVerfGE 35, 79/113; BVerfGE 47, 327/367.

44. BVerfGE 5, 85/146. See Malherbe (n 39, 1999) 346.

45. Obviously, the latter indicates that academic freedom has limits, the validity of which must be determined in accordance with s 36 of the Constitution.

46. Bray (n 39) 223 ff. From time to time, this is a prominent issue in American law—see O'Neil, "Academic freedom: Past, present and future," in Altbach et al., *American Higher Education in the Twenty-first Century* (1999), pp. 89–108; Olivas, "The legal environment: The implementation of legal change on campus," in Altbach et al., 216, 220–23.

47. Malherbe, (n 39, 1993) 365; (n 39, 1999) 347. The German federal constitutional court refers to *universitäts-typischen Angelegenheiten*—BVerfGE 15, 256/264.

48. *Widmar v Vincent*, 454 U.S. 263 (1981); *Regents of University of Michigan v Ewing*, 474 U.S. 214 (1985). See Chang (n 35) 31–35; Finkin, "On 'institutional' academic freedom," 1983, *Texas Law Review* 817 ff. For a recent account of the develop-

ment of institutional academic freedom, see Goring, "Affirmative action and the First Amendment: The attainment of a diverse student body is a permissible exercise of institutional autonomy," 1999, *University of Kansas Law Review*, 591: 601–13. See also Berdahl, Altbach, and Gumport, "Introduction," in Altbach et al., (n 47) 1 6, who distinguishes between academic freedom and substantive and procedural autonomy, the former indicating the what and the latter the how of academe.

49. BVerfGE 35, 79; see Maunz-Dürig (n 43) 145 ff.

50. This issue, and the unique nature of the university as an organ of State but still a bearer of the right to academic freedom, has been explained at length in Malherbe, (n 39, 1999). See also Rautenbach and Malherbe, *Constitutional Law* (2004) 78–79.

51. s 7(2) of the Constitution.

52. BVerfGE 35, 79/114; BVerfGE 67, 202/207. From cases such as these, it is evident that the courts in Germany accept the State's wide administrative and organisational powers in respect of higher education, as long as scholarly activity is left untouched. Any organisational changes must therefore be considered in view of the question to what extent it affects academic freedom and the ability of the institution to conduct scientific enquiry freely.

53. See, e.g., Malherbe, "The erosion of academic freedom in South Africa: Reflections on a battle forfeited," 2003, *Journal of South African Law*, pp. 213–40.

54. For recent contributions in this regard, see Neave, "Editorial: Academic freedom in an age of globalization," 2002, *Higher Education Policy*, pp. 331–35; Zusman, "Issues facing higher education in the twenty-first century," in Altbach et al. (n 47) 109–48; Altbach, "Harsh realities: The professoriate faces a new century," in Altbach et al. (n 47) 271–97; Glenn, "University mission and academic freedom: Are they irreconcilable?" 2000, *European Journal for Education Law and Policy*, 41–47; Dlamini, "University autonomy and academic freedom in transition: The British experience," 2001, *SA Public Law*, 343–61. See also earlier contributions such as Lowenthal, "The university's autonomy versus social priorities," in Seabury (ed.), *Universities in the Western World* (1975) 75–84; Shils, "The academic ethos under strain," in Seabury, 16–46; Macrae, "The British position," in Seabury, 176–80; Wahlbäck, "University autonomy in Sweden," in Seabury, 268–78; and those referred to by Malherbe (n 39, 1993).

55. Malherbe, "Die grondwetlike beskerming van godsdiensvryheid," 1998, *Journal of South African Law*, 680.

56. This aspect of the right is covered by section 18, which provides for the freedom of association, but even more expressly by s 31, which provides *inter alia* that members of a religious community may practise their religion together with other members of that community.

57. The discussion does not refer directly to the "Religion and Education" policy of the national Department of Education, although what is said here has specific implications for the policy. The policy has been discussed in depth elsewhere. See, e.g., Malherbe, "The constitutionality of government policy relating to the conduct of religious observances in public schools," 2002, *Journal of South African Law*, 391–418; Malherbe, "The unconstitutionality of government policy relating to religion and education," paper read at the eighth international conference of SAELPA on "Legal Risk

Management at School: Education Law and Policy Issues," 31 August–2 September 2003, Magoebaskloof, Limpopo Province.

58. See, e.g., Chandler et al., *Constitutional Law Deskbook: Individual Rights* (1993) 90 ff; Witte, J. and J. Green, "The American constitutional experiment in religious human rights: The perennial search for principles," in Van der Vyver, J. D. and Witte, J. (eds.), *Religious Human Rights in Global Perspective* (1996) 497 ff; Van der Vyver, J. D., "Introduction," in Van der Vyver and Witte, xi–xlvii; Witte, J., "The South African experiment in religious human rights," 1993, *Journal for Juridical Science*, 1 ff; Valente, *Law in the Schools* (1980) 109 ff; Underkuffler-Freund, L. S., "Religious guarantees in a pluralistic society: Values, problems and limits," 1997, *SA Public Law*, 32 ff.

59. *S v Lawrence; S v Negal; S v Solberg*, 1997 10 BCLR 1348 (CC), paras. 100–02; 116–18.

60. Malherbe (n 56) 703. See, in respect to Germany, Jarass, H. D. and Pieroth, P., *Gründgesetz für die Bundesrepublik Deutschland* (1995) 220 ff.

61. See Malherbe (n 56) 679–81.

62. 2002 4 SA 738 (C). See the comments by Roos, "The physical appearance of learners in public schools: *Antonie v Settlers High School* 2002 4 SA 738 (C)," 2003, *Journal of South African Law*, 792.

63. 2006 10 BCLR 1237 (N). This case is currently on appeal before the Constitutional Court.

64. *Christian Education South Africa v Minister of Education*, 2000, 10 BCLR 1051 (CC).

65. Act 66 of 1995.

66. Act 76 of 1998.

67. Sections 17 and 18 specify in detail what constitutes educator misconduct.

68. Education Laws Amendment Act 53 of 2000, Pretoria: *Government Gazette* 21783, 22 November 2000.

69. Labour Relations Act 66 of 1995, Schedule 8.

70. *Simela v MEC for Education, Eastern Cape*, 2001 9 BLLR 1085 (LC).

71. *MEC for Education & Culture v Mabika*, Unreported case No. D547/2003, Durban Labour Court, 2006.

72. *Hoffmann v South African Airways*, 2000 12 BLLR 1365 (CC).

73. Shisana, O., Peltzer, K., Zungu-Dirwayi, N., & Louw, J. S. *The Health of Our Educators: Focus on HIV/AIDS in South African Public Schools*. Cape Town: HSRC (2005) p. 355.

14

United States

Charles J. Russo

Introduction

The rights of public school teachers in the United States, which were modest until the advent of teacher activism and collective bargaining in the early 1960s, are governed by a complex array of state and federal laws. However, since non-public schools, which do not receive public funds, are governed largely by the law of contracts, with the federal or state governments having little to say about their employment rights, this chapter focuses on the rights of teachers in American public schools.

This chapter begins with a brief overview of the legal system in the United States before examining a variety of issues governing the substantive and procedural due process rights of teachers in elementary and secondary schools. It is important to note that as litigious as Americans are, it is probably safe to say that there are more cases in one year in the United States than there are in at least a decade or longer elsewhere. Thus, although footnotes often cite just one case, in many instances they could be replaced with multiple case names.

The American Legal System

The United States Constitution is the law of the land. As the primary source of American law, the Constitution provides the framework within which the entire legal system operates. Accordingly, all actions by the federal, state, and local governments, including state constitutions, statutes, regulations, and common law, are subject to the Constitution as interpreted by the Supreme Court.

As important as education is, it is not mentioned in the Constitution. Under the Tenth Amendment, according to which "[t]he powers not delegated to the United States by the Constitution, nor prohibited by it to the States, are reserved to the States respectively, or to the people," education is primarily the concern of individual states. Federal courts can intervene in educational disputes if a federal right is at issue, such as in *Brown v. Board of Education* (*Brown*).[1] In *Brown*, the Supreme Court struck down state-sanctioned racial segregation on the basis that officials in public school violated students' rights to equal protection under the Fourteenth Amendment to the United States Constitution.

Along with identifying the rights of Americans, the Constitution establishes three coequal branches of government. The legislative, executive, and judicial branches of government give rise to three other sources of law. The legislative branch "makes the law." Once bills complete the legislative process, they are signed into law by a Chief Executive, who has the authority to enforce them through regulations that are developed by personnel at administrative agencies who are experts in education.

The fourth and final source of law is judge-made or common law. Common law requires judges to "interpret the law," examining issues that may have been overlooked in the legislative or regulatory process or that may not have been anticipated when statutes were enacted. Common law involves the concept of precedent, the notion that a majority ruling of the highest court in a given jurisdiction is binding on lower courts within its jurisdiction. A ruling of the United States Supreme Court is thus binding throughout the nation, while a decision of a State Supreme Court is binding only in a given state.

The federal judiciary and most state court systems consist of three levels: trial courts, intermediate appellate courts, and courts of last resort. In the federal system, trial courts are known as federal district courts; state trial courts use a variety of names. Each state has at least one federal district court; some densely populated states, such as California and New York, have as many as four.

Trial courts typically involve a judge and a jury. The role of the judge, as trier of law, is to apply the law by deciding, for instance, whether evidence is admissible and instructing the jury on how the law should be applied in a case. Federal intermediate appellate courts are known as Circuit Courts of Appeal; there are 13 circuit courts; state intermediate appellate courts employ a variety of names. The highest court in the United States is the Supreme Court; while most states refer to their high courts as supreme courts, a variety of titles is in use.

Few school-related cases are directly under the jurisdiction of the federal courts. The vast majority of federal cases dealing with education involve a federal question, meaning that a dispute must be over the interpretation of the

United States Constitution, a federal statute, or a federal regulation. A party not satisfied with a ruling can appeal. Insofar as the Supreme Court receives almost 8,000 petitions per year and accepts fewer than 100 cases, it is clearly difficult for a dispute to reach the Supreme Court.[2] It is easier for an appeal in a state court to reach the court of last resort, especially where state law is at issue.

Employment Rights of Teachers

The primary source of law regulating the employment rights of teachers is established at the state level. Even so, federal law, especially in the area of anti-discrimination, has a major impact on the employment rights of teachers in public schools.

Teacher Certification

All jurisdictions require public, but not non-public, school teachers to have certification or licenses typically based on having completed professional preparation programs, achieving appropriate examination scores, and passing criminal background checks. States are moving away from certification as a kind of once-and-done permanence to teach and adopting licensure as a means of requiring teachers to complete ongoing professional development to maintain their jobs. Moreover, when faced with teacher shortages, states and sometimes local school boards can allow individuals to apply for temporary or emergency licenses or certifications.

Whether referred to as certification or licensure, since state endorsements are not written contracts under which teachers work, which typically delineate their job duties and rights in such areas as pay and evaluation, mere possession of credentials does not satisfy the statutory definition of a teacher since applicants must typically possess both valid certificates and perform the statutory duties of educators. Certification laws differ widely since legislatures place varying amounts of discretion in state and local school boards and accompanying agencies.

Local boards may require teachers to have additional qualifications such as extra course preparations[3] or certifications[4] as long as they are neither arbitrary nor capricious, are reasonably related to the jobs they seek, and are not barred by constitutional or statutory considerations. For example, in *Harrah Independent School District v. Martin*,[5] the Supreme Court affirmed that a board in Oklahoma was free not to renew the contract of a teacher who was aware of, but refused to comply with, a policy, enacted pursuant to state law, requiring her to complete continuing education requirements.

Certification or licensure requirements are subject to judicial scrutiny under federal and state anti-discrimination statutes and the Fourteenth Amendment. To this end, since the right to engage in a legitimate occupation is a liberty interest, state officials can only deny individuals jobs if reasonable standards protect public health, safety, and welfare.[6]

Employment is also sometimes denoted as a property right.[7] Even so, when public agencies act pursuant to objective criteria rather than discretionary standards, courts usually do not intervene on behalf of teachers. For instance, an appellate court in Pennsylvania dismissed the challenge of a teacher who failed the Praxis II test in Spanish Content Knowledge that was required for certification.[8] The Court explained that since the teacher had no expectation that she would have received a certificate, officials did not deprive her of any right or privilege, including the opportunity to litigate her disagreement.

In a preliminary question about teacher qualifications, in *Ambach v. Norwick*, the Supreme Court upheld a statute from New York that required candidates for jobs as public school teachers to be United States citizens.[9] The Court wrote that a state may regard teachers as having an obligation to promote civic virtues and understanding in their classes. More recently, a federal trial court in Georgia reached the opposite result.[10] The Court invalidated a state statute that precluded aliens from public employment as violating the Equal Protection Clause where there had been no finding that remaining in their jobs would have undermined a legitimate state interest. Other courts have refused to eliminate loyalty oaths,[11] residency requirements,[12] and mental and physical examinations for job candidates.[13]

If candidates meet the legal standards for certification, including successful completion of examinations,[14] state agencies may not arbitrarily reject their applications[15] or impose new conditions such as age requirements.[16] However, where the qualifications to obtain teaching certificates are clear and applicants who lack the basic requirements fail to correct their deficiencies by acquiring the necessary background, then they are not entitled to receive certificates.[17] Once teachers are employed, they are evaluated regularly, usually on multiple occasions, during their three- to four-year probationary periods of employment. Once teachers earn tenure, they are typically evaluated annually, often pursuant to provisions in their collective bargaining agreements.

Ideological–Constitutional Rights of Teachers

Aside from the fact that education is typically a concern of states rather than the federal government, three areas involving the federal constitutional rights of teachers come to the fore: the freedoms of religion, speech, and association, typically via memberships in unions or professional associations. Freedom of association also covers the personal lives of teachers away from work but, in the interest of space, is beyond the scope of this chapter. While public school teachers, like students, do not "shed their constitutional rights to freedom of speech or expression at the schoolhouse gate,"[18] there are limitations about what they can say and do with regard to religion and free speech, in particular, in schools.

Freedom of Religion

The Supreme Court interpreted the First Amendment Religion Clauses as imposing a "wall of separation" between "church and state." However, in perhaps its most important case involving the religious rights of public school employees, *Ansonia Board of Education v. Philbrook*,[19] the Court interpreted Title VII,[20] an expansive federal anti-discrimination statute,[21] as requiring school boards to make reasonable accommodations to meet the religious needs of staff, even if they are not the ones that the employees sought.[22]

One case involved the religious rights of teachers under the First Amendment and a collective bargaining agreement. An appellate court upheld the constitutionality of a provision in a bargaining contract that granted teachers up to three days per year for religious observances.[23] When board officials tried to have teachers use personal time rather than the days allotted in the contract, the Court noted that the provision did not violate the Establishment Clause since it neither impermissibly advanced religion by coercing union members to profess a belief nor imposed any requirements regarding which religious holidays might be invoked.

Another case highlighted the extent to which public employees can express their religious preferences in the workplace. The Ninth Circuit invalidated a prohibition against permitting an employee of the state department of education from displaying religious materials on the interior walls of his cubbyhole.[24] The Court observed that the restriction was unnecessary to serve the Department's interest in efficiency where there was no evidence of disruption in general or that any employee but the plaintiff engaged in the religious activity.

Claims of religious discrimination under Title VII are often unsuccessful when school officials provide legitimate, non-discriminatory reasons for acting. In such a case, a former high school paraprofessional sued his ex-principal, claiming that he was dismissed in violation of his right to his freedom to practice his Islamic faith and without due process.[25] In granting the principal's motion for summary judgment, a federal trial court held that the paraprofessional was unable to prove one of the elements of a prima facie case: that he performed his duties satisfactorily. The Court added that the principal did not violate the paraprofessional's right to due process because there was no evidence that he was personally involved insofar as the operative collective bargaining required only that the administrator refer the matter to the board's department of human resources, which notified him of his dismissal.

Religious disputes have also arisen over instructional issues. For example, an appellate court rejected the claim of a teacher who alleged that officials violated his rights to free speech by directing him not to talk about religion during the school day, during which he refused to teach about evolution,[26] while another court upheld a board's reassigning a teacher to teach a different biology course after he refused to teach about evolution.[27] In addition, the Seventh Circuit[28] affirmed that officials did not violate an individual's rights when they removed his name from an approved list of substitutes because he insisted on presenting his religious views in class.[29] These cases also stand clearly in line with the notion that since educators in K–12 schools lack academic freedom, they have no right to dictate the content of school curricula.

On another topic, many older cases dealt with whether public school teachers could wear distinctive religious garb. The disputes often arose over whether Roman Catholic nuns could wear their habits while teaching in public schools. In an early case, the Supreme Court of Pennsylvania affirmed the authority of a local board to hire Catholic nuns as teachers and to permit them to teach in their habits.[30] However, shortly thereafter, the legislature enacted a law specifically designed to prevent teachers from wearing any dress or insignia indicating membership in religious orders while at work. Deferring to legislative authority, the same court later upheld the law that banned nuns from teaching in their habits.[31]

The Supreme Court of Oregon, in a case involving a teacher who converted to the Sikh faith and wore white clothes, including a white turban, while teaching, posited that she was subject to a legislative ban on religious dress while performing teaching duties.[32] In dicta, the Court conceded that the prohibition would not likely have applied to incidental items such as a cross, Star of David, or ethnic or cultural dress.[33]

Two recent cases suggest that whether educators can wear religious symbolism depends on their obviousness and size. The federal trial court in Connecticut granted a school board's motion for summary judgment when officials told a substitute teacher either to cover a T-shirt with the message "Jesus 2000" on it or to go home and put on other clothes.[34] The Court ruled that officials did not violate the teacher's First Amendment rights to free exercise of religion or free speech. Conversely, a federal trial court in Pennsylvania granted an instructional assistant's motion for a preliminary injunction when she was suspended for refusing to follow board policy and remove or conceal a small cross that she wore on a necklace.[35] The Court agreed that the policy violated the Free Exercise Clause since its being directed only at religious exercise and symbolic expression made it impermissibly content and viewpoint based.

Free Speech Rights of Teachers

Concerns arise about the employment status of teachers who exercise their First Amendment rights to freedom of speech as private citizens. Beginning with *Pickering v. Board of Education of Township High School District* (*Pickering*),[36] the Supreme Court handed down a series of cases helping to clarify the parameters of this important topic.

At issue in *Pickering* was a school board's attempt to dismiss a teacher for writing a letter to a local newspaper which criticized its handling of a bond issue and its allocation of financial resources between the school's educational and athletic programs. In rejecting the board's claim that the letter was detrimental to the best interests of the schools, the Court wrote that the teacher's right to free speech was primary since this was a matter of public concern. In its rationale, in addition to recognizing that the teacher had the right to speak out on a legitimate matter of public concern as a private citizen, the Court commented that he did not have a close working relationship with those he criticized, that his letter did not have a detrimental impact on the district's administration, and that it did not negatively affect his regular duties.

The Supreme Court revisited the free speech rights of teachers in *Mt. Healthy City Board of Education v. Doyle* (*Mt. Healthy*),[37] when it considered the effect of including a constitutionally protected right as a factor in not renewing the contract of a non-tenured teacher. The board chose not to renew the contract of a teacher who had a record of being difficult in school despite his claim that it violated his rights because he called into a radio talk show and criticized a memo from his principal dealing with a faculty dress code.

In *Mt. Healthy* the Supreme Court rejected the Sixth Circuit's finding that including a protected activity as a substantial part of the justification for the non-renewal of a probationary teacher's contract entitled him to reinstatement with back pay. The Court conceded that where a teacher shows that protected conduct about a school matter was a substantial or motivating factor where a board chooses not to renew a contract, the board must be given the opportunity to show that it would have chosen not to re-employ in the absence of the protected conduct. On remand, the board reported that it would not have renewed the teacher's contract regardless of whether he placed the call to the radio talk show.[38]

Two years later, in *Givhan v. Western Line Consolidated School District* (*Givhan*),[39] the Court determined that the *Pickering* balancing test also applies to teachers who express themselves during private conversations with their supervisors. When officials chose not to renew the contract of a non-tenured teacher, she was informed that it was in response to, among other reasons, her allegedly making petty and unreasonable demands on the principal and addressing him in a manner variously described as insulting, hostile, loud, and arrogant. The teacher also complained that the board, which operated under a Court-ordered desegregation plan, was racially discriminatory in its employment policies and practices. In refusing to reinstate the teacher, the Court reasoned that the Fifth Circuit erred in declaring that educators were justified in not renewing her contract, suggesting that under *Mt. Healthy*, they may have had sufficient cause on other grounds that would have required further proceedings.

At issue in *Connick v. Myers* (*Connick*),[40] the Court's next case on employee speech, was whether *Pickering* protects public employees who communicate their views about workplace matters to peers. A former assistant district attorney challenged her dismissal on the day that she was scheduled for a transfer to another division because she circulated a questionnaire about office operations among staff.

In *Connick*, the Supreme Court distinguished *Givhan* in conceding that while the teacher's statements involved issues of public concern, the attorney's statements were primarily based on an internal disagreement with her supervisors and the questionnaire interfered with close working relationships. Pointing out that the attorney's dismissal did not violate her rights, the Court established a two-step test to evaluate whether speech is entitled to First Amendment protections. First, the Court explained that the judiciary must consider whether the speech involved a matter of public concern by examining its content and form along with the context within which it was expressed. Second, the Court posited that if speech does deal with a matter of public concern, the judiciary must balance employees' interests as citizens in speaking out on matters of public concern against those of employers in promoting effective and efficient public services.

Almost a decade later, in *Waters v. Churchill*,[41] a case involving a nurse who criticized internal policies at a public hospital, the Supreme Court, in a plurality opinion, reiterated that public employees who publicly dispute internal policies that are not of public concern may not be entitled to constitutional protection.

In a more recent application of the *Connick*'s principles, albeit again not in a school, in *Garcetti v. Ceballos* (*Garcetti*),[42] the Supreme Court affirmed that since a deputy district attorney's complaints about supervisors were not on matters of public concern, his speech was not entitled to First Amendment protection. At issue were a deputy district attorney's complaints about a supervisor in a dispute over a memorandum he wrote claiming that a police officer lied in his affidavit to secure a warrant. The Court held that since public employees who make statements pursuant to their official duties are not speaking as citizens for First Amendment purposes, the Constitution is unavailable to insulate their communications from employer discipline.

Among the many examples of subjects that met the criterion of public concern were cases school employees suffered adverse employment actions include criticisms of a medication policy,[43] a principal's failure to implement a school improvement plan,[44] a board's child abuse reporting policy,[45] a teacher's use of a racially derogatory word in class during a discussion on interracial marriage,[46] a secretary's questions about whether a board's awarding of a contract presented a conflict of interest,[47] a physical therapist's complaint that her school board did not do enough to meet the educational needs of students with disabilities,[48] and a teacher's report of financial improprieties by other school employees to her board.[49]

In a similarly large number of cases, courts refused to treat the speech of school employees as protected since it not only failed to involve matters of public concern but was also related to their official duties. Among these cases were instances criticizing a superintendent[50] or a board's hiring of a superintendent,[51] questioning class size policies,[52] challenging the non-renewals of teaching[53] and coaching contracts,[54] complaining about unfavorable evaluations,[55] claiming that school officials created a racially hostile work environment,[56] criticizing the quality of leadership and the education children received in a district,[57] and an athletic director/football coach's sending memoranda to the school's office manager and principal questioning the handling of school athletic funds.[58]

When teachers become involved in situations with political connotations, issues arise about how far school boards can go in enforcing rules prohibiting political activities by teachers in schools. For instance, the Seventh Circuit upheld a grant of summary judgment in favor of a school board in Indiana that chose not to renew the contract of a probationary elementary school teacher in Indiana who made her opposition to the war in Iraq known as part of a classroom discussion of current events.[59]

Although conceding that the war was a matter of public concern, the Sixth Circuit explained that the teacher had the right to express herself, as she was not disruptive. Still, the Court affirmed that the First Amendment did not protect the teacher since she departed from the board's approved curriculum, which allowed her to address controversies related to the war as long as she permitted students to speak out on all sides of the debate while keeping her opinion private. The Court concluded that the First Amendment does not permit educators in elementary and secondary schools who address captive audiences of students to cover topics or advocate perspectives that deviate from approved curricula, essentially reiterating the basic principle that educators in K–12 schools lack academic freedom.

The Supreme Court addressed a matter of speech that is related to employee rights of association and collective bargaining that segues into the next section. In *Texas State Teachers Association v. Garland Independent School District*,[60] the Court summarily affirmed that board policies allegedly denying faculty members the right to discuss teacher organizations during non-class time and preventing them from using school mail facilities to mention them were unconstitutional.

Freedom of Association—Unionization

Collective bargaining in public education, which began in earnest in the early 1960s, allows school boards and teachers to negotiate over terms and conditions of employment. Even so, the extent to which boards may engage in bargaining varies from one jurisdiction to the next. States have the power to permit teachers to engage in, or to refrain from, actions designed to bring about changes in employment conditions.

The Federal Constitution not only guarantees freedom of speech and of association but also restricts the conditions that can be placed on public employees. While the First Amendment does not require school boards to recognize or bargain with unions, it does protect teachers who join labor organizations[61] and cannot discipline them for doing so or for engaging in protected union activities.

In order to negotiate with their school boards, employee unions must organize bargaining units that are recognized as the exclusive bargaining agents of their members.[62] Once boards recognize unions, bargaining is limited to sessions with these exclusive bargaining agents.[63] In return, unions have the duty to represent all employees in good faith[64] during bargaining, even individuals who are not members who must pay so-called agency or representation fees.[65]

In order to avoid conflicts of interest, different bargaining units form around communities of interest such that teachers, typically referred to as professional staff, are in one unit, while other employees, usually referred to as classified staff, including office workers, maintenance staff, and the like, are in another. Managerial or administrative employees who work in personnel offices with information or others involved in bargaining are usually not permitted to form unions.[66] In fact, the Supreme Court of Nebraska decided that a union violated state law when it tried to include principals and supervisors in the same unit.[67]

Topics for bargaining are classified under three broad headings.[68] Mandatory topics include salaries and other terms and conditions of employment such as fringe benefits, sick days, and medical benefits. On the other hand, boards and unions are prohibited from bargaining on managerial prerogatives such as granting tenure,[69] creating school calendars,[70] and appointing principals[71] or department heads.[72] The third category, permissive topics, is most readily subject to judicial interpretation and includes such issues as drug testing,[73] the timing and effective dates of layoffs,[74] lump-sum payments for unused sick days,[75] and teacher requirements to take assessment tests before having their licenses renewed.[76]

Teacher evaluations highlight differences between substance and procedure. Whether, and by whom, evaluations are completed is often treated as policy matter excluded from bargaining.[77] While some courts treat the procedures used in the evaluation processes as subject to mandatory[78] bargaining, others view them as permissive.[79]

Although teachers clearly have the right to organize and bargain collectively in most states, questions arise over the extent to which school boards must allow unions to collect so-called fair share fees from non-members. Unions collect these fees in lieu of membership dues for the work they perform in bargaining on behalf of all employees, not just their members. The Supreme Court has addressed various aspects of this issue on four separate occasions in educational settings, restricting the unions in all of the cases.[80]

On another important topic, in *Perry Education Association v. Perry Local Educators' Association*,[81] the Supreme Court ruled that while a school board had to allow the representative of its employees access to its communication system, it did not have to make this available to a rival union that was seeking to replace the current representative. Three years later, in *Texas State Teachers Association v. Garland Independent School District*,[82] the Court affirmed that since a school board had not created either a public or limited public forum in its schools or mail facilities, denying a teacher organization access to them during school hours did not violate teachers' First Amendment rights since they had alternative means of communication available.

The ordinary means of redressing disputes relating to the administration of collective bargaining contracts is through grievances that, depending on state laws and local contracts, may pass through several stages before being subject to arbitration. Arbitration is properly used to denote the process whereby parties agree to be bound by the decision of a third party that they select. Insofar as arbitration is an alternative to judicial review, to the extent that courts are satisfied that arbitrators draw their judgments from the essence of the underlying bargaining agreements, more often than not they are content to leave the adjudications in place.

Arbitration differs from mediation, conciliation, fact-finding, or other forms of conflict resolution that do not culminate in legally binding outcomes. There is an important distinction between interest arbitration, which focuses on an agreement's terms, and rights or grievance arbitration that is concerned with a provision's application to an existing agreement. Grievance arbitration is common in both the public and private sectors. Including grievance arbitration clauses in bargaining contracts has spawned a great deal of litigation that is beyond the scope of this chapter.

A final form of dispute resolution occurs when contract negotiations break down and neither party is willing to compromise. At this point, the parties can declare an impasse[83] and, depending on the jurisdiction, proceed to mediation or fact-finding.[84] When breakdowns occur following the expiration of contracts, some courts agree that original agreements may be deemed to continue by the implied mutual assent of the parties,[85] while some,[86] but not all,[87] require boards to continue to pay step increases to employees.

Strikes are fairly common in the private sector. However, courts and legislatures ordinarily disapprove strikes by teachers. In the earliest case on this topic, the Supreme Court of Errors of Connecticut, although recognizing that educators had the right to bargain collectively, concluded that teacher strikes were illegal.[88] In addition to common law barriers against teacher strikes, courts overwhelmingly uphold statutory prohibitions against strikes[89] absent express legislative permission authorizing work stoppages.[90]

Courts can punish violations of orders to end strikes by placing unions and their leaders in contempt, even without jury trials.[91] If union officials violate court orders, they and their unions can be fined[92] and suffer the loss of dues "check-off" privileges.[93] Additionally, leaders can be imprisoned for contempt.[94] Teachers who participate in illegal strikes may face penalties including loss of pay,[95] having to reimburse boards for strike costs,[96] and dismissal.[97] However, the Supreme Court of Colorado affirmed that where a strike by public school teachers was legal, their board could not recover from them for tortious interference with their contracts between it and other teachers.[98]

Along with actual work stoppages, courts have also forbidden teachers from engaging in such activities as mass resignations[99] and absences to protest labor issues,[100] treating these as the equivalents of strikes. In a related concern, since unions have engaged in picketing as a form of protest when dealing with labor issues, the practice has generated litigation. If employees picket to induce breaches of contracts[101] or to obstruct government functions,[102] they can be restrained. Courts do not enjoin informational picketing unless it can be shown that it is likely to be disruptive.

Teacher Sanctions, Due Process, and Dismissals

Insofar as public school teachers can lose their jobs under two broad categories, namely not for cause, and for cause, this section examines legal issues surrounding dismissals.

Teacher Dismissal

Dismissal Not for Cause

Almost all states have statutes directly addressing the termination of teaching or other jobs in schools without fault on the part of individual employees, a practice commonly referred to as reduction-in-force (RIF). The grounds for RIF, the order in which employees are released, can "bump" others from their jobs, and call-back rights are matters of state law subject to modifications by board policies or collective bargaining agreements.

State laws typically permit RIFs due to declines in student enrollments, financial exigencies, elimination of jobs or programs, and board discretion. While courts ordinarily defer to the discretion of school boards on the need for RIFs, if challenged, officials must demonstrate that RIFs complied with state laws, board policies, or collective bargaining contracts. Courts also expect RIF policies to include descriptions of the criteria that boards use in selecting employees to be released, who makes the judgments, and how the criteria are weighed in implementing RIFs.

Once school boards decide to implement RIF of staff, they must establish the order of release. Insofar as RIFs are ordinarily based on seniority, courts typically treat seniority as a rational, but not exclusive, factor in selecting employees for RIF. Courts thus often interpret tenure statutes broadly as including seniority rights within the category of probationary employees, not just in tenured ranks. Additionally, courts have upheld board policies to rely on criteria such as race and gender as well as academic subject matter in high-demand areas, including science and mathematics, when implementing RIFs as long as they can demonstrate justifiable bases for acting, thereby granting protected individuals additional years of seniority in order to help them to preserve their jobs.

Courts place the burden of proving that positions are unnecessary on school officials when boards implement RIF. In evaluating seniority, absent modifications based on board polices or collective bargaining agreements, the first criterion is years of full-time service in the school system. Beyond that, the methods that boards rely on must be reasonable and not prohibited by state or federal law, such as dismissing individuals in such protected categories as race or gender.

By way of illustration, a case involving RIF, race, and seniority was days away from oral argument at the Supreme Court when the parties reached a settlement, thereby ending the litigation. At issue was a dispute from New Jersey wherein a school board, mistakenly believing that its affirmative action program required it to terminate the contract of a white, rather than an African American, teacher, due solely on race, dismissed the white woman even though the two had virtually identical credentials. The Third Circuit affirmed that since the RIF plan, which was adopted to promote racial diversity rather than remedy discrimination or its past effects in the district, violated the rights of non-minorities, it was unconstitutional.[103]

When tenured staff members are dismissed pursuant to RIFs, non-tenured employees usually can neither be retained nor may boards grant them the status of tenured staff. In other words, current employees who are about to have their jobs eliminated as part of RIFs are entitled to "bump" less senior staff members. "Bumping" is a term of art that makes it possible for employees with more seniority, and at least the same credentials, to retain the jobs for which they were certificated even if those positions are occupied by equally qualified staff members with less seniority.

Subject to board policies and collective bargaining agreements, RIF statutes usually stipulate that the jobs of certificated employees who have been released cannot be filled until they have first been offered their jobs back. State law, board policies, and bargaining contracts may even specify how much seniority individuals retain while on preferred eligibility, or call-back, lists. These laws, policies, and bargaining contracts may also specify how long former employees remain on preferred eligibility lists, typically for periods of two or three years, time frames that can be extended by bargaining agreements. Under preferred eligibility provisions, employees are usually called back to work in the order of seniority so that the first to be released from their jobs are usually the first to be called back.

Dismissal for Cause

Insofar as tenure statutes permit teacher contracts to continue without the express need for renewals, boards must follow specified procedures when they wish to dismiss tenured teachers. There are three basic elements in this form of due process: timely notice that dismissal is being contemplated, specification of charges, and hearings at which allegations are examined and judgments rendered on the records regarding teachers' future employment. Most statutes also include provisions for appeals that often result in judicial review.

Tenure statutes typically provide that tenured teachers may be dismissed only on specified grounds. Teachers who have not earned tenure can have their employment terminated for any lawful reason[104] without hearings.[105]

Conceding that states use a variety of terms for the same topics, the three sometimes-overlapping grounds for which teachers can be dismissed for cause are insubordination, which involves situations where teachers intentionally fail to comply with legitimate orders of supervisors or with valid rules and regulations of which they were, or reasonably should have been, aware; conduct unbecoming a professional, which increasingly has dealt with misconduct involving students; and incompetence, perhaps the most difficult of the three grounds to prove because teacher performance can be so difficult to measure.

State legislatures retain the authority to enumerate the grounds for which tenured teachers may be discharged. This means that local boards may not add reasons of their own choosing. Even so, most courts give broad interpretations to such words as incompetence, immorality, and conduct unbecoming a teacher.

Tenure statutes, local board policies, and collective bargaining agreements often require school officials to warn teachers before they initiate disciplinary actions for remediable offenses. Absent specific remediation provisions, boards are under no obligation to warn teachers and to offer them opportunities to correct their behavior.[106] When courts are convinced that misconduct can be corrected or punishments are disproportionate to offenses, they typically afford teachers opportunities to improve.

Procedural Due Process

In *Cleveland Board of Education v. Loudermill* (*Loudermill*),[107] the Supreme Court found that absent unusual circumstances, wherein they can be suspended with pay,[108] the Fourteenth Amendment requires school boards to provide educators who have property interests in their jobs, whether through tenure or unexpired contracts, to procedural due process, beginning with notice.[109] Depending on state law, tenured teachers are not necessarily entitled to full pre-termination hearings as long as they are afforded opportunities to have hearings after they are dismissed.[110]

Insofar as non-tenured teachers do not have the same property interests in their jobs and are not entitled to the same procedural protections as their tenured colleagues, it should not be surprising that jurisdictions have adopted statutes of varying degrees of specificity in creating due procedures dealing with the dismissals of teachers. Since the courts strictly enforce statutory due process rights, the failure of school boards to comply ordinarily renders adverse employment actions invalid.[111]

The Supreme Court's having not set a precise formula for due process in *Loudermill* aside, the heart of procedural due process is notice and a hearing at which teachers must have the chance to address the charges that they face.[112] Initial hearings are usually conducted by local school boards, hearing officers, or state administrative agencies. While hearings need not conform to strict judicial processes,[113] evidence that might not be admitted in court may be admissible as long as it does not violate the fundamentals of fair hearings.[114]

Notice

Teachers often challenge the adequacy of the notice that contains the charges they face. Teachers must be notified of all charges against them[115] with sufficient specificity,[116] including names, dates, facts, and other information that officials relied on in seeking to take adverse employment actions,[117] so that they can prepare responses.[118]

If charges against teachers involve a pattern of conduct, notice must include the time covered and specifics.[119] Officials must also afford teachers notice far enough in advance of disciplinary proceedings that they have adequate time to prepare defenses.[120] Thus, where state law required boards to give teachers written notice by a set date, the federal trial court in Vermont denied a board's motion for summary judgment where a non-tenured teacher claimed that the oral notice that she received almost two months late was insufficient to terminate her employment.[121]

To the extent that state statutes provide specifics with regard to notice, courts generally expect school officials to comply strictly with these requirements. When officials failed to comply with notice requirements, school employees have been reinstated as a matter of law[122] and may have been entitled to new contracts[123] or damages.[124] Where rights are limited by statute, such as when employees are placed on administrative leave,[125] where they engage in behavior that exceeds the limits of their employment,[126]or where they have other remedies available under collective bargaining agreements,[127] notice may not be required.

Hearings

Loudermill set the minimum requirements of due process that boards must provide teachers with property interests in their jobs before they can end their employment, noting that they are entitled to hearings of some sort before dismissal. The Court pointed out that informal hearings need not be elaborate since post-dismissal hearings should follow at which educators could present their cases.

Where statutes, contracts, or board policies call for pre-termination hearings, they must ordinarily precede individuals' removals from the payroll.[128] The absence of full adversarial pre-termination hearings does not per se invalidate board actions. Along with providing employees with appropriate notice of the charges that they face, board officials must present all of the evidence they relied on so that teachers can respond.[129] Although events are not automatically excluded from evidence if they occurred during previous school years, in order to be inadmissible, teachers must prove that the passage of time prejudiced their defenses such as when witnesses were unavailable or their memories were unclear.[130] If boards rely on past events, their notice must inform teachers of their intent to do so.[131]

Hearings may be open to the public or closed. At hearings, educators can question witnesses[132] and be assisted by counsel[133] but are not entitled to unlimited time to make their cases.[134] Boards must make particularized findings of fact based on a record[135] containing competent, probative, credible evidence.[136] While courts generally uphold administrative orders unless they are contrary to the manifest weight of evidence, there is an increasing judicial tendency to examine the evidence in cases involving adverse employment actions.

Insofar as some state statutes permit trials de novo to review dismissals and grant courts original jurisdiction, the adequacy of administrative hearings is not directly involved. Other statutes provide that although judicial review is of the record of hearings, courts are empowered to make additional inquiries or take additional testimony in their discretion.

As with notice requirements, if statutes or board policies prescribe details for conducting hearings, they must be strictly followed or they are likely to be rendered null and void. Pursuant to state statutory provisions or judicial orders,[137] when hearings are conducted before hearing officers rather than boards, teachers may be entitled to see, and respond to, reports before the meetings at which boards are to act.[138]

Emerging Issues

Perhaps the most significant emerging issue involving teachers concerns changes initiated by the No Child Left Behind Act,[139] an expansive and controversial federal statute that was enacted in 2002. Among the NLCB's more than three hundred pages, two sections in particular stand out: those on highly qualified teachers and accountability.

The NCLB and Highly Qualified Teachers

In requiring school boards to hire teachers who meet its "Highly Qualified Teacher (HQT)" mandate, the NCLB has not dramatically altered teacher preparation standards yet but has the potential to do so. Accordingly, the

NCLB divides teachers who must become HQTs into two groups, those new to the profession and those with experience.

New elementary school HQTs must meet two requirements. First, they must have at least a bachelor's degree. Second, they must demonstrate, by passing rigorous state, rather than federal, tests, that they have subject knowledge and teaching skills in reading, writing, mathematics, and other areas of basic elementary school curriculum.[140]

New middle and secondary HQTs must have at least a bachelor's degree and have demonstrated high levels of competency in each of the academic subjects in which they teach, either by passing rigorous state academic subject tests in each of the academic subjects they teach or by successfully completing, in each of the academic subjects they teach, academic majors, graduate degrees, course work equivalent to undergraduate academic majors, or advanced certifications in credentialing.[141]

The NCLB requires experienced teachers to have at least a bachelor's degree, meet the requirements for those new to the profession, and pass rigorous state tests or demonstrate competence in all academic subjects in which they teach. These competencies must be based on high objective uniform standards that are set by states for grade-appropriate academic subject matter knowledge and teaching skills; must be aligned with challenging state academic content and student academic achievement standards that have been developed in consultation with core content specialists, teachers, and administrators; must be created to offer objective, coherent information about individuals' attainment of content knowledge in the subjects in which they teach; must be applied uniformly to all in the same academic subject and grade level throughout states; must take into consideration the time teachers have been teaching in their academic subjects; must be made available to the public on request; and may involve multiple, objective measures of competency.[142]

As applied to special education teachers, the HQT provisions require school officials to "take measurable steps to recruit, hire, train, and retain highly qualified school personnel to provide special education and related services"[143] for students with disabilities; similar requirements apply to personnel who deliver related services and for paraprofessionals.[144] In order to be classified as HQT, subject area teachers must not only be certified fully in special education or pass state-designed special education licensure examinations but must also possess bachelor's degrees and demonstrate knowledge of each subject for which they are the primary instructors.[145]

Under the provisions relating to special education, which apply the same deadlines as for regular teachers,[146] then currently employed special education teachers were required to meet the standards even if they teach multiple subjects.[147] New special education teachers have until up to two years after they are hired to become HQTs in different subjects as long as they are fully certificated in at least one.[148]

Accountability

The accountability provisions in the NCLB do not have a direct impact on individual teachers but have the possibility of creating significant legal controversy. Under the NCLB, in the event that local schools fail to meet the law's requirement of annual yearly progress (AYP), which makes states and local school systems more accountable for student progress, the employment status of teachers could be in jeopardy.

If schools fail to meet their AYP goals, then significant accountability measures come into play. In schools that fail to meet their goals for two consecutive years, officials must develop a comprehensive plan with support from the state and or local education agencies.[149] In the most draconian option, in schools that serve children who are most at risk and that fail to reach AYP for two consecutive years, parents must be given the option of transferring their children to another school within the system.[150]

Second, parents must be informed that their children are entitled to state-approved supplemental educational services such as after-school or weekend tutoring;[151] these services can also be provided by private contractors rather than public school teachers. While neither of these options has yet to be applied, they would likely create considerable legal challenges, especially where teachers have acquired tenure, since such provisions would interfere with their pre-existing contracts.

Conclusion

As the environment in schools continues to evolve with the advent of charter and online schools, it will be interesting to observe how these reforms impact the rights of teachers. While the statutory rights of teachers are likely to remain unaffected, such major structural changes may influence the terms and conditions of teacher employment, meaning that this will certainly be an area to watch in coming years.

Notes

1. 347 U.S. 483 (1954).
2. Chief Justice John Roberts' *2007 Year-End Report on the Federal Judiciary* revealed that the total number of cases filed in the United States Supreme Court

increased from 8,521 filings in the 2005 term to 8,857 filings in the 2006 term—an increase of 4%. http://www.supremecourtus.gov/publicinfo/year-end/2007year-endreport.pdf

3. *Montgomery County Bd. of Educ. v. Messer*, 79 S.W.2d 224 (Ky. 1935).

4. *Cowen v. Harrison County Bd. of Educ.*, 465 S.E.2d 648 (W. Va. 1995).

5. 440 U.S. 194 (1979).

6. *Meyer v. Nebraska*, 262 U.S. 390 (1923).

7. See, e.g., *Leetham v. McGinn*, 524 P.2d 323 (Utah 1974); *Connecticut Educ. Ass'n v. Tirozzi*, 554 A.2d 1065 (Conn. 1989).

8. *Dauer v. Department of Educ.*, 874 A.2d 159 (Pa. Commw. Ct. 2005).

9. 441 U.S. 68, 76 (1979).

10. *Chang v. Glynn County Sch. Dist.*, 457 F. Supp.2d 1378 (S.D, Ga. 2006).

11. *Gough v. State*, 667 A.2d 1057 (N.J. Super. Ct. App. Div.1995).

12. *Wardwell v. Board of Educ. of City Sch. Dist. of City of Cincinnati*, 529 F.2d 625 (6th Cir. 1976); *Mogle v. Sevier County Sch. Dist.*, 540 F.2d 478 (10th Cir. 1976), *cert. denied*, 429 U.S. 1121 (1977); *Providence Teachers' Union Local 958 v. City Council of City of Providence*, 888 A.2d 948 (R.I. 2005).

13. *Sullivan v. River Valley Sch. Dist.*, 197 F.3d 804 (6th Cir. 1999), *cert. denied*, 530 U.S. 1262 (2000).

14. Courts typically uphold teacher competence examinations in the face of challenges. See, e.g., *United States v. State of S.C.*, 445 F. Supp. 1094 (D.S.C. 1977), *aff'd, sub nom. National Educ. Ass'n v. United States*, 434 U.S. 1026 (1978); *State v. Project Principle*, 724 S.W.2d 387 (Tex. 1987); *Association of Mexican-American Educators v. State of Cal.*, 231 F.3d 572 (9th Cir. 2000); *Allen v. Alabama State Bd. of Educ.*, 164 F.3d 1347 (11th Cir. 1999), *vacated*, 216 F.3d 1263 (11th Cir. 2000).

15. *Keller v. Hewitt*, 41 P. 871 (Cal. 1895); *State ex rel. Hopkins v. Wooster*, 208 P. 656 (Kan. 1922).

16. *State ex rel. Johnson v. Matzen*, 210 N.W. 151 (Neb. 1926).

17. *Bhatt v. New York State Educ. Dep't*, 843 N.Y.S.2d 737 (N.Y. App. Div. 2007).

18. *Tinker v. Des Moines Indep. Sch. Dist.*, 393 U.S. 503, 506 (1969).

19. 479 U.S. 60 (1986).

20. According to Title VII of Civil Rights Act of 1964, 42 U.S.C.A. § 2000e–2(a):

(a) Employer practices

It shall be an unlawful employment practice for an employer—

(1) to fail or refuse to hire or to discharge any individual, or otherwise to discriminate against any individual with respect to his compensation, terms, conditions, or privileges of employment, because of such individual's race, color, religion, sex, or national origin; or

(2) to limit, segregate, or classify his employees or applicants for employment in any way which would deprive or tend to deprive any individual of employment opportunities or otherwise adversely affect his status as an employee, because of such individual's race, color, religion, sex, or national origin.

Title VII does allow religiously affiliated non-public schools to impose special requirements for employees such as requiring them to be members of the faiths that maintain the institutions and to live in accord with their doctrinal precepts.

21. Although it is beyond the scope of this chapter, Title VII also provides extensive protection for employment discrimination against women in educational settings.

22. For a similar case, see *Bynum v. Fort Worth Indep. Sch. Dist.*, 41 F. Supp.2d 641 (N.D. Tex. 1999), rejecting a teacher's claim that he should not have been dismissed for refusing to work at least one weekend per month based on his religious beliefs where the board proved that requiring other employees to work in his place would have imposed an undue hardship on it.

23. *Maine-Endwell Teachers' Ass'n v. Board of Educ.*, 771 N.Y.S.2d 246 (N.Y. App. Div. 2004).

24. *Tucker v. California Dep't of Educ.*, 97 F.3d 1204 (9th Cir. 1996).

25. *Sharif v. Buck*, 338 F. Supp.2d 435 (W.D.N.Y. 2004).

26. *Peloza v. Capistrano Unified Sch. Dist.*, 37 F.3d 517 (9th Cir. 1994), *cert. denied*, 515 U.S. 1173 (1995).

27. *LeVake v. Independent Sch. Dist. No. 656*, 625 N.W.2d 502 (Minn. Ct. App. 2001), *review denied* (2001), *cert. denied*, 534 U.S. 1081 (2002).

28. *Helland v. South Bend Community Sch. Corp.*, 93 F.3d 327 (7th Cir. 1996).

29. See also *Williams v. Vidmar*, 367 F. Supp.2d 1265 (N.D. Cal. 2005), which largely rejected the claims of an elementary school teacher who alleged that officials violated his rights by not permitting him to use supplemental classroom materials with religious content and talking about religion with his students.

30. *Hysong v. School Dist. of Gallitzin Borough*, 30 A. 482 (Pa. 1894). For a similar case, see *Rawlings v. Butler*, 290 S.W.2d 801 (Ky. 1956).

31. *Commonwealth v. Herr*, 78 A. 68 (Pa. 1910). For a similar result, *see O'Connor v. Hendrick*, 77 N.E. 612 (N.Y. 1906); *Zellers v. Huff*, 236 P.2d 949 (N.M. 1951).

32. *Cooper v. Eugene Sch. Dist. No. 4J*, 723 P.2d 298 (Or. 1986), *appeal dismissed*, 480 U.S. 942 (1987).

33. See also *Mississippi Employment Securities Comm'n v. McGlothin*, 556 So. 2d 324 (Miss. 1990), *cert. denied*, 498 U.S. 879 (1990), holding that officials could not dismiss a teacher who was a member of the African Hebrew Israelites out of Ethiopia faith for insubordination when she wore a religious head wrap to school. But see *United States v. Board of Educ. for Sch. Dist. of Philadelphia*, 911 F.2d 882 (3d Cir. 1990), rejecting the claim of a female Muslim teacher who adhered to the religious conviction that she should, when in public, cover her entire body except face and hands.

34. *Downing v. West Haven Bd. of Educ.*, 162 F. Supp.2d 19 (D. Conn. 2001).

35. *Nichol v. ARIN Intermediate Unit 28*, 268 F. Supp.2d 536 (W.D. Pa. 2003).

36. 391 U.S. 563 (1968).

37. 429 U.S. 274 (1977).

38. *Doyle v. Mt. Healthy City Sch. Dist. Bd. of Educ.*, 670 F.2d 59 (6th Cir. 1982).

39. 439 U.S. 410 (1979).

40. 461 U.S. 138 (1983).

41. 511 U.S. 661 (1994).

42. 547 U.S. 410(2006).

43. *Johnsen v. Independent Sch. Dist. No. 3 of Tulsa County*, 891 F.2d 1485 (10th Cir. 1989).

44. *Harris v. Victoria Indep. Sch. Dist.*, 168 F.3d 216 (5th Cir. 1999), *reh'g and reh'g en banc denied*, 336 F.3d 343 (5th Cir. 1999), *cert. denied*, 528 U.S. 1022 (1999).

45. *Calvit v. Minneapolis Pub. Schs.*, 122 F.3d 1112 (8th Cir. 1997).

46. *Labalokie v. Capital Area Intermediate Unit*, 926 F. Supp. 503 (M.D. Pa. 1996).

47. *Kirchmann v. Lake Elsinore Unified Sch. Dist.*, 67 Cal. Rptr. 2d 268 (Cal. Ct. App. 1997).

48. *Ryan v. Shawnee Mission U.S.D. 512*, 416 F. Supp.2d 1090 (D. Kan. 2006).

49. *Peres v. Oceanside Union Free Sch. Sch. Dist.*, 209 F. Supp.2d 15 (E.D.N.Y. 2006).

50. *Burkybile v. Board of Educ. of Hastings-On-Hudson Union Free Sch.*, 411 F.3d 306 (2d Cir. 2005), *cert. denied*, 126 S. Ct. 801 (2005).

51. *Vukadinovich v. Board of Sch. Trustees of Michigan City Area Schs.*, 978 F.2d 403 (7th Cir. 1992), *cert. denied*, 510 U.S. 844 (1993).

52. *Cliff v. Board of Sch. Commr's of City of Indianapolis*, 42 F.3d 403 (7th Cir. 1994).

53. *Padilla v. South Harrison R-II Sch. Dist.*, 181 F.3d 992 (8th Cir. 1999), *reh'g and reh'g en banc denied*, 192 F.3d 805 (8th Cir. 1999); *Alba v. Ansonia Bd. of Educ.*, 999 F. Supp. 687 (D. Conn. 1998).

54. *Lancaster v. Independent Sch. Dist. No. 5*, 149 F.3d 1228 (10th Cir. 1998).

55. *Fales v. Garst*, 235 F.3d 1122, 1124 (8th Cir. 2001).

56. *Wallace v. School Bd. of Orange County*, 41 F. Supp.2d 1321 (M.D. Fla. 1998).

57. *McCullough v. Wyandanch Union Free Sch. Dist.*, 187 F.3d 272 (2d Cir. 1999), *on remand*, 132 F. Supp.2d 87 (E.D.N.Y. 2001).

58. *Williams v. Dallas Indep. Sch. Dist.*, 480 F.3d 689 (5th Cir. 2007).

59. *Mayer v. Monroe County Community Sch. Corp.*, 474 F.3d 477 (7th Cir. 2007).

60. *Texas State Teachers Ass'n v. Garland Indep. Sch. Dist.*, 784 F.2d 1113 (5th Cir. 1986), *aff'd*, 479 U.S. 801 (1986).

61. *Stellmaker v. DePetrillo*, 710 F. Supp. 891 (D. Conn. 1989).

62. *Appeal of Londonderry Sch. Dist.*, 707 A.2d 137 (N.H. 1998).

63. *Independence-Nat'l Educ. Ass'n v. Independence Sch. Dist.*, 162 S.W.3d 18 (Mo. Ct. App. 2005), *transfer denied* (2005), *on subsequent appeal*, 223 S.W.3d 131 (Mo. 2007).

64. See, e.g., *Leer v. Washington Educ. Ass'n*, 172 F.R.D. 439 (W.D. Wash. 1997); *Fratus v. Marion Community Schools Bd. of Trustees*, 749 N.E.2d 40 (Ind. 2001).

65. *O'Brien v. City of Springfield*, 319 F. Supp.2d 90 (D. Mass. 2003).

66. *Barrington Sch. Comm. v. Rhode Island State Labor Relations Bd.*, 608 A.2d 1126 (R.I. 1992); *Chicago Teachers Union v. Illinois Educ. Labor Relations Bd.*, 695 N.E.2d 1332 (Ill. App. Ct. 1998).

67. *Papillion/La Vista Schs. Principals and Supervisors Org. v. Papillion/LaVista Dist. No. 27*, 562 N.W.2d 335 (Neb. 1997).

68. See *Colonial Sch. Bd. v. Colonial Affiliate, NCCEA/DSEA/NEA*, 449 A.2d 243 (Del. Super. Ct. 1982).

69. *Cohoes City Sch. Dist. v. Cohoes Teachers Ass'n*, 390 N.Y.S.2d 53 (N.Y. 1976); *Mindemann v. Independent Sch. Dist. No. 6 of Caddo County*, 771 P.2d 996 (Okla. 1989).

70. *Kenai Peninsula Borough Sch. Sch. Dist. v. Kenai Peninsula Educ. Ass'n*, 572 P.2d 416 (Alaska 1977); *Public Employee Relations Bd. v. Washington Teachers' Union Local 6*, 556 A.2d 206 (D.C. 1989).

71. *Berkshire Hills Reg'l Sch. Dist. Comm. v. Berkshire Hills Educ. Ass'n*, 377 N.E.2d 940 (Mass. 1978).

72. *Maine Sch. Admin. Dist. No. 61 Bd. of Dirs. v. Lake Region Teachers Ass'n*, 567 A.2d 77 (Me. 1989).

73. *Drivers, Chauffeurs and Helpers Local Union No. 639 v. District of Columbia*, 631 A.2d 1205 (D.C. 1993).

74. *West Bend Educ. Ass'n v. Wisconsin Employment Relations Comm'n*, 357 N.W.2d 534 (Wis. 1984).

75. *Perrenod v. Liberty Bd. of Educ. for Liberty Cent. Sch. Dist.*, 636 N.Y.S.2d 210 (N.Y. App. Div. 1996).

76. *Massachusetts Fed'n of Teachers v. Board of Educ.*, 767 N.E.2d 549 (Mass. 2002).

77. *Bethlehem Township Bd. of Educ. v. Bethlehem Township Educ. Ass'n*, 449 A.2d 1254 (N.J. 1982).

78. *Arlington Community Sch. Dist. v. Iowa Pub. Employment Relations Bd.*, 392 N.W.2d 495 (Iowa 1986); *City of Beloit by Beloit City School Bd. v. Wisconsin Employment Relations Comm'n*, 242 N.W.2d 231 (Wis. 1976).

79. In *re Pittsfield School Dist.*, 744 A.2d 594 (N.H. 1999).

80. *Abood v. Detroit Board of Educ.*, 431 U.S. 209 (1977); *Chicago Teachers Union, Local No. 1, AFT, AFL-CIO v. Hudson*, 475 U.S. 292 (1986), *on remand*, 922 F.2d 1306 (7th Cir. 1991), *cert. denied*, 501 U.S. 1230 (1991); *Lehnert v. Ferris Faculty Ass'n*, 500 U.S. 507 (1991); *Davenport v. Washington Educ. Ass'n*, 127 S. Ct. 2372 (2007).

81. 460 U.S. 37 (1983), *on remand*, 705 F.2d 462 (7th Cir. 1983).

82. 784 F.2d 1113 (5th Cir.1986), *aff'd*, 479 U.S. 801 (1986).

83. For cases discussing impasse, see, e.g., *Mountain Valley Educ. Ass'n v. Maine Sch. Admin. Dist. No. 43*, 655 A.2d 348 (Me. 1995); *State ex rel. Boggs v. Springfield Local Sch. Dist. Bd. of Educ.*, 694 N.E.2d 1346 (Ohio 1998).

84. See, e.g., Ohio Rev. Code Ann. 4117.14 (C) for an example of a statute dealing with breakdowns in bargaining.

85. *State ex rel. Boggs v. Springfield Local Sch. Dist. Bd. of Educ.*, 757 N.E.2d 339 (Ohio 2001), *reconsideration denied*, 761 N.E.2d 49 (Ohio 2002).

86. *Board of Trustees of Univ. of Me. Sys. v. Associated Colt Staff of Univ. of Me. Sys.*, 659 A.2d 842 (Me. 1995).

87. *Board of Educ. of Township of Neptune in County of Monmouth v. Neptune Township Educ. Ass'n*, 675 A.2d 611 (N.J. 1996).

88. *Norwalk Teachers' Ass'n v. Board of Educ.*, 83 A.2d 482 (Conn. 1951).

89. *Anchorage Educ. Ass'n v. Anchorage Schl. Dist.*, 648 P.2d 993 (Alaska 1982); *Warwick School Comm. v. Warwick Teachers' Union, Local 915*, 613 A.2d 1273 (R.I. 1992).

90. *Jefferson County Bd. of Educ. v. Jefferson County Educ. Ass'n*, 393 S.E.2d 653 (W.Va. 1990).

91. *Rankin v. Shanker*, 295 N.Y.S.2d 625 (N.Y. 1968).

92. *Wilmington Fed'n of Teachers v. Howell*, 374 A.2d 832 (Del. 1977); *Labor Relations Comm'n v. Fall River Educ. Ass'n*, 416 N.E.2d 1340 (Mass. 1981).

93. *Buffalo Teachers Fed'n v. Helsby*, 676 F.2d 28 (2d Cir. 1982).

94. In *re Block*, 236 A.2d 589 (N.J. 1967).

95. *Head v. Special Sch. Dist. No. 1*, 182 N.W.2d 887 (Minn. 1970), *cert. denied*, 404 U.S. 886 (1971); *Board of Educ. of Marshallton–McKean Sch. Dist. v. Sinclair*, 373 A.2d 572 (Del. 1977).

96. *Passaic Township Bd. of Educ. v. Passaic Township Educ. Ass'n*, 536 A.2d 1276 (N.J. Super. Ct. App. Div. 1987).

97. *Hortonville Joint School District No. 1 v. Hortonville Education Ass'n*, 426 U.S. 482 (1976).

98. *Martin v. Montezuma–Cortez Sch. Dist. RE-1*, 841 P.2d 237 (Colo. 1992).

99. *Board of Educ. of the City of N.Y. v. Shanker*, 286 N.Y.S.2d 453 (N.Y. App. Div. 1967).

100. *Pruzan v. Board of Educ. of City of N.Y.*, 217 N.Y.S.2d 86 (N.Y. 1961).

101. *Board of Educ. of Martins Ferry City Sch. Dist. v. Ohio Educ. Ass'n*, 235 N.E.2d 538 (Ohio Common Pleas. 1967).

102. *State v. Heath*, 177 N.W.2d 751 (N.D. 1970).

103. *Taxman v. Board of Educ. of the Township of Piscataway*, 91 F.3d 1547 (3d Cir. 1996), *cert. granted*, 521 U.S. 1117 (1997), *cert. dismissed*, 522 U.S. 1010 (1997).

104. *Haviland v. Yonkers Pub. Schools*, 800 N.Y.S.2d 578 (N.Y. App. Div. 2005).

105. *Von Gizycki v. Levy*, 771 N.Y.S.2d 174 (N.Y. App. Div. 2004).

106. *Roberts v. Lincoln County Sch. Dist. No. One*, 676 P.2d 577 (Wyo. 1984).

107. 470 U.S. 532 (1985), *on remand*, 763 F.2d 202 (6th Cir. 1985), *on remand*, 651 F. Supp. 92 (N.D. Ohio 1986), *aff'd*, 844 F.2d 304 (6th Cir. 1988), *cert. denied*, 488 U.S. 941 (1988), *cert. denied*, 488 U.S. 946 (1988).

108. See *Bauman v. Board of Educ. of Watkins Glen Cent. Sch. Dist.*, 800 N.Y.S.2d 461 (N.Y. App. Div. 2005).

109. See, e.g., *Tweedall v. Fritz*, 987 F. Supp. 1126 (S.D. Ind. 1997), judging that one-day notice was sufficient where a teacher was accused of touching students inappropriately).

110. See, e.g., *Baird v. Board of Educ. for Warren Community Unit Sch. Dist.*, 389 F.3d 685 (7th Cir. 2004).

111. *Jackson v. El Dorado Sch. Dist.*, 48 S.W.3d 558 (Ark. Ct. App. 2001); *Neshaminy Fed'n of Teachers v. Neshaminy Sch. Dist.*, 462 A.2d 629 (Pa. 1983).

112. *Bertolini v. Whitehall City Sch. Dist. Bd. of Educ.*, 744 N.E.2d 1245 (Ohio Ct. App. 2000), *stay denied*, 739 N.E.2d 817 (Ohio 2000), *appeal not allowed*, 742 N.E.2d 146 (Ohio 2001); *Post v. Salem-Keizer Sch. Dist.*, 45 P.3d 116 (Or. 2002).

113. *Knox County Bd. of Educ. v. Willis*, 405 S.W.2d 952 (Ky. 1966); *Cope v. Board of Educ. of Town of W. Hartford*, 495 A.2d 718 (Conn. Ct. App. 1985).

114. *Carangelo v. Ambach*, 515 N.Y.S.2d 665 (N.Y. App. Div. 1987), *appeal denied*, 522 N.Y.S.2d 109 (N.Y. 1987).

115. *Clark County Sch. Dist. v. Riley*, 14 P.3d 22 (Nev. 2000).

116. *Washington v. Independent Sch. Dist. No. 625*, 590 N.W.2d 655 (Minn. Ct. App. 1999).

117. *Blackburn v. Board of Educ. of Breckinridge County*, 564 S.W.2d 35 (Ky. Ct. App. 1978).

118. *Cliff v. Board of Sch. Commrs of City of Indianapolis*, 42 F.3d 403 (7th Cir. 1994), *reh'g and suggestion for reh'g en banc denied*, 42 F.3d 403 (7th Cir. 1994); *Rubin v. Lafayette Parish Sch. Bd.*, 649 So. 2d 1003 (La. Ct. App. 1994), *writ denied*, 654 So. 2d 351 (La. 1995).

119. *Allen v. Texarkana Pub. Schs.*, 794 S.W.2d 138 (Ark. 1990).

120. *Clark County Sch. Dist. v. Riley*, 14 P.3d 22 (Nev. 2000).

121. *Latouche v. North Country Union High Sch. Dist.*, 131 F. Supp.2d 568 (D. Vt. 2001).

122. *Morrison v. Board of Educ. of Weatherford Pub. Schs.*, 47 P.3d 888 (Okla. Ct. Civ. App. 2002).

123. *State ex rel. Chapnick v. East Cleveland City Sch. Dist. Bd. of Educ.*, 755 N.E.2d 883 (Ohio 2001).

124. *McDaniel v. Princeton City Sch. Dist. Bd. of Educ.*, 45 Fed.Appx. 354 (6th Cir. 2002).

125. *Pavlik v. Chinle Unified Sch. Dist. No. 24*, 985 P.2d 633 (Ariz. Ct. App. Div. 1999).

126. *McGehee v. DePoyster*, 708 So. 2d 77 (Miss. 1998).

127. *Rich v. Montpelier Supervisory Dist. (Rich)*, 709 A.2d 501 (Vt. 1998).

128. *Vanelli v. Reynolds Sch. Dist. No. 7*, 667 F.2d 773 (9th Cir. 1982).

129. *Haddock v. Board of Educ., Unified Sch. Dist. No. 462, Cowley County*, 661 P.2d 368 (Kan. 1983).

130. *Tomczik v. State Tenure Comm'n*, 438 N.W.2d 642 (Mich. Ct. App. 1989).

131. *Allen v. Texarkana Pub. Schs.*, 794 S.W.2d 138 (Ark. 1990).

132. *Gibson v. Caruthersville Sch. Dist. No. 8*, 336 F.3d 768 (8th Cir. 2003).

133. *Coleman v. Reed*, 147 F.3d 751 (8th Cir. 1998).

134. *Halpern v. Board of Educ. of City of Bristol*, 703 A.2d 1144 (Conn. 1997), *cert. denied*, 523 U.S. 1138 (1998).

135. *Harmon v. Mifflin County Sch. Dist.*, 713 A.2d 620 (Pa. 1998); *Barnett v. Board of Educ. of Town of Fairfield*, 654 A.2d 720 (Conn. 1995).

136. *Jones v. Sully Buttes Schs.*, 340 N.W.2d 697 (S.D. 1983).

137. *Winston v. Board of Educ. of Borough of S. Plainfield*, 309 A.2d 89 (N.J. Super. Ct. App. Div. 1973), *aff'd*, 319 A.2d 226 (N.J. 1974); *Powell v. Brown*, 238 S.E.2d 220 (W.Va. 1977).

138. *Buck v. Board of Educ. of City of N.Y.*, 553 F.2d 315 (2d Cir. 1977), *cert. denied*, 438 U.S. 904 (1978).

139. 20 U.S.C.A. §§ 6301 *et seq.* For a more thorough discussion of this law, see C. Daniel Raisch & Charles J. Russo (2006), "The No Child Left Behind Act: Federal Over-Reaching or Necessary Educational Reform?" *Education Law Journal, Vol. 7, No. 4*, 255–65.

140. 20 U.S.C.A. § 7801(23)(B)(i).

141. 20 U.S.C.A. § 7801(23)(B)(ii).

142. 20 U.S.C.A. § 7801(23)(C).

143. 20 U.S.C.A. § 1412(a)(14)(C)(D).

144. 20 U.S.C.A. § 1412(a)(14)(B).

145. 20 U.S.C.A. § 1402(10)(B).

146. 20 U.S.C.A. § 1412(a)(14)(C).
147. 20 U.S.C.A. § 1402(10)(D)(ii).
148. 20 U.S.C.A. § 1402(10)(D)(iii).
149. 20 U.S.C.A. §§ 6316(b)(1)(A), (c)(4).
150. 20 U.S.C.A. § 6316(b)(5)(A).
151. 20 U.S.C.A. § 6316(b)(5)(B).

15

Analysis and Reflections

Jan DeGroof and Charles J. Russo

In various national and international legal instruments, the right to education is recognised and generally accepted as a universal fundamental right in society. Respect for basic rights is a long-established tenet in most countries. Worldwide, there is already a considerable catalogue of measures which concern teachers. Attention is increasingly focused on teachers' rights. In all the countries covered in this book, teachers have clearly established rights that, to a large extent, provide them with strong protection in varying degrees and areas.

At first sight, the countries addressed in this book seem to live up to the obligations imposed by the national governments or decentralised public authorities such as provinces or states. At the same time, educational policy is considered mainly an area of national, public concern, regardless of whether it is dealt with centrally at the national level, as it is in most of the countries discussed in this book, or at the provincial–state level, as in Canada and the United States. The fundamental role of teachers is thus rightly seen as "complementary" to that of their governments that are in charge of public service.

The various international instruments that were reviewed in Chapter 1 are legally binding in various degrees in the countries examined in this book. These instruments grant teachers a number of rights which are explicitly recognised and confirmed by formal ratification.

In all of the countries reviewed in this book, the rights of teachers have been ensured for at least the last decade, and typically much longer, by legislation through, for instance, administrative, employment, federal, provincial, and special acts relating to education; by state laws; and by means of employment agreements, regardless of whether they are collective, and policies of local educational agencies or boards. To this end, there is a clear desire to guide transitions, via the teachers' functions, toward democracy and participation, protecting teachers from discrimination on such grounds as religion, race, and culture. In fact, laws in such countries as Canada, Germany, the Netherlands, and the United States are particularly clear in this regard.

Education is often regarded as a sovereign task. Accordingly, teachers generally have the status of civil servants. Teachers also have different rights, depending on whether they work in private schools, where their rights are based primarily on contract rather than public law. While these rights and duties often differ according to employment in private or public schools, there is typically a strong aspiration to achieve equality and equal legal protection in most countries.

Internal evaluation frameworks of teachers comply with quality standards. This means that teachers are required to display high standards of competence and performance. Teachers are evaluated on their professional competency, job performance, skills, and attitudes. As in most countries, since teacher education varies according to the level of one's education, evaluation must be adjusted accordingly.

In Belgium and France, for example, state inspectors evaluate teachers in both public and private schools. In Germany, internal and external evaluations have yet to be developed; this stands in stark contrast to nations such as Singapore and, to a lesser extent, the United States, where teachers, or at least those who have not acquired tenure, are supervised regularly. In the Netherlands, when there is a conflict between teachers and school boards concerning assessments of teachers' competence, absent clear indications that individuals acted against formal and procedural regulations or that their decisions are not evidently arbitrary, courts typically assume that they acted correctly. In some countries, teacher evaluations are increasingly oriented toward evaluation by students, especially in higher education institutions.

Governments impose specific tasks on teachers while stipulating the prerequisites for employment. In general, applicants must be of good character, be fit to be teachers, conduct themselves in a way upholding the integrity of the public service, and possess the required competences, knowledge, skills, and attitudes. Governments, as the employers of teachers, respect human rights thanks to prohibitions against discrimination based on gender, race, ethnicity, disability, age, political engagements, religion, and other grounds. Of course, these prohibitions protect both teachers and students.

In New Zealand, the Teachers' Council may take into account relevant matters when evaluating whether applicants are satisfactorily prepared to teach. However, they must take applicants' qualifications into consideration. As such, the Teachers' Council is empowered to make regulations with regard to teacher misconduct or incompetence. In order to guarantee the neutral character of state education, the competent government agencies in New Zealand (and elsewhere) prescribe regulations on the qualifications which teaching staff must fulfill.

It is striking that in some countries, including South Africa, schools employ only teachers who are registered with the appropriate national agencies and hold certificates for teaching positions. In New Zealand, like many states in the United States, teachers must maintain, or update, their practising certificates while they are employed. In New Zealand, for example, teachers must renew their certificates every three years. In Singapore, the "Education Act" sets out the conditions for teacher registration; it also governs the regulations concerning, among other things, school staff and teacher qualifications to ensure a good standard of teaching. Individuals who wish to teach in Canadian public schools also need teaching certificates, licenses, or other type of teacher accreditation. The same applies for teachers in South Africa.

In Singapore, individuals who lack teaching qualifications can apply for jobs as teachers. These applicants then must complete a special training course under strict conditions. Whenever qualified teachers are unavailable, the Canadian Ministry of Education has the power to grant temporary licenses on an exigency basis. In the United States, individual states and local school boards can grant emergency licenses and certifications to deal with teacher shortages subject to a variety of conditions.

In England and Wales, legally qualified teachers also receive registrations, while individuals who lack qualifications are allowed to teach in certain circumstances. Moreover, England and Wales permit teachers to be employed by teacher supply agencies. These teachers do not have contracts of employment that entitle them to the rights of teachers under government-controlled contracts in public and private schools and can be employed other than under contracts of employment. While this is often the case for short-term cover in England and Wales, these teachers have far fewer legal rights, and they cannot easily stand for their rights.

Public school teachers in Brazil can be admitted only through qualifying examinations which entitle them to tenured positions after three years, a length that is similar to the probationary status of most public school teachers in the United States. The promotion of teachers in Malaysia is subject to their successfully passing of examinations; they must also have completed probationary periods of one to three years.

Established teachers in France, as civil servants, are recruited by competitive examinations that allow them to prove that they have the appropriate educational qualifications. In addition, non-established teachers in France are recruited by contracts for set periods of time, while doctoral candidates can gain experience for their subsequent careers by giving educational guidance to students. German applicants must first pass state teacher examinations and, after two years, they must pass an additional examination. In China, graduation from a specialised teacher education program is not a prerequisite to obtain a teacher licenses, and individuals who have not obtained the required teacher education might receive licenses after passing teacher qualification tests.

Insofar as most teachers in Singapore are civil servants, the terms and conditions of their employment are incorporated in the contracts they sign with the government. Teachers who are employed in China also work under contracts that they sign with their schools. The rights of public school teachers in Malaysia are grounded in contracts which, for instance, bind them to teach for periods of five years after graduation. Teachers in Malaysia can be offered permanent positions after three years.

If school officials in Belgium demand commitments from their teachers with respect to specific educational projects, they must be part of their contractual commitment declarations. In Brazil, the careers, salaries, professional status, and benefits of public school teachers are established by law, not by contract, but the parties must reach a mutual agreement on a voluntary and equal basis.

Contracts in Brazil contain some required components, such as their length, descriptions of the teaching positions and their responsibilities, working conditions, and possibilities for contract modification, renewal, termination, and violations. If school officials in Brazil do not approve teachers' resignations, then employees can still terminate their contracts after working for six additional months.

Teachers in private schools in France are under partnership contracts with the State, some of which are totally independent of the State while others are in public law situations, even though school officials have great powers of control and decision over the activities of teachers. As in Belgium and the United States, the State in France cannot impose the appointments of teachers to non-governmental or private schools. When public school teachers in France are engaged under permanent contracts, they are, in a way, protected, but they do not benefit from the same security of employment or from pension regulations as civil servants. Contractual teachers in private schools in France that operate under partnership contracts have the same rights as public teachers regarding working conditions, social benefits, and training opportunities as far as they are equally qualified. The training and conditions of employment of private school teachers in Germany may not be inferior to that of teachers in public schools.

In Dutch primary and secondary schools as well as in institutions for vocational training, teachers must have diplomas testifying that they address expected requirements. More specifically, these teachers must demonstrate pedagogical–didactic knowledge, insight, and competences as well as professional competence; these requirements are further defined in a governmental decree.

There is a legal distinction between the treatment of part-time or fixed-term contracts and full-time or permanent contracts in England and Wales; these contracts contain detailed provisions on duties and working time. In China, attention focuses on transfers from permanent placement of teachers toward employment on the basis of contracts. A far-reaching restriction on teachers' basic rights is to be found in German private schools, where contracts may restrict the rights of their teachers.

A novel approach has appeared in New Zealand, where officials introduced a *Code of Ethics* which stipulates teachers' obligations to society. The Code also asks teachers to support policies and programmes which promote equality of opportunity for all, to work collegially to develop schools and centres which model democratic ideals, to teach these widely accepted values, and to encourage learners to apply them and critically appreciate their significance. In a certain way, this can be seen as an instrument used by the authorities to guide society. In Singapore, teachers, as civil servants, are expected to act within the policies governing public officers. Moreover, South Africa has a *Code of Conduct* for educators, the preferred term there, that expects individuals to demonstrate the desired conduct toward learners (or students), parents, and others, requiring them to act in a manner that enhances the dignity and status of the teaching profession. South Africa prefers the term *educator* to *teacher* because it denotes obligation that is wider that merely engaging in teaching of learning outcomes for learners.

Teacher trainees in Singapore who do not meet the requirements of their training must reimburse the government for the training costs; a similar provision in Malaysian law was upheld in the face of a judicial challenge. After terminating their contracts, Chinese teachers may also have to reimburse the government for their training expenses. Students in China, like in Malaysia, who receive tuition fees or scholarships are legally obligated to work as teachers for five years.

Canada, England and Wales, and the United States have recently started requiring criminal record checks as a pre-condition of employment. In England and Wales, in particular, applicants need criminal record certificates before they can be employed. Teachers in New Zealand have the burden of reporting any criminal convictions to school officials, while teachers in Malaysia must take oaths that they have not committed criminal offences.

In Belgium the private lives of teachers can lead to sanctions only if their actions influence their educational relationships with students, peers, or their schools. German teachers can invoke the same rights of privacy that they enjoy outside school. At school, German teachers must ensure that these rights do not conflict with their educational tasks. In Canada the privacy rights of teachers in Catholic schools are constrained. Further, Canadian teachers, as public servants, are, it seems, never off duty and are subject to public and judicial scrutiny.

French teachers are strongly protected when students who are under their supervision suffer injuries. In fact, direct action against teachers before courts for a lack of supervision has been made impossible. If teachers in Germany cause damage or injuries to students, they can be liable for damages through legal actions in civil courts.

In some of the countries discussed in this book, teachers seem to show little enthusiasm for the practice of assembly or union membership or they may not be encouraged to join such associations, as, for instance, in Malaysia. There is a difference in countries which regard most teachers to be civil servants. In England and Wales the role of teachers' unions has weakened over the last years, as the rights of teachers there have become more individual and less collective. The government in England and Wales reduced the autonomy of teachers by imposing detailed requirements on them and the conditions of their employment.

On the other hand, there are several teachers' unions in, for instance, Singapore, where most teachers are union members. The legal circumstances of public teachers in Germany are also regulated by state-level collective bargaining agreements. In South Africa teachers who are employed by the State have collective bargaining rights, while teachers in private schools have to negotiate the terms of their employment on an individual basis.

Insofar as nearly all teachers in public schools in Canada are unionized, their rights and obligations are governed by collective agreement between their unions and employers. However, teachers in private schools in Canada are rarely unionized. As union members, teachers in Canada can be sanctioned for failing to comply with the bylaws and policies of their unions. Unions are also a powerful force in public education in the United States, as teachers in the majority of states belong to unions that enter into collective bargaining agreements on their behalf with their employers.

Teachers in Canadian schools who are not Canadian citizens need employment authorizations from the government before they can become members of teachers' federations. On the related question of citizenship, the situation in the United States varies, as the Supreme Court ruled that it could be a precondition for employment in an older case but a more recent lower court judgment reached the opposite result.

In France, Catholic private schools and their unions have reached agreements on the training conditions of teachers. In New Zealand, teachers who are covered by collective agreements are not subject to performance-related pay. In this context, it is worth referring to the competency-based system in Singapore, which links teachers' rewards to reviewed performance and evidence of ongoing professional development. In Great Britain, the union did not accept a national agreement because of its concerns about performance-related payment. Performance-based salaries are still subject to discussion in Germany.

The Ministry of Education advanced a remarkable initiative in Singapore to organise annual legal awareness seminars for school leaders. Teachers, on the other hand, still have little understanding of the legislation that has an impact on their job. This special training on skills and knowledge in legislative matters aims at achieving more understanding of issues that have an impact on the teaching profession.

Although lifelong appointments are typical for the civil service, teachers in private schools in Belgium and Germany can also receive permanent appointments. On a related matter, private schools in Belgium must pay their teachers at least as much as the equivalent of public school teachers. Brazil guarantees equal rights for tenured and non-tenured teachers, where, in terms of retirement, there is a difference between those who worked in private and public schools.

Teachers in private schools in China must be licensed and must be given the same rights as teachers in public schools regarding their professional development, titles, and employment. In China, there is a gender difference in retirement ages which has been legally challenged as alleged gender discrimination. Retired teachers in China receive pensions for the rest of their lives, as in Malaysia, while in Brazil teachers are entitled to retirement pensions after specified periods during which they contributed to government pensions; men and women are treated differently under Brazil's retirement provisions.

Local education authorities of publicly funded state schools in Great Britain have the right to employ teachers in any schools under their power. A similar development is taking place in Germany, where teachers can be transferred to other schools against their wills. In Malaysia, teachers do not have the right to be assigned to particular schools, as officials in the Ministry of Education can post them to any schools they like. Moreover, Malaysian teachers cannot claim the right of non-transferability, and there are no legal provisions that allow them to appeal such decisions in courts.

The word *freedom* means different things to different people or institutions. While most countries guarantee the right to freedom of speech in their constitutions, the practical outcomes differ substantially.

In the United States, teachers are free to speak out as private citizens on matters of public concern, even if these issues affect the schools at which they are employed. However, American teachers cannot speak out on political issues in class to the extent that doing so deviates from approved curricula because teachers in elementary and secondary schools, unlike those in higher education, lack academic freedom. At the same time, while teachers in the Netherlands have very limited rights in this regard, the situation may change due to growing dissatisfaction with pedagogical innovations in the 1990s that have been detrimental to the teaching profession.

Teachers' freedom of personal, political, moral, or religious beliefs in New Zealand must be manifested as conduct harmful to the interests of children in order to be justifiably limited by the State. In addition, there is no justification for an association between "unpopular belief" and unfitness to teach. As the government in New Zealand defines the education guidelines and content of the curriculum, there is no academic freedom for teachers to depart from or augment the curriculum. Even so, while teachers in New Zealand have the right to freely express themselves, the content of their lessons must be relevant to the learning outcomes, and they are not allowed to further political or religious agendas in class.

As laws are being introduced seeking to restrict their dress, teachers in the Netherlands appear be able to dress in distinctive religious garb such as Islamic headscarves or burqas. At the same time, Dutch teachers may neither express their religious opinions too fervently nor try to convert students in violation of the principle of neutrality, which demands reticence in matters of religion. Dutch teachers who violate this prohibition may be fired. Teachers in the Netherlands retain the freedom to establish and have religions, including the right to change religions or not to have one, as well as the freedom to behave in accordance with specific religions or to profess or propagate religions in rituals, cults, and clothing. Of course, these freedoms must be practiced outside, rather than in, classes where students are present for instruction.

Political propaganda is prohibited in Singapore, as textbooks are controlled by the Ministry of Education. Teachers' freedom in Singapore is controlled by the government, as there are severe restrictions on communication matters such as publications and cooperation on broadcast. Conversely, while Dutch law does not place such restrictions on teachers, it does not, as noted above, grant them unfettered rights to express their political views in classes. Dutch teachers are free to express their political views outside school within specified parameters that are far from clear.

In Canada, the Provincial Ministries of Education issue instruments of control such as guidelines and curricula. In China and South Africa, teachers are encouraged to engage in research, exchange academic outcomes, and join professional academic societies. South African teachers can express their academic freedom wherever the explorations that arise in their mind lead them to do so.

A strict distinction in France focuses on the freedom of opinion and the freedom of speech. To the extent that teachers as civil servants have moral obligations, they must be completely neutral in expressing their views. A proselytising attitude is strictly forbidden in French primary and secondary education. Sanctions are justified for French teachers in public schools and for teachers in private schools under partnership contracts, although the schools have to respect the teachers' freedom of conscience.

Teachers in primary and secondary education in England and Wales do not have the right to academic freedom in either private or public schools. In public schools, teachers are allowed to express their views within specified constraints. Teachers in Germany have no right to academic freedom as well, since school officials set the curricula. However, German teachers have individualized rights to methodological freedom, which means that even though they cannot choose the textbooks, they are free to organize the instruction they provide. There is a remarkable freedom of speech in Germany concerning political education, where teachers must communicate political facts because they have to stand up for the principles of democracy. Moreover, teachers in Germany must express their own opinions and make contributions to the shaping of the political opinions of their students, although they cannot openly come out of any political party.

Academic freedom in Malaysia is guaranteed in terms of the freedom to speak freely and to use appropriate teaching methods and materials as long as they do not criticize the national curriculum. It is striking that in Malaysia, there is no litigation regarding freedom of speech and expression. Although Malaysian teachers have religious freedom, they are prohibited from taking part in politics or displaying any symbols associated with political parties. Malaysian teachers are also prohibited from making oral or written public political statements, acting as agents for candidates in elections, and contesting for posts or holding positions in political parties. These restrictions only apply to graduate teachers, as non-graduate teachers can publicly become members of political parties. In Germany, on the other hand, since the political engagement of teachers is regarded as valuable and useful, it is encouraged.

In New Zealand, conflicts might arise between personal religious commitments and the duty to teach impartially. Teachers in Singapore and the United States, based on the notion of the "wall of separation between church and state," are strictly prohibited from engaging in any form of religious proselytising. The standard used in Singapore is one which puts the emphasis on the national interest of maintaining the multicultural and multi-religious harmony in society. Students in Singapore cannot be engaged in religious activities against their wish. Further, contrary to many other countries, attendance at religious activities cannot be set as a condition for students to be admitted to schools in Singapore.

South African teachers in public and private schools have the right to join others in manifesting their beliefs as long as attendance is voluntary. In China, religion and education are strictly separated. As in Singapore, Chinese teachers are prohibited from using religion to interfere with education. In Belgium, the Netherlands, and the United States, religiously affiliated private schools can demand ideological commitments on the part of their staffs. Unlike the United States, the subsidized Belgian schools must employ staff members with equivalent qualifications to those in public schools. Free Belgian educational institutions have the freedom to employ teachers with a view to achieve their own educational objectives. Church institutions in Belgium are legally entitled to sanction the authority of religious instruction. The same applies to teachers in schools in England and Wales that are supported by churches or religions.

Teachers in England and Wales cannot offend the religions to which the schools are linked. Additionally, these schools have specific regulations on the appointments and dismissals of teachers of religious education. In fact, schools with religious character can even require given sexual orientations as a determining requirement for employment. Similarly, officials at religious schools in the Netherlands may differentiate in hiring on the basis of religion or belief when individuals' religions or beliefs constitute a genuine occupational requirement. On the other hand, in Germany, schools that are attended, for instance, by a majority of Catholic students are not permitted to give preference to Catholic teachers since religious affiliation is not a determining factor in teacher employment. In a slightly different vein, students in Brazil have a free choice of religious education, where some teachers in public schools are prepared by churches or religious entities.

A recent, much-discussed topic worldwide is whether teachers are allowed to reveal their own religious affiliations explicitly by, for instance, wearing veils or religious symbols. Teachers are not allowed to conduct visible private worship at school in China, France, Great Britain, and the United States, but they can do so in South Africa. Religious education forms part of the curriculum in Great Britain.

Teachers in public schools in countries that include religion as the study of faith (as opposed to theist objective study as if it were history or literature) in the curriculum have the right to opt out of teaching religious education because of their own religious opinions. Although there is legislation on religious discrimination, these teachers are not similarly protected in schools with certain religious characteristics.

In stark contrast to the United States, religious freedom in public schools is extensive in Germany. Teachers in Germany are allowed to practice their beliefs in school, and while they can profess their beliefs in class, they cannot disparage or slight other religions. However, as in France and the United States, female teachers in Germany cannot wear headscarves in class because it is seen as the profession of a political creed that violates the duty of civil servants to exercise restraint in political manners. In Malaysia teachers can express their religion through their practices, but the status of religious clothing is uncertain. Malaysian teachers have a constitutional right to profess, practice, and propagate their religion as long as their actions do not threaten the public order or morality because, as public servants, they cannot place their personal interests over their public duties.

Pedagogical freedom is an important regulation to maintain pluralism in educational provisions in Belgium, where teachers have to implement the pedagogical projects of their schools. It is important to note that Belgian teachers also have the right to have their own teaching styles. As in other countries, teaching staffs in Belgium are becoming increasingly involved in school management and policy-making since the exercise of the pedagogical freedom is seen as a collective right. The same applies to teachers in China, who can voice their opinions and suggestions on teaching and who can participate in the management of schools.

In Brazil, teachers are entitled to the right of pluralism of pedagogic ideas and conceptions as they are asked to participate in the elaboration of the schools' pedagogic plans. This legislative measure has resulted in an increased (pedagogic) participation of the teachers in Brazil, thereby expanding their rights. Chinese unions are supposed to organize teachers to participate in democratic decision making in their schools. Additionally, Chinese teachers are entitled to conduct educational activities and have the right to select instructional methods, but this right is limited because they cannot decide on the curriculum.

German legislation contains no specific teachers' rights on pedagogic freedom. The freedom of science applies only to university teachers. Teachers in Germany are allowed to invoke their right of religion, free speech, and association. Teachers with civil service status in Germany have no right to strike, while teachers with public-sector status have this right. In a related concern, public school teachers in the United States are generally forbidden from striking or engaging in concerted activities such as work slowdowns. As there are no legal regulations on the educational duties of German teachers, their duties are partly developed by school inspection authorities, and they have the freedom to maintain personal approaches.

All of the countries reviewed in this book afford teachers opportunities to offer their own defences in disciplinary proceedings which ministries of education, school governing bodies, local educational agencies, or school boards bring against them for a variety of infractions. Teachers who are dissatisfied with the decisions of the local teacher councils or school governing bodies can appeal to, for instance, a national court in New Zealand or a local educational agency in China. As schools in China are defined as public service units instead of government agencies, teachers do not have the right to administrative or judicial review. Conversely, as public servants, this means that administrative courts in the Netherlands are competent to resolve cases between teachers and public schools.

In New Zealand, employers can institute disciplinary or competence proceedings against staff. Teachers in Singapore have the right to appeal their performance evaluations. German applicants have the right to a judicial review of hiring decisions. In Malaysia, teachers need permission from the government before they can legally proceed in matters related to their employment, but they have a constitutional right to be heard before being dismissed.

Teachers in the United States, especially those who have achieved tenure, have extensive rights to substantive and procedural due process, including three basic elements: timely notice that dismissal is being contemplated, specification of charges, and a hearing at which the allegations are examined and a judgment rendered on the record regarding a teacher's future employment.

In some countries, difficulties have surfaced concerning the gender-based access to the teaching profession. Due to a shortage of male teachers, the government of New Zealand recently offered men special incentives to seek teacher training qualifications. Germany and the United States explicitly prohibit discrimination on gender grounds. Further, in Germany it is prohibited to give women preference for senior positions until they account for the same percentage as men in these jobs.

Singapore is a strong multicultural and ethnically diverse country. Still, English is the common language and the official teaching language since it serves as a unifying force for the different ethnic groups. In Brazil, to the contrary, native communities can use their maternal native languages and their proper learning processes even though the regular teaching is practiced in the Portuguese language. At the same time, the Brazilian government is seeking to professionalize teaching through specific training and publicly recognise native teaching.

A great deal is still expected from training and professional development programmes. In Singapore, teacher training is considered a priority, as the government both provides and facilitates a broad range of professional development through training courses, annual monetary contributions, trained mentors, and development and career plans. Singapore also provides an online forum for teachers as a platform to express their views. In this context, it is also worth mentioning the objective of the Brazilian government to allocate 60% of its resources for better teacher salaries.

The situation in China, as is increasingly the case in the United States, requires teachers to complete continuing education or further training on a regular basis. Chinese teachers must receive at least 120 hours of in-service training and 240 hours of training for every five years they teach; requirements vary from one state to the next in the United States. In Malaysia, teachers can receive financial grants or scholarships if they wish to improve their qualifications. On the other hand, German teachers do not have the right to continuing or advanced training.

In summary, this book has striven to cover a wide array of activities in the field of teachers' rights. Teachers in general have legal rights to employment, freedom of speech and religion, and freedom of association. Many times these rights are restricted to protect the public or national order. While the legal framework is often extended, the rights of teachers are nevertheless often strictly bound in some countries.

What nations must achieve is freedom from fear, intimidation, and inferior education, especially as teachers and their school employers are increasingly faced with the pressure of public accountability for student performance. We are also convinced that equality must be guaranteed as far as the expression of teachers' views are concerned. Clearly, legal systems can play an important role in this process.

Our aim was to shed light on the rights, duties, and new challenges that teachers confront as we have stressed the importance of respecting their fundamental rights. Yes, teachers are already legally protected in many ways. However, many rights, such as gender equity and freedom of speech, need to become more explicit and legally enforceable for teachers. As the authors of the South African chapter expressed, there might even be a worldwide concern that education is seen by governments primarily as an instrument to pursue State-determined objectives rather than a service by which the State empowers its citizens to achieve their highest potential.

As teachers are increasingly being viewed as coaches or role models rather than as teaching civil servants, an approach that has led to a backlash in the Netherlands, changes are likely to be made in existing school curricula. Thus, it is important that education officials hire dedicated and motivated teaching staff.

We hope this book will contribute to and provide an impetus in the debate on the rights of teachers worldwide. Inspired by what the contributors have written, we hope that law makers, policy makers, and educational leaders can proceed to outline new visions of developments for the rights of teachers that culminate in increased student achievement even as these changes are driven by national, rather than international, priorities.

About the Contributors

Hongqi Chu is a professor of education and the Dean of the College of Education Administration, Beijing Normal University, as well as director of the National Training Center for Primary School Principals in China. In 1994 Chu earned his Ph.D. from BNU and during 2002–2003 conducted research as a Senior Visiting Scholar at Indiana University. His research focuses on education policy and law, education administration, and educational history. Chu has published four single-authored monographs, 15 co-authored monographs, and more than 70 theses. He is also currently the editor of *Chinese Educational Administration Review* and *Educational Development Review*.

Jan DeGroof is founder and chairman of both the European Association for Education Law and Policy and the Interuniversity Centre for Education Law; he is also a co-founder of the Russian and the South African Associations for Education Law and Policy. One of the leading education law specialists worldwide, DeGroof helped organize and chaired the First World Conference on the Right to Education in Amsterdam–The Hague in 2004. DeGroof is a professor at the College of Europe in Bruges, Belgium, and the University of Tilburg, the Netherlands; formerly, he was a professor at Ghent University in Belgium. He is also government commissioner for the universities of the Flemish Community in Belgium. Previously, he was Chef de Cabinet of the Flemish Minister for Education and Training. DeGroof is often entrusted with international assignments and acted as an expert for OECD, EU, Council of Europe, and UNESCO while also fulfilling missions with Max Van Der Stoel, former High Commissioner for National Minorities of the OVSE, chiefly in the Balkan region. He publishes extensively in the field of international law, public law, education rights, and education law and policy and is author or co-author of various books, chapters, and academic articles. He is also Visiting Professor at several universities worldwide and is often invited as a guest speaker at international symposia on educational rights and policy. DeGroof is founder and editor in chief of the *European Journal for Education Law and Policy,* now transformed into the *International Journal for Education Law and Policy.*

Greg M. Dickinson, B.A. (Hon.), LL.B., Ed.D., of the Bar of Ontario, is a professor in the Faculty of Education, The University of Western Ontario, London, Canada, where he has specialized in education law for more than twenty-five years. Dickinson has also been a faculty member in the Faculty of Law and director of the Clinical Legal Education Program. He has been the editor in chief of *Education & Law Journal* (Thomson Carswell) since 1988 and the director of the Althouse Press since 2002. Dickinson is a co-author and co-editor of several books, including *Rights, Freedoms and the Education System in Canada* (1989), *Understanding the Law* (1989, 1996), and *Beyond the "Careful Parent": Tort Liability in Education* (1998), and he is the author of numerous book chapters and articles on education law. His article "The Right to Education in Canada: A Difficult Beast to Tame" represented Canada in the special issue on the right to education in the inaugural issue of *International Journal for Education Law and Policy* (2005).

Tie Fatt Hee, B.A., Dip. in Ed., M.Ed., LL.B., LL.M., SJD., is an associate professor at the University of Malaya in Kuala Lumpur, Malaysia. He was admitted as an advocate and solicitor to the High Court of Malaya in 1994 after completing his Bachelor of Law degree from the University of London and the Certificate in Legal Practice. He is a regular speaker at the Australia and New Zealand Education Law Association conference.

Sean Kinsler holds the degrees of M.A. (Hon.) and LL.B. (Hon.) from the University of Auckland and is Assistant Crown Counsel at the Crown Law Office in Wellington, New Zealand. His research interests are in public law, the law of contracts, and the history of Western philosophy.

André Legrand, was professor of public law in the University of Nanterre (France) and is now retired. He was *recteur d'académie* in Limoges and Rennes and, next, director in the French Ministry of Education for secondary and primary education. He is also a former president of the University of Nanterre and president of the Conference of the French University Presidents. He has written many articles and several books about French and foreign constitutional and administrative law, civil rights, and education law and policy. His latest book is *L'école dans son droit*, published in 2005.

Rassie Malherbe is a professor of public law at the University of Johannesburg, South Africa, and specializes in constitutional law, human rights, education law, and statutory interpretation. He is a graduate of the University of Stellenbosch (LL.B., 1975) and the Rand Afrikaans University (LL.D., 1992). He publishes widely, both nationally and internationally, and is the author and co-author of numerous textbooks, articles, and case notes in the fields of constitutional law, human rights, and education law. He is an executive member of the South African Education Law and Policy Association and of the Inter-University Education Law and Policy Centre in Pretoria, and he is a member of the editorial committee of the *Journal for South African Law*. He served as an adviser during the South African constitution-making process in the early nineties.

Nina Beatriz Stocco Ranieri is a lecturer in the Department of State Law of the Faculty of Law of the University of São Paulo (USP) and in the Institute of International Relations, where she is vice-coordinator of the undergraduate course. She is also an attorney-at-law in the Legal Department at USP and a member of the Brazilian Bar Association. She currently works for the State of São Paulo Government as Special Legal Advisor to the Governor. She has a B.A. degree in Law and an M.A. degree in Constitutional Law from the Pontifícia Universidade Católica de São Paulo (PUC/SP), and she has a Ph.D. in State Law from the Faculty of Law, USP. She is the author of the following books: *Autonomia Universitária (University Autonomy), Educação Superior, Direito e Estado (Higher Education, Law and the State),* and the organizer of *Autonomia Universitária na USP, de 1934 a 2004 (University Autonomy at USP from 1934 to 2004)*; she has also written articles on public law and educational law. She was a member of the Superior Council of Juridical and Legislative Matters of the Federation of Industries of the State of São Paulo (2003–2004), a councilor of the Brazilian Bar Association (São Paulo Section) and a member of its Commission for Juridical Instruction (2001–2003), and the Coordinator of Permanent Courses of the Superior School of the Bar Association (2001/2005). She was Chief of Staff to USP's Dean (1997–2001), Chief of Staff of the São Paulo State Secretary for Science and Technology (2001–2003), and Secretary General of USP (2003–2005). She was also an advisor to the Brazilian Ministry of Education (1995–1996) and to the Brazilian Mission at the United Nations (October 2004).

Ingo Richter, president of the Irmgard Coninx Foundation, studied law at the universities of Göttingen, Munich, Hamburg, and Paris. He earned his doctorate in Law at Hamburg University (1965); Docteur de Law l'Université de Paris (1966). From 1967 to 1979 he was head of the Department of Law and Administration at the Max-Planck-Institute for Educational Research, Berlin; from 1975 to 1979 he was a professor of law at the Free University of Berlin; and from 1979 to 1993 he was a professor of public law at the University of Hamburg. He also taught at the universities of Bordeaux, Rostock, Hastings, and Chicago. From 1993 to 2002 he was chairman and head of Deutsches Jugendinstitut in Munich. From 1999 to 2001 he was chairman of the 11th Government Commission on Children and Youth. Moreover, since 1977 he has been editor of the educational law journal *Recht der Jugend und des Bildungswesens.* His areas of research include constitutional and administrative law; educational politics and law, with a particular focus on school law and the law of further education; social policy and law, with a particular focus on children and youth law; and labor law, with a particular focus on youth in training and work.

Paul Rishworth is a professor of law and Dean of the Faculty of Law at the University of Auckland. He was a founding member of the New Zealand chapter of the Australia and New Zealand Education Law Association and teaches elective papers in rights and freedoms, equality and anti-discrimination law, education law, and South Pacific legal studies. He is a joint author of *The New Zealand Bill of Rights* (2003) and has published widely on human rights law and education law in New Zealand.

J. P. Rossouw has twenty years' experience as a teacher and twelve years' experience as lecturer at the North-West University in Potchefstroom, South Africa. He is an associate professor in education law and specializes in labor law, sport law, values in education, and learner discipline. He is the author or co-author of six books in education law and various articles in accredited journals, and he has read academic papers at international conferences in a number of countries. Professor Rossouw has received research grants from the National Research Foundation; the Queensland University of Technology in Brisbane, Australia; the Secretariat of the Commonwealth, London; and the North-West Department of Education. He has visited Australia (2004), the United States (2006), and the United Kingdom (2008) for lectures, research at schools, and conference presentations. He serves on the executive committees of the South African Education Law Association (SAELA) and Centre for Education Law and Policy, and he is the editor of *Sui Generis,* the SAELA journal.

Anne Ruff, LL.B., LL.M., Cert. Ed., Barrister, was a Principal Lecturer in Law at Middlesex University, London, U.K., until January 2006 and remains a Visiting

Senior Lecturer. She established an education law module as well as provided teaching, writing, and research on aspects of education law, discrimination law, and the law of contract. Her publications include *Education Law Text Cases and Materials* (Oxford University Press) and chapters on the school curriculum and on staffing in *Butterworths Education Law Manual* (Tottel Publishing). She is a contributing editor to the *Education Law Journal*. She is a trained special educational needs (SEN) mediator and works occasionally for the London SEN Mediation Service. She also chairs school admission and exclusion appeal panels and is a part-time chairperson of social security appeal tribunals.

Charles J. Russo, M.Div., J.D., Ed. D., is the Joseph Panzer Chair in Education in the School of Education and Allied Professions and Adjunct Professor in the School of Law at the University of Dayton. The 1998–1999 president of the Education Law Association and 2002 recipient of its McGhehey (Achievement) Award, he has published in excess of 650 publications, including 30 books. He speaks extensively on issues in education law in the United States and overseas and has spoken at education law conferences in Australia–New Zealand, Canada, Europe, Malaysia, and South Africa. He worked in Sarajevo, Bosnia, and Herzegovina with the Office of the Ombudsman on matters pertaining to civil rights and religious freedom as well as with the Faculty of Education on improving schooling in Bosnia. He also worked with officials at South East European University in Tetovo, Macedonia. In addition to having spoken in twenty-two different nations on six continents, he has taught summer courses in England and Spain and served as a Visiting Professor at Queensland University of Technology in Brisbane, Australia (and has been appointed to a similar capacity at the Law Faculty of the University of Newcastle, Australia); the University of Sarajevo, Bosnia; South East European University, Macedonia; the Potchefstroom Campus of North-West University in Potchefstroom, South Africa; and the University of Malaya in Kuala Lumpur, Malaysia. In May 2004 he received the award of Philosophiae Doctor, Honoris Causa, from Potchefstroom University (now the Potchefstroom Campus of North-West University) in Potchefstroom, South Africa, in recognition of his contribution to the study of education law. Before joining the faculty at the University of Dayton as professor and chair of the Department of Educational Administration in July 1996, he taught at the University of Kentucky in Lexington, Kentucky, and at Fordham University in his native New York City.

Mônica Sifuentes has been a federal judge in Brasília since 1993 and has additional service in the Federal Court of Appeal. She is also a professor of education law at the University of Brasília (UNB) and of constitutional law at the Master's Course of Constitutional Law of Instituto Brasiliense de Direito Público (IDP-Brasília). Sifuentes earned a B.A. in Law, and a master's degree in Economic Law from the Federal University of Minas Gerais/Brazil, and a Ph.D. in Constitutional Law from the Faculty of Law of the University of Lisbon. The author of the books *The Access to the Basic Education in Brazil: A Development's Right* (2001) and *Súmula Vinculante—A Study about the Normative Power of the Tribunals* (2005), she has also written articles in the areas of public law, access to justice, human rights, and educational law and policy while contributing to newspapers and other publications. Sifuentes participated as a Brazilian representative at the "Experts' Consultation on the Operational Definition of Basic Education" on December 17–18, 2007, a meeting at UNESCO headquarters on the operational definition of basic education that was proposed during the workshop on "Challenges and Perspectives of Law and Education" in São Paulo in December 2006. Sifuentes coordinated two international seminars on education law in the Council of the Federal Justice, Brazil, in 2004 and 2005. She currently works in a Permanent Group of Studies about the Hague Convention of 1980, on the Supreme Court of Brazil, and since September 2006 has been designated Liaison Judge in Brazil for the Hague Conference on Private International Law in cases of child abduction.

Marius Smit, B. Com., LL.B., LL.M., is a practicing attorney, notary, and conveyancer and is also a qualified educator. He lectures in education law at the Faculty for Education Sciences at North-West University, Potchefstroom Campus. He has published articles in academic journals and has co-authored books in the field of education law. Smit serves as a member of the executive of SAELA (South African Education Law Association) and as a member of a school governing body responsible for disciplinary and legal matters. He is studying toward a Ph.D. in Education Law and has a special interest in comparative education law.

Kenneth Stott is the Provost at the Fraser Coast campus of the University of Southern Queensland. He has also served as Pro Vice Chancellor and Acting Dean of Education. Stott, who is one of the world's top researchers in education leadership, previously held a senior appointment in Singapore, where he worked for 16 years. Stott has co-authored a number of books, many of which have won international acclaim, including titles in management, team building, strategic planning, and change leadership. He is well known for his ability to challenge mainstream management thinking and to provoke new ways of approaching change in complex environments. Stott's recent work on encountering an uncertain future is considered to be at the vanguard of leadership thought. He lives in Queensland with his wife, a lawyer, school teacher, and specialist in Education Law, and their two young children.

Mui Kim Teh is both a lawyer and an educator. She is a registered barrister-at-law in London and was an Advocate and Solicitor of the Supreme Court of Singapore. She was a lawyer in Singapore before moving to Australia. Earlier in her career, Teh was both a teacher and a department head in Singapore schools. She is currently based at the University of Southern Queensland in Hervey Bay, where she is a part-time law lecturer and where she is completing her doctorate in International Education Law.

Ben P. Vermeulen is a professor of constitutional and administrative law at the Vrije Universiteit, Amsterdam; professor of education law, Vrije Universiteit, Amsterdam, and Radboud Universiteit, Nijmegen; member of the Onderwijsraad (Education Council), the permanent advisory board of the Minister of Education; and member of the Adviescomissie Vreemdelingenzaken (Immigration Council), the permanent advisory board of the Minister of Immigration and Integration. He has written extensively on fundamental rights, constitutional freedoms, education law, and asylum law.

Ran Zhang is a Ph.D. candidate in Educational Policy Studies and Educational Psychology at Indiana University, Bloomington. She has contributed a chapter on China to *The Educational Rights of Students: International Perspectives on Demystifying the Legal Issues* and co-edited two issues of *Chinese Education and Society* on new trends in student rights litigation in China. In 2007, Zhang received a doctoral dissertation improvement grant from the U.S. National Science Foundation (Law and Social Sciences Program) to conduct her dissertation fieldwork on the legal rights consciousness of Chinese college students. She received undergraduate degrees in law and economics from Beijing University.

www.ingramcontent.com/pod-product-compliance
Ingram Content Group UK Ltd.
Pitfield, Milton Keynes, MK11 3LW, UK
UKHW012037150926
475560UK00001B/48

9 781578 869343